SHOPPING AND TRAVELING IN EXOTIC THAILAND

Impact Guides available through your local bookseller or directly from Impact Publications:

- ***SHOPPING AND TRAVELING IN EXOTIC ASIA: Hong Kong, Thailand, Malaysia, Singapore, and Indonesia***
- ***SHOPPING AND TRAVELING THE EXOTIC CARIBBEAN: The Bahamas, Bermuda, Barbados, Dominican Republic, Haiti, Jamaica, St. Martin/ Sint Maarten, St. Thomas, and Puerto Rico***
- ***SHOPPING AND TRAVELING IN EXOTIC HONG KONG***
- ***SHOPPING AND TRAVELING IN EXOTIC INDONESIA***
- ***SHOPPING AND TRAVELING IN EXOTIC SINGAPORE AND MALAYSIA***
- ***SHOPPING AND TRAVELING IN EXOTIC THAILAND***
- ***SHOPPING IN EXCITING AUSTRALIA AND PAPUA NEW GUINEA***
- ***SHOPPING IN EXOTIC PLACES: Hong Kong, Korea, Thailand, Indonesia, and Singapore***
- ***SHOPPING THE EXOTIC SOUTH PACIFIC: Australia, New Zealand, Papua New Guinea, Fiji, and Tahiti***

Available in Fall, 1992:

- ***SHOPPING AND TRAVELING IN EXOTIC INDIA***
- ***SHOPPING AND TRAVELING IN EXOTIC MOROCCO***
- ***SHOPPING AND TRAVELING THE EXOTIC PHILIPPINES***

SHOPPING & TRAVELING IN EXOTIC THAILAND

Your Passport to Exciting Bangkok, Chiangmai, and Beyond

Ronald L. Krannich, Ph.D.
Caryl Rae Krannich, Ph.D.

IMPACT PUBLICATIONS
Woodbridge, VA

SHOPPING AND TRAVELING IN EXOTIC THAILAND

Library of Congress Cataloging-in-Publication Data

Krannich, Ronald L.
Shopping and traveling in exotic Thailand / Ronald L. Krannich, Caryl Rae Krannich.
p. cm.
Includes index.
ISBN 0-942710-55-X: $13.95
1. Shopping—Thailand—Guide-books. 2. Thailand—Description and travel—1976—Guide-books. I. Krannich, Caryl Rae. II. Title. III. Title: Shopping and traveling in exotic Thailand.
TX337.T5K72 1992
380.1'45'00025593—dc20 91-38264
CIP

Cover designed by ABS Graphics, 8564 Custer Court, Manassas, VA 22111, Tel. 703/361-7415.

For information on distribution or quantity discounts, call 703/361-7300 or write to: Sales Department, IMPACT PUBLICATIONS, 4580 Sunshine Court, Woodbridge, VA 22192. Distributed to the trade by National Book Network, 4720 Boston Way, Suite A, Lanham, MD 20706, 301/459-8696.

CONTENTS

LIABILITIES AND WARRANTIES

While the authors have attempted to provide accurate and up-to-date information in this book, please be advised that names, addresses, and phone numbers do change, and shops and restaurants do move, go out of business, or change ownership and management. We regret any inconvenience such changes may cause to your travel and shopping plans.

Inclusion of shops, shippers, restaurants, hotels, tour groups, and other hospitality providers in this book in no way implies guarantees nor endorsements by either the authors or publisher. The information and recommendations appearing in this book are provided solely for your reference. The honesty and reliability of shops and shippers is best ensured by **you**—ask the right questions and require the proper receipts and documents. The book provides numerous tips on how you can best experience a trouble-free adventure as well as ensure against dishonesty, misrepresentation, and misunderstanding when shopping and traveling in Thailand.

PREFACE

Exotic Thailand offers wonderful traveling and shopping opportunities for those who know what to look for, where to go, and how to properly travel and shop its many cities, towns, and villages. We discovered this years ago. During the past 25 years we have repeatedly returned as students, scholars, development workers, businesspeople, advisors, tourists, and curious travelers to further discover this ever-changing and delightful country as well as explore its many hotels, restaurants, shopping centers, arcades, department stores, shophouses, factories, markets, and villages. Thailand remains one of our favorite Asian destinations. Its people and products continue to enrich our lives.

Thailand offers visitors many shopping opportunities for gems, jewelry, clothes, arts, antiques, handicrafts, and home decorative items. From each trip shoppers return home with unique and quality items to enhance their homes and wardrobes. If approached properly, we believe Thailand may well become one of your favorite travel and shopping destinations.

What has particularly impressed us about Thailand in recent years are the many wonderful shopping alternatives it presents to visitors. While it continues to offer interesting sightseeing and cultural opportunities, Thailand's shopping particularly intrigues us. Indeed, we find Thailand to be one of the best kept shopping secrets in all of Asia. Numerous shops in Bangkok and Chiangmai offer a dazzling array of Thai and Burmese arts, antiques, woodcarvings, ceramics, furniture, and home accessories to complement contemporary most Western homes.

Shopping in Thailand is different from shopping in Hong Kong, Tokyo, Seoul, or Singapore. If you don't know what to buy, where to go, or how to shop in Thailand, you can easily miss some of the best shopping in Asia as you end up with only silk and a few tourist trinkets—popular items which may not integrate well with many Western wardrobes and homes. This is unfortunate for Thailand has much more to offer you.

While Thailand is still exotic to us, it no longer presents the mystery and confusion that often confronts first-time visitors. It is an increasingly modern, convenient, and comfortable country to visit. More and more people speak English, the transportation and health systems are good, the food and hotels are outstanding, service is exceptional, prices are still reasonable, and the people are interesting and delightful to meet.

We wrote this book as part of a larger writing endeavor on shopping and traveling in Asia and the Pacific. This fifth volume in our "Impact Guides" series reflects several years of living, working, and traveling in Thailand. Especially during the past 10 years, we have witnessed the virtual transformation of shopping choices with selections of greater quality products and compatibility with Western design tastes. Thailand is well on its way to becoming a shopper's paradise with its numerous unique and tasteful products.

As you will quickly discover, this is not a typical travel guide to Thailand. Indeed, we are not interested in duplicating the efforts of others. The chapters that follow present a particular perspective on traveling in Thailand. We decided to write more than just another descriptive travel guide primarily focusing on hotels, restaurants, sightseeing, and entertainment and with only a few paragraphs or pages on shopping. We take shopping as our central focus in an effort to best enjoy a travel process that includes meeting new people, experiencing interesting cultures, and acquiring quality products.

While our primary focus is on shopping, the book goes beyond other shopping guides that only concentrate on the "whats" and "wheres" of shopping. In addition, the book is much more than just a shopping guide to Thailand. In many respects it is a complete travel guide in which shopping takes center stage in the travel process.

Our experience convinces us that there is a need for a different type of travel book on Thailand. The book should outline the "how-tos" along with the "whats" and "wheres" of shopping in Thailand. Such a book should both educate and guide you through Thailand's shopping and travel mazes. Consequently, this book focuses on the shopping **process** as well as provides you with the necessary shopping **details** for making informed shopping choices in specific shopping areas, arcades, centers, department stores, markets, and shops.

Rather than just describe the "what" and "where" of travel and shopping, we include the critical **"how"**—what to do before you depart on your trip as well as while you are in Thailand. We believe you and others are best served with a book that leads to both **understanding** and **action**. Therefore, you will find little in these pages about the general history, culture, economics, and politics of Thailand; these topics are covered well in other types of travel books.

The perspective we develop throughout this book is based on our belief that traveling should be more than just another adventure in eating, sleeping, sightseeing, and taking pictures of unfamiliar places. Whenever possible, we attempt to bring to life the fact that Thailand has real people and interesting products that you, the visitor, will find exciting. This is a country of talented artists, craftspeople, traders, and entrepreneurs who offer you some wonderful opportunities to participate in their society through their shopping processes. When you leave Thailand, you will take with you not only some unique experiences and memories but also quality products that you will certainly appreciate for years to come.

We have not hesitated to make qualitative judgments, including many frank observations, about shopping and traveling in Thailand. If we just presented you with shopping information, we would do you a disservice by not sharing our discoveries, both good and bad. Indeed, it would be irresponsible for us to just describe the "what" and "where" of shopping in Thailand by presenting "the facts" without making judgments on what you should or should not do about Thailand's shopping weaknesses and potential problems, such as rip-offs, touts, and commissions.

Above all, we believe you could use a **good friend** when you travel to Thailand. Hopefully this book will become your best and most trusted friend as you navigate the many promises and pitfalls of shopping and traveling in Thailand.

While we know our judgments may not be valid for everyone, we offer them as **reference points** from which you can make your own decisions. Our major emphasis throughout this book is on **quality shopping**. We look for shops that offer excellent quality and styles which we think are appropriate for Western homes and wardrobes. If you share our concern for quality shopping, you will find many of our recommendations useful for your own shopping purposes.

Buying quality items does not mean you must spend a great deal of money on shopping. It means that you have taste, you are selective, you buy what fits into your wardrobe and home. If you shop in the right places, you will find quality products. If you understand the shopping process, you will get good value for your money. While shopping for quality may not be cheap, it need not be expensive. But most important, shopping for quality in Thailand is fun and it results in lovely items which can be enjoyed for years to come.

Throughout this book we have included "tried and tested" shopping information. We make judgments based upon our experience—not on judgments or sales pitches from others. We acquired some fabulous items, and gained valuable knowledge in the process. However, we could not make purchases in every shop nor can we guarantee that **your** experiences will be the same as ours. Shops close, ownership or management changes, and the shop you visit may not be the same as the one we shopped. So use this book as a start, but ask questions and make your own judgments before you buy.

This book was originally published in 1989 as ***Shopping in Exotic Thailand***. The book quickly found a dedicated audience of travelers who thoroughly enjoyed their Thailand shopping adventure. Their many letters and telephone calls confirmed what we suspected—there was a need for a different type of travel book that emphasized the "how-tos" of traveling and shopping in Thailand. Indeed, we were gratified to meet some of our readers—from budget to up-scale travelers—using our book in Bangkok and Chiangmai when we revisited several of our recommended shops in 1989, 1990, and 1991. They shared our interest in acquiring good quality products. Better still, they validated much of our "how-to" advice and recommendations. In addition to our shopping tips, they especially liked our hotel and restaurant recommendations. Some left Thailand fat, happy, and broke—the ultimate signs of a truly wonderful travel and shopping adventure! And many enjoyed their trip so much that they are going back to Thailand this year to pick up where they left off.

This book is a revision of our earlier book. It reflects many changes occurring in Thailand's travel and shopping scene during the past three years. We've included more shops, hotels, and restaurants in this present volume. We think you will be especially pleased with our new hotel and restaurant recommendations. Like many of our readers, you may find Thailand both a shopping and gastronomic delight centered around fabulous hotels!

We wish to thank the many individuals and organizations that contributed to this book. Thai Airways took us safely around Thailand and Thai Airways International pampered us all the way home. This fine airline has a well deserved reputation for convenience, comfort, and service. It's a great airline on which to both begin and end your Thailand adventure. Thai Airways also offers some excellent value package deals, the "Royal Orchid Holidays," which we describe in Chapter Two.

The government tourist organization—Tourism Authority of Thailand (TAT)—was helpful in ensuring the success of this project. We are confident their offices will assist you in any way possible to ensure that your trip to Thailand will be one of your most rewarding adventures. In Chapter Two we include contact information on the TAT offices found throughout the world as well as within Thailand.

Whatever you do, enjoy Thailand. Its people, products, and service will charm you. While you need not *"shop 'til you drop"* in Thailand, at least shop it well and with the confidence that you are getting good quality and value for your money. Don't just limit yourself to small items that will fit into your suitcase. Be adventuresome and consider acquiring larger items that can be safely, conveniently, and inexpensively shipped to your home.

We wish you well in your travel and shopping adventure to Thailand. The book is designed to be used on the roads, streets, and lanes of Bangkok, Chiangmai, Chiangrai, Maesai, Lampang, Lamphun, Mae Hong Son, Ayuthaya, Pattaya, and Phuket. If you plan your journey according to the first five chapters, handle the shopping process according to the next two chapters, and navigate the cities and towns based on the remaining eight chapters, you should have a marvelous time. You'll discover some exciting places, acquire some choice items, and return home with fond memories of exotic Thailand. You, too, may return home fat, happy, and broke as well as experience that unexplained urge to return to Thailand next year. If you put this book to use, it will indeed become your best friend—and passport—to shopping and traveling in exotic Thailand. Enjoy!

Ronald L. Krannich
Caryl Rae Krannich

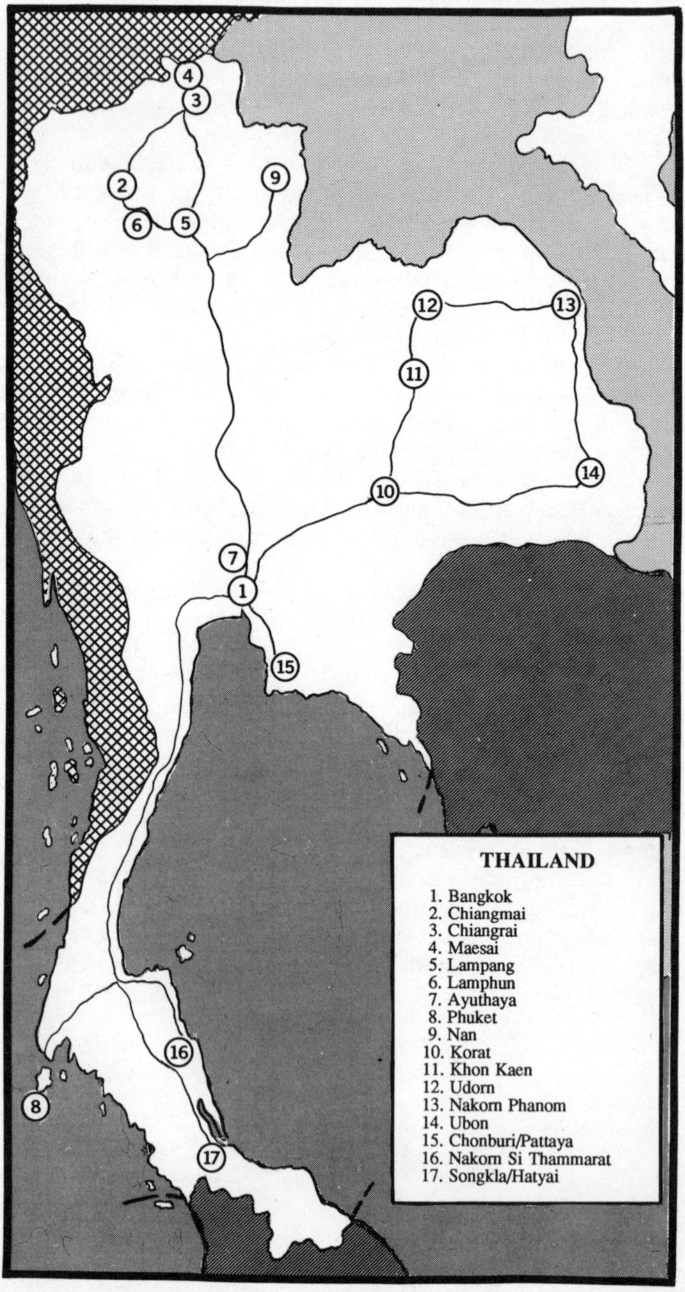
THAILAND
1. Bangkok
2. Chiangmai
3. Chiangrai
4. Maesai
5. Lampang
6. Lamphun
7. Ayuthaya
8. Phuket
9. Nan
10. Korat
11. Khon Kaen
12. Udorn
13. Nakorn Phanom
14. Ubon
15. Chonburi/Pattaya
16. Nakorn Si Thammarat
17. Songkla/Hatyai

1 WELCOME TO THAILAND

Welcome to one of the world's most exotic and charming places. You've made a wise decision in selecting Thailand as your next travel and shopping destination. This is still one of the world's most exotic places. It yields some very exciting travel and shopping experiences which you will remember for years to come.

If this is your first visit to Thailand, you're in for a real treat. You will discover an intriguing land of exceptionally friendly and gracious people, talented craftspeople, bustling cities and towns, picturesque countrysides, idyllic beaches and villages, colorful festivals, exciting cuisine, gorgeous hotels, and fascinating cultures. It's a land where you can literally *"shop 'til you drop"* and still want to come back for more. Thailand will surely touch you forever with its people, places, products, prices, and many varied pleasures.

From the chic boutiques, dazzling jewelry stores, awe inspiring antique shops, and colorful markets of Bangkok to the dusty shophouses and cluttered factories of Chiangmai, Chiangrai, Maesai, Lampang, Lamphun, Mae Hong Son, Ayuthaya, Pattaya, and Phuket, let us take you on a shopping and travel adventure of a lifetime as we fly, drive, and walk to some of the world's most exciting places. Come with us and we will share with you a Thailand largely absent in the enticing tourist brochures, travel books, and advertisements aimed at bringing you to another mystical, mysterious, and magical world of Southeast Asia!

A TRIP WELL WORTH TAKING

Thailand is one of the world's most interesting, yet largely undiscovered, travel and shopping destinations. Known as the "Land of Smiles," for its friendly and jovial people, and the "Land of the Free," for its ability to avoid Western colonization, Thailand is a delightful place to shop, sightsee, and indulge your gastronomic and entertainment fancies. Visit Thailand and you will certainly return home with wonderful memories and a treasure-trove of products to enhance your home and wardrobe.

Thailand proudly displays its long historical, cultural, and religious traditions to visitors. Better still, it offers shoppers a unique variety of quality arts and handicrafts expressive of these traditions. Particularly sensitive to foreigners, the Thai are gracious hosts who genuinely want you to enjoy your every moment in their charming and colorful country. When you visit Thailand, you will encounter a kaleidoscope of wonderfully exotic travel experiences. If you miss Thailand, you will miss a truly fascinating shopping adventure.

GETTING TO KNOW YOU

We highly recommend Thailand for many reasons. Offering a great deal to international shoppers, Thailand is one of today's best kept shopping secrets. The people are friendly, delightful, and relatively honest to deal with. Thai service is simply outstanding—the best you will encounter in all of Asia. You will be pampered with polite, considerate, and spontaneous people who are genuinely concerned that you, their guest, are *"having a good time"* in their country. Thais put their best face forward for your convenience and enjoyment. If you come directly from Hong Kong—where the people tend to be more formal, reserved, and at times rude—Thailand is a paradise of personable people who try hard to make your visit most enjoyable.

But Thailand is best appreciated by travelers who love spontaneity, a bit of painless adventure, and can tolerate charming chaos. It is for those who are open to new experiences rather than tourists who seek to reconfirm their notion that the world should always be well organized and orderly—

just like back home. The Thais do not organize themselves like many Westerners, nor do they disorganize themselves like many of their neighbors. Thais generally lack strong and efficient organization, but they prize individualism, tolerate the unique, and permit a high degree of individual autonomy. It is a country of spontaneous and makeshift organization, where everything seems to be in the process of being completed—or further complicated. It has a certain worn, dilapidated, make-shift, yet charming look about it, in spite of impressive new high-rise office buildings, hotels, and banks that punctuate its ever changing urban landscapes with innovative and adventure-some Thai architecture.

CHARMING CHAOS

Thailand exhibits a certain degree of disorderliness, chaos, unpredictability, and adventure that also makes it such a delightful and charming place to visit—once you overcome your initial reluctance to venture forward into its many congested roads, streets, and lanes. Indeed, you first become disoriented by the visual chaos of its streets. Then you become captivated by the serendipity, charm, contrasts, contradictions, and spontaneity of the Thai who seem to adjust so well to everyday inconveniences with their *mai pen rai* ("never mind") attitude toward daily inconveniences inherent in their country of muddling chaos.

Thailand, its people, and its products grow on you—if you let them. But you must first be open to them rather than force them into preconceptions or a tidy plan to be quickly followed. While Hong Kong's and Singapore's do-it-yourself organization and conveniences allow you to quickly implement your shopping plans, Thailand is not designed for people in a hurry. In Thailand you need time, flexibility, a sense of humor, and a little help to get things done. Going from one point to another in Bangkok, for example, can become a nightmare of traffic congestion, requiring you to rethink what may become an unrealistic plan.

Thailand will charm you with its many pleasures. While your memories of Hong Kong will center primarily on your purchases, the crowds, the harbor views, and the efficiency of the city and its people, your memories of Thailand will turn to its gracious people, fine food and service, unique shopping, beautiful hotels, glittering temples in the midst of chaotic neighborhoods, a charming river and canals graced with lumbering barges, and numerous funny and serendipitous experiences. After a while you forget the heat and pollution and mainly recall the positives of this exotic and friendly country—its people, products, and pleasures.

Whatever you do, don't miss Thailand. It's a very special country. The shopping is marvelous and you will enjoy its wonderful people. But you must approach Thailand right, shop it properly, and give it enough time to grow on you. Like many other travelers who have discovered the delights of this country, you should leave Thailand with a very special set of memories and wonderful buys that once again confirm the wisdom of traveling and shopping in exotic places!

SURPRISING COMMUNITIES

Shopping in Thailand primarily involves making trips to shopping centers, hotel shopping arcades, department stores, shophouses, factories, and markets located in and around Thailand's two major cities—Bangkok and Chiangmai. These are the country's centers for fashion, design, production, trade, marketing, transportation, and communication. Here you will also find Thailand's best travel amenities—fine hotels, restaurants, entertainment, and tourist sights. At the same time, you will discover some unique shopping opportunities in small towns and villages where you can purchase local products either not available in the city shops or less expensive than elsewhere. Most of these towns and villages are located in the northern region within a one to four hour drive of Chiangmai. Overall, you will quickly discover the best shopping for quality, design, and uniqueness is found in Bangkok and Chiangmai.

Bangkok, a bustling city of nearly 7 million people, is a shopper's paradise. Stroll through the Peninsula Plaza, River City Shopping Complex, World Trade Center, Thaniya Plaza, and Oriental Plaza and you will quickly discover some of the best quality shopping in all of Southeast Asia. Shop after shop offer exquisite jewelry, clothes, antiques, art, and home decorative items for discerning shoppers with an eye for quality. Venture into the Weekend Market, Pratunam, Thieves Market, Chinatown, and the vendor stalls that line Silom, Suriwongse, and Patpong roads and you will find great bargains on inexpensive clothes, souvenirs, and copy watches, handbags, briefcases, belts, and shirts. The city brims with thousands of shops that will literally keep you busy shopping for days.

Chiangmai, Thailand's second largest city of less than 200,000 people, is located approximately 700 kilometers north of Bangkok. This is a city of legendary charm and beauty. Chiangmai is to Thailand what Bali is to Indonesia—a truly unique cultural center which is also one of Asia's major cottage industry centers for handcrafted items. Known for its gentle and friendly people, beautiful scenery, pleasant winter climate, and diverse attractions, Chiangmai is a shopper's paradise for antiques and locally produced as well as imported Burmese handcrafted products that make lovely home decorative items: woodcarvings, textiles, furniture, silver, basketry, celadon, lacquerware, and umbrellas. Explore the small shops and stalls in the downtown Night Bazaar and the factories along nearby Chiangmai-Sankamphaeng Road and in Hang Dong and you will leave Chiangmai with a treasure-trove of lovely handcrafted items at inexpensive prices that may astound you. Indeed, you will be shopping in many of the same places dealers from Bangkok and abroad come to buy items for their shops.

Chiangrai, Maesai, Lampang, and Lamphun are within one to four hours driving distance from Chiangmai. Each of these communities offers unique handcrafted items either produced locally or imported from Burma. Chiangrai is especially noted for its handicrafts and antiques. The border town of Maesai is a center for gems, handicrafts, and antiques that regularly cross the border from Burma. Here you will find some of the best buys in all of Thailand on Burmese tapestries, puppets, baskets, gems, and jewelry. But you had better know your gems and jewelry before making any such purchases. Lampang is one of Thailand's major centers for producing the famous blue and white ceramics. More than 50 factories turn out a wide range of unique ceramics.

Mae Hong Son, until recently a small, sleepy, and isolated provincial town near the Thai-Burmese border, is located west of Chiangmai, approximately 40 minutes by air or 11 hours by road. A favorite destination for adventuresome travelers who enjoy trekking in the picturesque surrounding hills and mountains, it is a culturally rich area long influenced by the Burmese and Shan. It is also home for numerous hilltribes such as the Karen, Lahu, and Meo. A few downtown shops offer excellent buys on Burmese lacquerware, textiles, and hilltribe clothes and handicrafts.

Ayuthaya, located 86 kilometers north of Bangkok, is one of Thailand's most important historical areas and popular tourist attractions. Amidst its many temples and monuments are several shops offering excellent quality handicrafts, antiques, art, and stone sculptures. Nearby Bansai is home for Her Majesty the Queen's Royal Folk Arts and Crafts Centre where student's produce unique handicrafts and wooden products.

Pattaya, a bustling seaside resort town located southeast of Bangkok, has long served as Thailand's center for sun, surf, and sex. Amidst the many hotels, restaurants, and bars you will find numerous shops offering everything from resortwear and copy watches to handicrafts and jewelry.

Phuket, located approximately 900 kilometers south of Bangkok, is Thailand's premier resort island. Beautiful beaches, lovely scenery, terrific seafood restaurants, and an easy-going atmosphere make this a delightful place to visit for a few days of rest and relaxation. Phuket also offers many shopping opportunities for handcrafted items. While most products are imported from Bangkok and Chiangmai, Phuket also produces local jewelry, textiles, and handicrafts of interest to many visitors.

APPROACH IT RIGHT

If approached in the right manner, Bangkok, Chiangmai, and beyond offer wonderful shopping opportunities not found in other Asian cities and countries. To be most rewarding, shopping in Thailand must be approached differently from other places in Asia. For example, as a rapidly developing Third World country which has recently entered the fringes of the Newly Industrialized Countries (NICs), Thailand has a long, continuous, and proud history, traditions, and culture. These are clearly expressed in Thailand's art and handicrafts. Moreover, since the neighboring countries of Burma, Laos, and Cambodia are largely closed to tourists and businesspeople, Thailand functions as the major Asian middleman for acquiring and marketing beautiful arts, antiques, and handicrafts—most of which are compatible with contemporary Western homes—from these surrounding countries.

Thailand is also one of the world's leading producers of inexpensive reproductions and copies of antiques, designer label clothes, and accessories. Although the quality of copies varies greatly—from outstanding to poor—individuals not interested in paying high prices for authentic and copy-protected goods will indeed find Thailand to be a shopper's paradise! Knowing about such products in Thailand, you are well advised to develop a shopping strategy that will put you in the right place to buy such unique products.

Wherever you go in Thailand, you will find plenty of unique shopping opportunities. Thai craftspeople are still some of Asia's most talented and prolific artisans who produce good quality products at inexpensive prices. Our recommendation: **shop in Thailand as soon as possible before the craft skills decline in response to its rapidly developing urban economy and prices increase due to rising labor costs.**

FOCUS ON QUALITY AND VALUE

Shopping and Traveling in Exotic Thailand is designed to provide you with the necessary **knowledge and skills** to become an effective shopper throughout Thailand. We especially designed the book with two major considerations in mind:

- Do quality shopping for items that have value.
- Discover unique items that can be integrated into your home and/or wardrobe.

As you will quickly discover, this is not a book on how to find great bargains in inexpensive Thailand, although we do show you how to bargain as well as where and how to find bargains. Nor are we preoccupied with shopping in weekend and night markets for cheap goods—places we often find disappointing and, with a few exceptions, a waste of precious travel time. And we are not particularly interested in shopping for expensive name-brand luxury goods imported from Europe or manufactured in Bangkok under licensing arrangements which are beginning to appear in Bangkok shops in response to the shopping preferences of Japanese, Taiwanese, and Korean tourists and Bangkok's wealthy residents. These items tend to be overpriced and reflect an "imported" shopping culture of little appeal to us since we are primarily interested in finding quality local products expressive of local cultures.

While you will find bargains in Thailand and prices still seem inexpensive, this book primarily focuses on **quality shopping for unique items that will retain their value.** As such, we are less concerned with shopping to save money and to get great bargains than with shopping for local products that can be taken home, integrated into one's wardrobe and home decor, and appreciated for years to come. Rather than work with a cheap tailor or purchase an inexpensive piece of jewelry or art, we prefer finding the best of what there is available and selectively choose those items we both enjoy and can afford. If, for example, you buy one finely tailored suit, a single piece of exquisite jewelry, or a special work of art that can be nicely integrated into your wardrobe or home, chances are these purchases will last much longer, and you will appreciate them for many more years to come than if you purchased several cheap pieces of jewelry or tourist kitsch that quickly loose their value and your interest.

Our general shopping rule is this: **A "good buy" is one that results in the exchange of money for something that has good value; when in doubt, go for quality because quality items will hold their value and you will enjoy them much more in the long run.**

Indeed, some of our most prized possessions from Thailand are those we felt we could not afford at the time, but we purchased them nonetheless because we knew they were excellent quality items and thus they had great value. In retrospect our decisions to buy quality items were wise decisions because these items are things we still love today.

We have learned one other important lesson from shopping abroad: **Good craftsmanship everywhere in the world is declining** due to the increased cost of labor, lack of interest among young people in pursuing the traditional crafts, and erosion of traditional cultures. Therefore, any items that require extensive hand labor and traditional craft skills—such as woodcarvings, textiles, silver and bronze work, ceramics, furniture, basketry, tribal artifacts, and handcrafted jewelry—are outstanding values today because many of these items are disappearing as fewer craftspeople are trained in producing quality arts and crafts. As elsewhere in the world, the general trend in Thailand is to move from producing high quality arts and crafts to creating fakes and copies as well as to mass producing contemporary handicrafts for tourists and export markets.

Throughout this book we attempt to identify the best quality shopping in Thailand. This does not mean we have discovered the cheapest shopping or best bargains. Our search for unique shopping and quality items that retain their value in the long run means many of our recommended shops may initially appear expensive. But they offer top value that you may not find in many other shops.

SELECT YOUR CITIES

If you decide to include all of the shopping places outlined in this book, you will want to start your shopping adventure in Bangkok. However, should you enter Thailand after first visiting Singapore and Malaysia, you may want to initially stop in Phuket and then proceed on to Bangkok before going on to Chiangmai and the North.

We recommend initially spending at least three days in Bangkok where you will have a chance to survey shops, products, prices, and shipping arrangements prior to visiting other areas of the country. If you plan to make many purchases that would require a sea freight shipment from Thailand—at least one cubic meter in volume—Bangkok will become your central shipping point. It's best to begin making shipping arrangements in Bangkok before venturing on to other parts of the country where you may make additional large purchases that will need to be consolidated into a single sea freight shipment from Bangkok.

We recommend making Chiangmai your next stop after Bangkok. This is Thailand's craft center where you will find many items appearing in shops of Bangkok and Phuket for sale in the Night Bazaar and in the numerous factory shops in and around Chiangmai. If you visit Phuket before Chiangmai, you may discover you are purchasing many items made in Chiangmai at twice the Chiangmai prices. From Chiangmai you can rent a car to visit Chiangrai, Maesai, Lampang, and Lamphun. If you wish to visit Mae Hong Son, it's best to fly from Chiangmai rather than make the grueling 11 hour drive.

You will probably want to return to Bangkok for a few days before continuing on to Ayuthaya, Pattaya, or Phuket. From Phuket you can travel to Malaysia, Singapore, Indonesia, or the Philippines. These countries also offer wonderful shopping opportunities. Should you decide to include these countries in your trip, we recommend three other volumes in our "Impact Guides" series: ***Shopping and Traveling in Exotic Singapore and Malaysia***, ***Shopping and Traveling in Exotic Indonesia***, and ***Shopping and Traveling the Exotic Philippines***.

COMPARE CITIES, PRODUCTS, AND PRICES

You may or may not get better buys on handcrafted items in northern Thailand than in Bangkok. The theory that goods are always cheaper at the production source is not always true. While many of the handcrafted items in Bangkok are made in Chiangmai, they are not necessarily available in Chiangmai to most visitors. Many Bangkok shops work directly with factories in Chiangmai by having pieces commissioned to their own design and color specifications. On the other hand, many dealers from Bangkok buy handcrafted items off the open market in Chiangmai—the Night Bazaar, Chiangmai-Sankamphaeng Road, and Hang Dong—places you are likely to visit. In these cases you might be able to buy the same handcrafted items in Chiangmai for one-half the price asked by shops in Bangkok.

In general, however, we find shops in Bangkok tend to have the best quality items; their buyers seem to pick the best of what is available in Chiangmai and other areas in the North. Designs and displays in Bangkok shops are far superior to any found in shops outside Bangkok. Considering the costs of traveling to Chiangmai, as well as the cost of shipping items from Chiangmai to Bangkok, you may do just as well by making purchases in Bangkok. Our general rule for comparative shopping in Bangkok, Chiangmai, and other areas in Thailand is this: **If you see something you love, buy it now; if you wait to find it elsewhere, chances are you won't find a comparable item, and the one you left behind may be gone when you return.** Visit Chiangmai and other areas in Thailand if you have the time. You will find many lovely items in Chiangmai which are not available in Bangkok. Better still, the prices in Chiangmai are very good if you know how to properly shop this city and its hinterland.

ORGANIZE FOR THAILAND

The chapters that follow take you into the best of shopping in Bangkok, Chiangmai, Chiangrai, Maesai, the Golden Triangle, Lampang, Lamphun, Mae Hong Son, Ayuthaya, Pattaya, and Phuket. In so doing, we've attempted to construct a complete **user-friendly book** that first focuses on the shopping process. The book also offers extensive details on the "how," "what," and "where" of shopping in Thailand. It purposely includes a sufficient level of redundancy to be informative, useful, and usable.

The chapters are organized as one would organize and implement a travel and shopping adventure to Thailand. Each chapter incorporates basic details, including names and addresses, to get you started in some of the best shopping areas and shops in each city or town.

Indexes and table of contents are especially important to us and others who believe a travel book is first and foremost a guide to unfamiliar places. Therefore, our index includes both subjects and shops: the shops are printed in bold for ease of reference; the table of contents is elaborated in detail so it, too, can be used as another handy reference index for subjects and products. By using the table of contents and index together, you can access most any information from this book.

The remainder of this book is divided into four parts and 13 additional chapters which look at both the process and content of shopping in exotic Thailand. The next four chapters in Part I—**"Traveling Smart"**—assist you in preparing for your Thailand shopping adventure by focusing on the "how-tos" of traveling. Chapter Two, "Know Before You Go," takes you through the basics of getting to and enjoying your stay in Thailand, including international and domestic transportation and the promises and pitfalls of local travel. Chapter Three, "Prepare For Your Adventure," surveys key pre-trip preparation concerns—costs, customs regulations, money management, packing, and shipping arrangements. Chapter Four, "Arrival and Survival," takes you into Thailand and examines major concerns in getting around with ease—customs, immigration, money, transportation, tours, food, restaurants, accommodations, and safety. Chapter Five, "Pleasures, Pains, and Enjoying Your Stay," prepares you for both the positives and negatives of traveling in Thailand.

Part II—**"Shopping Well"**—introduces Thailand's world of shopping by examining critical "what" and "how" questions. Chapter Six, "Shopping Rules, Bargaining Skills, and Tailoring Tips," prepares you for Thailand's distinct shopping culture where knowing important shopping rules, pricing practices, bargaining strategies, and tailoring considerations are keys to becoming an effective shopper. Chapter Seven, "Major Shopping Choices," surveys the major products you will encounter in your Thailand shopping adventure.

The chapters in Part III—**"Surprising Bangkok"**—examine the "how" and "where" of shopping in Bangkok. Here you will learn how and where to best shop for different products as well as enjoy your stay in one of Asia's most exotic cities. This chapter identifies names, addresses, and telephone numbers of Bangkok's top quality shops.

Part IV—**"Exotic Chiangmai and Beyond"**—focuses on the "how," "what," and "where" of shopping in Chiangmai as well as five other northern towns—Chiangrai, Maesai, Lampang, Lamphun, and Mae Hong Son. It also examines the shopping delights of Ayuthaya, Pattaya, and Phuket. The two chapters in this section take you on the road to discover handcrafted items produced in factories as well as available in small shops and stalls along the Thai-Burmese border, next to temples, and near gorgeous beaches.

The book concludes in Chapter Fifteen with a brief discussion of resources relevant to pre-trip planning as well as sources for importing Thai products for business purposes. Here we discuss the importance of reviewing travel resources, examining tour group options, visiting shops in the U.S. selling Thai products, and identifying wholesalers in Thailand who are eager to work with foreign businesses.

BEWARE OF RECOMMENDED SHOPS

Throughout this book we concentrate on providing you with the necessary knowledge and skills to become an effective shopper in Thailand. We prefer not recommending and listing specific shops and services—even though we have favorite shops we use when shopping in Thailand. We know the pitfalls of doing so. Shops that offered excellent products and service during one of our visits, for example, may change ownership, personnel, and policies from one year to another. In addition, our shopping preferences may not be the same as your preferences.

Our major concern is to outline your shopping options in Thailand, show you where to locate the best shopping areas, and share some useful shopping strategies that you can use anywhere in Thailand, regardless of particular shops we or others may suggest. Armed with this knowledge and some basic shopping skills, you will be better prepared to locate your own shops and determine which ones offer the best products and service in relation to your own shopping and travel goals.

However, we also recognize the "need to know" when shopping in exotic Thailand. Therefore, throughout this book, we list the names and locations of various shops we have found to offer good quality products. In some cases we have purchased items in these shops and can also recommend them for service and reliability. But in most cases we surveyed shops to determine the type and quality of products offered without making purchases. To buy in every shop would be beyond our budget, as well as our home storage capabilities!

When we do list specific shops we do so only as **reference points** from which to start your shopping. We do not guarantee the quality of products or service. In many cases we have found our recommendations to be shops of exceptional quality, honesty, and service. We believe you should have the advantage of this information, but we also caution you to again evaluate the business by asking the necessary questions.

If you rely solely on our listings, you will miss out on one of the great adventures of shopping in Thailand—discovering your own special shops that offer unique items, exceptional value, and excellent service.

Should you encounter problems with these recommendations, we would appreciate hearing about your experiences. We can be contacted in care of our publisher: Impact Publications, 4580 Sunshine Court, Woodbridge, VA 22192. While we cannot solve your problems, future editions of this book will reflect the experiences—both positive and negative—of our readers. We appreciate your thoughtful observations and comments.

EXPECT A REWARDING ADVENTURE

Whatever you do, enjoy your shopping and travel adventure to Thailand. This is a very special country that offers unique items that can be purchased and integrated well into many Western homes and wardrobes.

So arrange your flights and accommodations, pack your credit cards and traveler's checks, take your sense of humor, wear a smile, and head for one of the world's most delightful shopping and travel destinations. You should return home with much more than a set of photos and travel brochures and a weight gain attendant with new eating habits. You will acquire some wonderful products and accumulate many interesting travel and shopping tales that can be enjoyed and relived for a lifetime.

Shopping and traveling in exotic Thailand only takes time, money, and a sense of adventure. Take the time, be willing to part with some of your money, and open yourself to a whole new world of shopping in exotic places. If you are like us, your shopping adventure will introduce you to an exciting world of quality products, friendly people, and interesting places that you might have otherwise missed had you passed through these places only to eat, sleep, see sights, and take pictures. When you travel and shop in exotic Thailand, you learn about some exciting places by way of the people, products, and pleasures that define this country's urban and rural cultures.

PART I

TRAVELING SMART

2 KNOW BEFORE YOU GO

The more you know about Thailand before you depart on your adventure, the better prepared you should be to enjoy its many shopping and travel pleasures. However, the pace of change in Thailand is so rapid that it becomes increasingly difficult to give an accurate snapshot of today's Thailand. At best we can provide you with an orientation that should be useful in preparing for Thailand's changing realities.

NEW AND CHANGING REALITIES

Rapid changes are especially evident in Thailand's economic and tourist infrastructure. Just two years ago Thailand's booming tourist industry was the envy of most countries. During most of the year hotel occupancy rates were in the 90 to 100 percent range; the domestic airline was normally fully booked on the Bangkok-Chiangmai run; and inbound tour services, shops, and restaurants reported a booming business.

Unfortunate for tourists, the Thai tourist industry responded to the boom by steeply increasing hotel prices—in some cases doubling and tripling room rates within a 12-month period. Within a two-year period Thailand's tourist infrastructure had become severely strained as millions of tourist flocked to discover what was reputed to be one of Asia's best kept, and inexpensive, travel secrets. Tourists were advised to book their hotels and domestic flights well in advance.

But as prices sharply increased, Thailand began to lose one of its major attractions—its reputation as an inexpensive to reasonably priced destination. Hotel prices peaked in late 1990 with some deluxe hotels charging US$230 per night double occupancy.

The worldwide recession of early 1991 coupled with the Iraq-Kuwait war in the Middle East brought a terrible shock to the booming Thai tourist industry. It literally went bust in early 1991 as hotels experienced record low occupancy rates; in peak season, when hotels were normally fully booked, many major hotels reported 30 to 40 percent occupancy rates. At the same time, more new hotels where opening in anticipation of accommodating the 12,000+ visitors attending the annual World Bank meeting in Bangkok and a continuing booming tourist industry. The World Bank group came and went but the tourist industry has yet to return to the booming 1989 and 1990 period.

The good news for tourists is that airline seats and hotel rooms are now much easier to find and hotel rates have fallen accordingly. Thailand's most serious tourist problem remains Bangkok's continuing nightmare of traffic congestion accompanied by noxious fumes and air pollution.

If there is one thing you will find most unattractive about Thailand, it is Bangkok's terrible traffic and pollution. The inability, or unwillingness, of the government to resolve these problems is legend. Indeed, recently it further exacerbated the problems by drastically lowering import duties on automobiles which, in turn, has resulted in a large influx of automobiles onto Bangkok's already gridlocked roads, streets, and lanes. Consequently, **where you stay** in Bangkok will make a significant difference in how much you enjoy this city as wel as your impression of Thailand. If you stay near the central shopping areas, you can walk to most places and thus avoid the hassles of being continuously stranded in creeping traffic.

BOOMING ECONOMY, BURSTING INFRASTRUCTURE

Please keep in mind that Thailand is an advanced Third World nation quickly entering the ranks of the Newly Industrialized Countries (NICs), such as Hong Kong, South Korea, Taiwan, and Singapore. As such, it exhibits a booming economy centered in and around Bangkok, a rapidly expanding middle class and affluent upper class, and a severely strained infrastructure trying to cope with unexpected domestic consumer demands as well as one of the world's most rapidly developing tourist industries.

The infrastructure problem is evident everywhere, from crowded port and shipping facilities to overloaded transportation, communication, and energy systems. Experiencing one of Asia's most remarkable economic boom cycles, Thailand's overheated economy has been advancing at unprecedented levels as it enters into a new era of industrialization and tourism. It has recently come in for a soft landing attendant with the recession of 1991.

You will be visiting a very different Thailand than we knew 5, 10, or 20 years ago. Today's Thailand is undergoing dramatic economic, social, cultural, and political changes. Increasingly playing important political and economic roles throughout Asia, today's Thailand still exhibits some rough edges which contribute to its exotic image and, in turn, appear as inconveniences for many foreign visitors.

We do not hesitate to strongly recommend what has become our favorite travel destination. We have traveled to and from Thailand numerous times during the past three decades, lived and worked in its many cities, towns, and villages, and ventured into nearly every one of its 73 provinces. Nonetheless, Thailand always surprises us with its changes from year to year. Despite rising costs, it continues to be a good travel buy. It's a convenient country to get to and, except for Bangkok's horrendous traffic and some overloaded tourist facilities, it's a relatively convenient country to get around in.

LOCATION AND AREA

Thailand is located in the heart of mainland Southeast Asia, south of China, west of Laos and Cambodia, east of Burma, and north of Malaysia and Indonesia. Extending approximately 1000 miles from north to south and 500 miles from east to west, Thailand's nearly 200,000 square miles make this country approximately the size of France or the state of Texas. Its population of 57 million is primarily rural (83 percent).

The largest city is the capital, Bangkok, with a population of nearly 7 million. The second largest city, Chiangmai in the North, has a population of nearly 200,000. These two cities are the primary destinations for most tourists and the areas for the most exciting shopping adventures. Except for a few beach resorts in the Southeast and South and a few towns in the North, other cities and towns are relatively nondescript small towns primarily functioning as administrative and commercial centers for Thailand's highly centralized government.

CLIMATE, SEASONS, AND WHEN TO GO

Thailand is primarily an equatorial and tropical monsoonal country where the climate is often hot and humid. For many visitors from temperate climates, Thailand appears to have three similar seasons: hot, hotter, and hottest!

But in reality there are three distinct seasons which vary somewhat in different parts of the country. The hot season occurs between March and May, with temperatures ranging from 86F to 104F. The rainy season begins in May and lasts through October. A highly unpredictable season, it is marked by frequent rains, high humidity, and sporadic flooding in Bangkok. March through June can be the most miserable months of the year; the hot and rainy seasons meet in what is often an oppressive combination of hot and sticky days and nights, where the only relief is escape into air-conditioned buildings or your hotel swimming pool.

Thailand's cool season begins in November and ends in February. The temperatures are pleasant, skies are clear, and the humidity is relatively low. During the cool season temperatures are known to drop into the low 30s(F) in the North, but normally the temperatures are in the low to mid-80s in throughout Thailand. This is the best season to visit Thailand and, accordingly, it is the peak tourist season for visitors.

Thailand's year-round tropical climate is relatively easy to prepare for in terms of clothing. You should take lightweight clothes, preferably loose fitting cottons, for most of the year. If you plan to visit during the cool season and travel to the North, be sure to pack a sweater, jacket, warm socks, and gloves. While it rarely freezes, the combination of cool temperatures and high humidity can be extremely chilling.

If you visit Thailand during the hot and humid season, be sure to pace yourself. Limit the amount of walking you do, slow your walking pace, and relax in the air-conditioned comfort of hotels, department stores, restaurants, and shops. The easier you take Thailand, the easier it will be on you.

GETTING THERE

Getting to Thailand is relatively convenient. Most visitors enter Thailand by way of Bangkok International Airport, located just north of Bangkok. Serviced by 49 international airlines, this new airport is efficient.

Air connections to Bangkok are relatively good. It is best to fly the Pacific route if you originate in the U.S. or Canada. From New York City, you can fly directly to Bangkok in about 24 hours—depending on the airline and routing. It's a long one-day journey, but it goes surprisingly fast if you take a good book with you and plug in the head phones for viewing what hopefully may be some good movies!

The national carrier, Thai Airways International, is a fine airline and a great way to introduce you to Thailand. The airline has a well deserved reputation for excellent service and safety. From the moment you enter the plane to when you deplane, you will be pampered with Thai-style service. The airline flies to 72 cities in 37 countries. In North America, Thai originates in Toronto, Seattle, and Los Angeles. It regularly services numerous cities in Europe, Asia, and Australia. If flying Thai Airways International, it's convenient to ticket your domestic transportation on Thai Airways at the same time. The domestic fleet uses airbuses on many of the busiest routes. Their fleet is sparkling clean and the flight attendants give gracious service.

While we usually arrive by air, a wonderful way to enter Thailand is by **train**. One of the world's most delightful and romantic rail trips originates in Singapore, transverses the length of the Malay Peninsula, enters southern Thailand, and ends at the Hualampong Railway Station in Bangkok. Along the way you may wish to stop in Kuala Lumpur and Penang—two large Malaysian cities offering some good shopping opportunities for Malay handcrafted and duty-free items. The Singapore-Bangkok Express takes about 54 hours. Along the way you will get a quick glimpse of rural and urban Southeast Asian life. The first-class accommodations are more than adequate, but you are well advised to take along some snacks and buy bottled drinks, fruits, and well cooked foods from vendors at the various stops along the way. This trip is best enjoyed in the privacy of your own air-conditioned sleeping compartment. It's worth paying a little extra to really enjoy this wonderful rail trip.

You can also drive a **car** from Singapore to Bangkok, but we do not recommend such an adventure, especially through southern Thailand. The road systems are excellent in Singapore and Malaysia and good in Thailand, but the rules of the road—or lack thereof—change dramatically as soon as you enter Thailand. Indeed, many Malaysians go through culture shock in Thailand, much of which is directly attributed to Thai driving habits. Malays fear driving in Thailand where only one rule seems to govern roads: the faster and more aggressive the better. Unless you have adapted to the Thai defensive driving style, driving in many parts of Thailand is simply dangerous. And should you get into an accident, you will likely be detained. This could mean an interruption to your otherwise marvelous trip.

Finally, you can enter Thailand by **bus**, but only from the South. There are no rail or road connections operating from Burma, Laos, or Cambodia. The tour buses in the South are relatively convenient and efficient. However, their small seats make them uncomfortable for many Westerners, and they are dangerous with accidents frequently occurring. Unless you want to live dangerously on the edge of Thailand's local transportation system, we recommend avoiding buses. Whenever possible, fly or take the train in Thailand.

Package tours are available to Thailand, but they are not as numerous as those to Hong Kong or Singapore. Many are package tours to Hong Kong and Singapore with three to four-day extensions to Bangkok and Chiangmai. This is unfortunate. While these are good values for your money, three to four days in Thailand simply are not enough. Thailand should be more than an after-thought or a brief add-on. It deserves major attention as a primary travel and shopping destination in its own right. It has much more to offer than many of the more popular tourist destinations in Asia. We suggest a minimum of seven days to tour and shop Bangkok properly. Better still, plan at least an 11-day trip—seven days in Bangkok and four days in Chiangmai. You'll need this much time to shop and enjoy the sights.

Should you decide to do Thailand **on your own**, you can easily arrange your own transportation and accommodations. We recommend booking your hotels in advance—especially if you are arriving during the peak tourist season. Once you arrive, you will find numerous tour services available to assist you with your stay. Most, however, focus on seeing sights in and around Bangkok. None of these services focus on shopping. With this book and a few other key resources, you will be well prepared to shop Thailand on your own and have a marvelous time doing so.

COSTS AND PACKAGE TOURS

Thailand is one of those wonderful places where you can easily travel on a limited budget or splurge to your heart's content. The country is still a favorite destination for budget travelers who manage to travel on US$10 to US$20 a day by staying in guest houses and hotels for US$5 to US$10 a night and eating well from small restaurants and food stalls for US$5 to US$8 a day. On the other hand, you will find some of the world's best hotels in Bangkok with rooms going for US$100 to US$250 a night. You can dine at some of Asia's finest restaurants for US$20 to US$40 per person.

Your biggest expense is likely to be for the shopping treasures you discover in Thailand. Here, we cannot give you specific guidelines other than the general observation that you should take enough cash, personal checks, and traveler's checks, as well as sufficient credit limits on your credit cards, in anticipation of finding plenty of treasures in Thailand. If you love good quality jewelry or are a serious collector of art, antiques, and home decorative items, you may quickly find yourself in financial trouble given the large number of quality items you will probably want to buy in Bangkok and Chiang-mai!

Since Thailand is now a major travel destination, many tour packages include Thailand in their Asian itineraries. These packages range from the inexpensive (US$1120 for 6 days) to expensive (US$5000+ for 15 days) inclusive of international airfare. Asian Dreams (800/628-0600), Four Winds Travel (800/248-4444), Pacific Bestours (800/562-0208), TBI (800/223-0266), and Visitours (800/367-4368) are some of the better known such tours.

Thai Airways offers some great value tour packages called the "Royal Orchid Holidays." They include international transportation and local arrangements. The packages are very flexible, enabling individuals to structure their own visit to Thailand without having to join an organized tour group. You can go with the basic 6-day package for $1120, which includes round-trip airfare from the United States (west coast), first-class accommodations, transfers, American breakfast, and a half-day tour of Bangkok. Once in Thailand, you can join numerous local tours. You can also add on to these tours by including other destinations in Thailand or other cities in Asia. For further information, including a brochure outlining various options, contact your travel agent or call Thai Airway at 800/426-5204 (punch "4" or ask for the "Tour Department").

If you want to travel deluxe class and money is no object, try the organized package tours offered by Abercrombie & Kent (800/323-7308) and Travcoa (800/992-2003).

If in doubt about your travel and tour options to Thailand, contact your local travel agent for information on special air fares as well as these and other package tours.

DOCUMENTS

Thailand is a relatively easy country to get into and out of if you plan to be there less than two months. Most foreign nationals who plan a week or two in Thailand need only a valid passport and a confirmed ticket for onward passage. Upon arrival you receive a 15-day "transit visa" which normally cannot be extended. If you plan to stay longer, you should apply for a 60-day "tourist visa" from a Thai embassy or consulate prior to departing for Thailand.

CONVENIENCE

Thais have an insightful saying about the relative comfort and convenience of their country: *"Thailand is comfortable but not convenient; the West is convenient but not comfortable."* There is some truth to their comparisons. Thailand is an easy-going, laid-back country where life can be very *sabai* ("comfortable") both physically and mentally. Thailand at times is *mai saduak* ("inconvenient") because of its weak and often makeshift organization, bordering on a kind of charming and exotic Third World chaos. Not everything seems to work according to plan, but it works nonetheless. In Bangkok the traffic is terrible, the pollution is noxious, and the crowds in local shopping centers can be overbearing. The city has too many people trying to go to too many different locations.

Thailand has little of the orderliness and efficiency associated with Hong Kong and Singapore. This is a "muddle-through" country where life is one constant serendipitous affair. The country works, but not at peak performance. Yet, you can get around Bangkok. Minimize the pollution by taking only air-conditioned vehicles, and shop outside the congested shopping centers used primarily by locals. Thai service tends to off-set the daily inconveniences of getting things done in Bangkok. If all else fails, you should adopt the relatively stressless *maj pen rai* ("never mind") attitudes of the Thai for dealing with daily inconveniences. This is the "comfort" side of the ubiquitous Thai "comfort/convenience" equation.

The transportation and communication facilities outside Bangkok are relatively convenient, although they are overloaded at times due to the recent surge in economic development. Three of Thailand's greatest strengths are its excellent road, rail, and air systems. English language newspapers are found in most medium-sized towns and cities. Local tours and English-speaking guides can be easily arranged through hotels and agencies in response to your individual needs. Good food and drinks are plentiful everywhere you go. Thailand's major inconveniences are heat and humidity and Bangkok's traffic and pollution.

RESOURCES AND RECOMMENDED READINGS

Numerous useful travel resources are available on Thailand, but they are not well distributed outside Thailand. Thus, you will have difficulty finding good information to plan your trip prior to arriving in Bangkok.

Most of these resources are maps and travel guides focusing on sightseeing, restaurants, hotels, culture, and crafts. Much of what is written about Thailand for tourists and budget travelers is centered on accommodations, restaurants, and the typical tourist attractions found in Bangkok and Chiangmai—questions already addressed by package tours.

For an overview of Thailand, examine the ***APA Insight Guide: Thailand*** and the ***APA Cityguide: Bangkok***. Heavy on color photography, these books give a brief overview of the history and culture of the country as well as insightful summaries of travel to the various regions. The final *"Guide in Brief"* sections provide useful information on hotels, climate, language, and holidays. Read these books before going to Thailand; they are big, bulky, and heavy—not good travel companions.

Most major travel guides in Asia and Southeast Asia devote a brief chapter to Thailand. The chapters give a basic sketch of hotels, restaurants, and sightseeing opportunities. The best of these guides are Fodor's ***Southeast Asia***, Fielding's ***Asia***, Moon's ***Bangkok***, and American Expresses' ***Hong Kong, Singapore, and Bangkok***. Baedeker produces a city guide entitled ***Bangkok***. For budget travelers, the Lonely Planet's volume—***Thailand: A Travel Survival Guide***—gives good advice on how to do Thailand on the cheap. Also look for two new Southeast Asian guides with sections on Thailand: Arthur Frommer's ***Southeast Asia*** and Moon's ***Southeast Asia***. Gault Millau's new ***The Best of Thailand*** is an ambitious attempt to identify Thailand's best restaurants, hotels, and shops. However, we believe it omits many of Thailand's best places and elevates some mediocre ones. Many of these guides are available in local bookstores or they can be ordered through direct-mail by calling or writing the following excellent travel bookstores: **Traveller's Bookstore** (22 W. 52 St., New York, NY 10019, Tel. 212/664-0995), **Book Passage** (51 Tamal Vista Boulevard, Corte Madera, CA 94925, Tel. 800/321-9785), or **Travel Books Unlimited** (4931 Cordell Ave., Bethesda, MD 20814, Tel. 800/220-2665 or 301/951-8533).

Once you arrive in Thailand, you will find several useful local guides and maps. One of the first resources you must buy is Nancy Chandler's illustrated ***Map of Bangkok*** and/or ***Map of Chiangmai***. Both of these colorful maps are filled with useful information on shopping areas, shops, sights, hotels, restaurants, recreation, and transportation. These maps are widely available in major bookstores and hotel sundry shops. Chandler's maps will quickly become your most important travel companion for Bangkok and Chiangmai. If you are coming from the United States, you can acquire the latest editions of these maps by writing to: Nancy S. Chandler, 432 Eldridge Avenue, Mill Valley, CA 94941. Enclose a check for $6.50 ($5.00 plus $1.50 postage and handling) for one map or $12.50 ($10.00 plus $2.50 postage and handling) for both maps made payable to Nancy S. Chandler. California residents should add 6.5% state sales tax. If you need more than two maps, write for information on quantity purchases. The maps are also available through MapLink (25 East Mason Street, Santa Barbara CA 93101, Tel. 805/965-4402).

One of the best local guides to Bangkok is the ***Bangkok Guide*** published by the Australian-New Zealand Women's Group. Designed for expatriates living in Thailand, it's filled with useful information on living and shopping in Thailand. It includes everything from where to buy ballet shoes to how to shop for jewelry. It also includes a copy of Nancy Chandler's ***Map of Bangkok***. If you buy this book, you need not buy the map separately. The book is available in major bookstores in Bangkok, with the best supply found in Asia Books at 221 Sukhumvit Road (between Soi 15 and 17). Also look for Pat Nervo's ***Factory Outlet Shopping Bangkok Style*** which is available at Asia Books. This mistitled book is primarily an annotated listing of all types of shops. Thailand has a few markets, but it simply does not have factory outlets in the sense of Hong Kong. You will be disappointed if you buy this book in expectation of visiting factory outlets in Bangkok! It's primarily a colorful annotated guide to shops in Bangkok, Chiangmai, and a few other areas, including many of the best which are neither factory outlets nor bargain hunter's paradises.

A great deal of tourist literature is available at the airport, hotels, and travel agents in Bangkok. Thailand's national tourism organization, the Tourism Authority of Thailand (TAT), publishes a bi-monthly ***Official Shopping Guide***. This guide lists TAT member shops which display the official TAT insignia, a blue emblem with a figure of a market woman sitting between two baskets. These shops have been screened by the Committee on Thai Handicraft Shop Standard Promotion for their honesty and reliability. Should you have any problems with these shops, TAT will help you resolve them. TAT also prints numerous handouts on individual cities, festivals, and tours, such as the Elephant Roundup in Surin and the Rocket Festival in Yasothon, as well as sponsors a few tours. You may wish to visit their office at Ratchadamnoen Nok Avenue (Tel. 282-1132 thru 7) to pick up literature as well as talk to officials concerning various tours sponsored by TAT. In Chiangmai you may want to visit the TAT office at 105-1 Chiangmai-Lamphun Road, just south of the Narawat Bridge, or call them at 248604 or 248607.

Most major hotels will have copies of several free weekly and monthly publications designed to assist you during your stay in Thailand. These include ***Lookeast: Your Complete Guide to Bangkok and Thailand***; ***Thaiways: A Tourist Companion***; and ***Where***. If you make the Oriental Plaza one of your first shopping stops, you can pick up copies of these publications at the information desk located at the front entrance. However, the informative ***Lookeast*** magazine is increasingly difficult to find in Bangkok.

Two English-language newspapers are published in Bangkok and are widely available in major cities and towns throughout the country: ***The Bangkok Post*** and ***The Nation***. In addition to providing basic coverage of international news, these newspapers include calendars of upcoming events, performances, and specialized tours sponsored by such organizations at TAT, The Siam Society, and the National Museum.

Since the most useful travel guides, books, maps, and magazines on Thailand are difficult to find outside Thailand, or are too academic and specialized for travelers, your best starting point for background reading before arriving in Thailand is the ***APA Insight Guide: Thailand*** and ***APA Insight Cityguide: Bangkok***. Remember, these are not practical trip planning guides—they give you a sense of *"setting"* with their lovely color photographs and discussions of history and culture. Like most other volumes in the APA Series, this one is available worldwide through APA Publications in Singapore or through Prentice-Hall in the United States. For more practical travel information in planning your trip, you may want to survey the various Asian travel guides published annually by Fodor's, Fielding, Baedeker, American Express, Lonely Planet, Frommer, and Moon.

As soon as you arrive in Thailand, you should make a quick trip to the best of Bangkok's bookstores—**Asia Books**. The three branches of this store have excellent collections of general and specialized resources on Thailand. The main Asia Books store is located at 221 Sukhumvit Road, between Soi 14 and 17 (Tel. 252-7277 or 250-1833). It is conveniently located just east of the huge Ambassador Hotel restaurant and shopping complex on Sukhumvit Road. Its branch stores are found on the second floor of the pleasant Peninsula Plaza shopping arcade on Rajadamri Road, next to the Regent Hotel (Tel. 253-9786 thru 8)—a great place to start your whole shopping adventure in Thailand—and in the Landmark Plaza (attached to the Landmark Hotel on Sukhumvit Road) and in the new Thaniya Plaza (between Silom and Suriwongse Roads near Patpong).

Other good bookstores in Bangkok include **D.D. Books** (32/9-10 off Soi 21 Sukhumvit Rd., Tel. 258-3703), the **Bookseller** (81 Patpong Rd., Tel. 233-9632 or 233-1717), **Robinson Book City Yajimaya** (222 Soi 1 Siam Square, Tel. 251-5433 and 250-0710), and the bookstores in the five branches of the **Central Department Store**, but especially their major distribution center on Silom Road.

When you visit these bookstores or your hotel newsstand and sundry shop, you should look for copies of ***Sawadii*** and ***Living in Thailand*** magazines. You should also find copies of two books on Thailand which make wonderful light reading: Carol Hollinger's ***Mai Pen Rai*** and William Warren's ***Jim Thompson: The Legendary American of Thailand***—both of which can be found in some libraries abroad or obtained through the publisher, Houghton-Mifflin (Boston). If you fall in love with Thai food, these bookstores also stock a good collection of English-language Thai cookbooks, many of which are written for Western kitchens.

If you are interested in arts and crafts but know little about Thailand, don't worry. Once you arrive in Thailand you can quickly learn a great deal about traditional Thai arts, crafts, culture, and religion. One of the best books covering all areas of Thai arts and culture is the special bicentennial issue of ***Sawadii*** magazine—***Sawaddi Special Edition . . . A Cultural Guide to Thailand***. A collection of important articles on different facets of Thai art and culture, this book is available at some bookstores in Bangkok or directly from the American Women's Club of Thailand, 33 Rajadamri Road—a short walk from the Peninsula Plaza and Regent Hotel. Two special issues of ***Arts in Asia*** magazine are devoted to Thai arts and handicrafts: May-June 1978 and November-December 1982 (***Bangkok Bicentennial Issue***). For additional information on Thai arts and handicrafts, visit **The National Museum** (next to Thammasat University and across from Pramane Ground on Naprathat Road). A good way to see and understand this interesting museum is to take the special one-hour English-language tours available at 9:30am, Tuesday through Thursday:

Tuesday:	*Thai Art and Culture*
Wednesday:	*Thai Buddhism*
Thursday:	*Early Thai Art*

The Siam Society also has displays, as well as a great deal of literature and special tours, on Thai arts and crafts. You may want to include their library and museum on your tour of Bangkok: The Siam Society, 131 Soi Asoke, Sukhumvit Road, Tel. 258-3491 or 391-4401.

Many visitors become fascinated with the hilltribe handicrafts. For excellent introductions into the hilltribes and their handicraft traditions, look for these two books in Bangkok's major bookstores: Paul and Elaine Lewis' ***Peoples of the Golden Triangle*** (London: Thames and Hudson), and Margaret Campbell's ***From the Hands of the Hills*** (Hong Kong: Media Transasia).

If you are interested in shopping for home decorative items in Thailand, be sure to get a copy of ***Thai Design*** (Bangkok: Asia Books). This beautifully illustrated book is filled with examples of Thai architecture as well as demonstrates the tasteful use of Thai home decorative items, especially antiques, woodcarvings, and handicrafts. You will find other books that specialize on different types of Thai handcrafted items, from textiles to pottery. For those interested in Lao textiles now widely available in Thailand, be sure to pick up a copy of Patricia Cheesman's ***Lao Textile: Ancient Symbols—Living Art*** (Bangkok: White Lotus Co.). If your interests include Burmese lacquerware, look for Sylvia Fraser-Lu's ***Burmese Lacquerware*** (Bangkok: The Tamarind Press). An excellent resource for understanding the unique Burmese tapestries called ***kalagas*** is Mary Anne Stanislaw's ***Kalagas: The Wall Hangings of Southeast Asia*** (Menlo Park, CA: Ainslie's). Most of these books are available at Asia Books as well as at a few antique and home decorative shops such as the Elephant House in Bangkok. In the United States, many of these and other books on Thailand are available through Oceanie-Afrique Noire (9 East 38th St., New York, NY 10016, Tel. 212/779-0486) or the Cellar Book Shop (18090 Wyoming, Detroit, MI, 48221, Tel. 313/961-1776). Write or call them for copies of their most recent catalogs. If you are in the Washington, DC area, be sure to visit the Banana Tree (1129 King St., Alexandria, VA 22314, Tel. 703/836-4317). This shop carries a good selection of books on Thailand amongst its many quality arts, antiques, and home decorative items from Thailand.

TOURISM AUTHORITY OF THAILAND

The Tourism Authority of Thailand (TAT) is Thailand's official government agency responsible for promoting tourism. This organization has offices throughout the world which provide information on traveling to Thailand. They also maintain branch offices in nine of Thailand's 73 provinces. If you contact their offices, they can provide you with brochures and answer any questions you might have concerning travel to Thailand. The TAT overseas offices are found in:

AUSTRALIA: Royal Exchange Bldg., 12th Floor
56 Pitt Street
Sydney 2000
Tel. (02) 277-549, 277-540

HONG KONG: Fairmont House, Room 401
8 Cotton Tree Drive
Central
Tel. (5) 868073

JAPAN:	Hibiya Mitsui Bldg. 1-2 Yurakucho 1-Chome Chiyoda-ku, Tokyo 100 Tel. (03) 580-6776-7
	Hirano-Machi Yachiyo Bldg., 5th Floor 2-8-1 Hirano-Machi Higashi-Ku, Osaka 541 Tel. (06) 231-4434
MALAYSIA:	c/o Royal Thai Embassy 206 Jalan Ampang Kuala Lumpur Tel. 2480958
SINGAPORE:	c/o Royal Thai Embassy 370 Orchard Rd. Singapore 0923 Tel. 2480958
FRANCE:	Office National du Tourisme de Thailande 90 Avenue des Champs Elysees 75008 Paris Tel. 4562-8656 FAX (331) 45637888
ITALY:	Ente Nazionale per il Turismo Thailandese Via Barberini, 50 00187 Roma Tel. (06) 4747410, 4747660 FAX (396) 4747660
UNITED KINGDOM:	49 Albemarle Street London WIX 3 FE, England U.K. Tel. (01) 499-7670 FAX (01) 6295519
GERMANY:	Thailandisches Fremdenverkehrsburo Bethmann Str. 58/IV D-6000 Frankfort/M.1 Tel. (069) 295-704

U.S.A.

5 World Trade Center
Suite No. 2449
New York, NY 10048
Tel. (212) 432-0433
FAX (212) 9120920

3440 Wilshire Blvd., Suite 1101
Los Angeles, CA 90010
Tel. (213) 392-2353
FAX (213) 380-6476

Once you arrive in Thailand, you may want to visit the head TAT office which is found on Ratchadamnoen Nok Avenue (Tel. 282-1143 thru 7 or FAX 662-280-1744), just opposite the United Nations complex. This office also sponsors tours to different provinces. The local and regional TAT offices are found at:

CENTRAL REGION:

KANCHANABURI
Saeng Chuto Road
Amphur Muang
Kanchanaburi 71000
Tel. (034) 511200

PATTAYA
382/1 Chaihat Road
South Pattaya 20260
Tel. (038) 428750, 429113

NORTHERN REGION:

CHIANGMAI
105-1 Chiangmai-Lamphun Rd.
(just south of the Narawat Bridge)
Amphur Muang
Chiangmai 50000
Tel. (053) 248604, 248607

PITSANULOK
209/7-8 Surasi Trade Center
Boromtrailokanat Road
Amphur Muang
Phitsanulok 65000
Tel. (055) 252742, 252743

NORTHEAST REGION:	NAKHON RATCHASIMA (KORAT) 2102-2104 Mittraphap Rd. Tambon Nai Muang Amphur Muang Nakhon Ratchasima 30000 Tel. (044) 243427, 243751
	UBON RATCHATHANI Sala Prachakhom Si Narong Rd. Amphur Muang Ubon Ratchathani 34000 Tel. (054) 255603
SOUTHERN REGION:	PHUKET 73-75 Phuket Road Amphur Muang Phuket 83000 Tel. (076) 212213, 211036
	HAT YAI 1/1 Soi 2 Niphat Uthit 3 Rd. Hat Yai, Songkhla 90110 Tel. (074) 243747, 245986
	SURAT THANI 5 Talat Mai Rd. Ban Don Amphur Muang Surat Thani 84000 Tel. (077) 282828, 281828

While most of these offices are organized to promote tourism by dispensing information on local attractions, they also can assist you should you have any problems with local shops.

3 PREPARE FOR YOUR ADVENTURE

While Thailand is a relatively comfortable and convenient place to travel, it requires some basic pre-trip preparation if you plan to shop this country properly. You will especially want to anticipate the most important aspects of any trip to this part of the world by budgeting overall costs, checking on customs regulations, managing your money, gathering essential shopping information, packing right, and anticipating shipping alternatives and arrangements.

MINIMIZE UNCERTAINTY

Preparation is the key to experiencing a successful and enjoyable shopping adventure in Thailand. But preparation involves much more than just examining maps, reading travel literature, and making airline and hotel reservations. Preparation, at the very least, is a process of minimizing uncertainty by learning how to develop a shopping plan, manage your money, determine the value of products, handle customs, and pack for the occasion. It involves knowing what products are good deals to buy in Thailand in comparison to similar items back home. Most important of all, preparation helps organize and ensure the success of all aspects of your adventure.

MAKE A PLAN

Time is money when traveling abroad. If you plan to include all shopping areas identified in this book, you will need to do some detailed planning. Given the near full capacity operation of many Thai Airways routes, we highly recommend making all domestic air reservations at least two months in advance of your arrival in Bangkok. This is especially important if you plan to visit Chiangmai.

The better you plan and use your time, the more time you will have to enjoy your trip. If you want to use your time wisely and literally hit the ground running, you should plan a detailed, yet tentative, schedule for each day. Begin by doing the following:

- Identify each city, town, and area you intend to visit.
- Block out the number of days you plan to visit in each area.
- List those places you feel you "must visit" during your stay.
- Leave extra time daily for unexpected discoveries.

Keep this plan with you and revise it in light of new information.

At a minimum, we recommend 5-7 days in Bangkok; 3-5 days in Chiangmai; 2-3 days if your itinerary includes Chiangrai, Maesai, Lampang, and Lamphun; and 2-4 days for Phuket. You may also want to include another week or two in order to visit other areas, such as Mae Hong Son, Tak, and Phitsanoluk in the North; Sukhothai, Rathburi, and Kanchanaburi, and Pattaya in the Central region; Nakorn Ratchasima (Korat) and Khon Kaen in the Northeast; and Nakorn Si Thammarat, Songkla, and Hatyai in the South. While these areas do not offer as many shopping opportunities as the main areas covered in this book, they are interesting areas to visit and they do offer some shopping opportunities. The Tourism Authority of Thailand will be able to give you information on these areas. The head office in Bangkok sometimes sponsors tours to these and other locations outside the major tourist destinations of Bangkok, Chiangmai, and Phuket.

CREATE YOUR OWN GOOD LUCK

Thailand is a very special place where you are likely to encounter a great deal of good luck. It's a great place for dashing well designed plans, altering expectations, and experiencing serendipity. The funniest and most unexpected events usually arise in Thailand to make any travel and shopping adventure to this country a most rewarding and memorable one.

But just how much pre-trip planning should you do? Our experience has taught us that planning is fine, but don't overdo it and thus ruin your trip by accumulating a list of unfulfilled expectations. Planning needs to be adapted to certain realities which often become the major highlights of one's travel and shopping experiences.

Good luck is a function of good planning: you place yourself in many different places to take advantage of new opportunities. You should be open to unexpected events which may well become the major highlights of your travel and shopping experiences.

If you want to have good luck, then plan to be in many different places to take advantage of new opportunities. Visit, for example, many different shopping centers, hotel shopping arcades, factories, and markets in both Bangkok and Chiangmai if you want to experience a truly rewarding shopping adventure. Expect to alter your initial plans once you begin discovering new and unexpected realities. Serendipity—those chance occurrences that often evolve into memorable and rewarding experiences—frequently interferes with the best-laid travel and shopping plans. Welcome serendipity by altering your plans to accommodate the unexpected. You can do this by revising your plans each day as you go. A good time to summarize the day's events and accomplishments and plan tomorrow's schedule is just before you go to bed each night.

Keep in mind that your plan should be a means to an end—experiencing exciting travel and shopping—and not the end itself. If you plan well, you will surely experience good luck on the road to a successful adventure in Thailand!

CONDUCT RESEARCH AND NETWORK FOR INFORMATION AND ADVICE

Do as much research as possible before you depart on your Thailand adventure. A good starting place is the periodical section of your local library. Here you may find a few magazine and newspaper articles on travel and shopping in Thailand. Several travel magazines and newspapers as well as the travel sections of major newspapers, such as the *New York Times* and the *Los Angeles Times*, run special sections on shopping around the world. Occasionally an article will appear on shopping in Thailand.

You should also write, call, or fax the Tourism Authority of Thailand nearest you for information on shopping and travel to Thailand. See pages 30-31 in Chapter Two for contact information on these offices. We also recommend **networking for information and advice**. You'll find many people, including relatives, friends, and acquaintances, who have traveled to Thailand and are eager to share their experiences and discoveries with you. They may recommend certain shops where you will find excellent products, service, and prices. Ask them basic "who," "what," "where," "why," and "how" questions:

- **What** shops did you particularly like?
- **What** do they sell?
- **How** much discount could I expect?
- **Whom** should I talk to?
- **Where** is the shop located?
- **How** do I get what I want?
- **Is** bargaining expected?

Once you arrive in-country, be sure to contact the local TAT offices. Of the cities outlined in this book, only Bangkok, Chiangmai, and Phuket have TAT offices. However, Lampang also operates its own tourist promotion office separate from TAT. Local municipal (*tesaban*) and provincial (*changwat*) offices may be able to assist you, although most are not organized to assist tourists. Nonetheless, if you have questions, someone in these offices will attempt to assist you with information. Most cities and towns also have local branches of the Lions, Rotary, and Jaycees whose members will be more than happy to meet and assist fellow members from other countries.

CHECK CUSTOMS REGULATIONS

It's always good to know customs regulations **before** leaving home. If you are a U.S. citizen planning to return to the U.S. from Thailand, the United States Customs Service provides several helpful publications which are available free of charge from your nearest U.S. Customs Office, or write P.O. Box 7407, Washington, D.C. 20044.

- ***Know Before You Go*** (Publication #512): outlines facts about exemptions, mailing gifts, duty-free articles, as well as prohibited and restricted articles.

- ***Trademark Information for Travelers*** (Publication #508): deals with unauthorized importation of trademarked goods. Since you will find many copies of trademarked items in Thailand, this publication will alert you to potential problems with custom inspectors prior to returning home.

- ***International Mail Imports*** answers many travelers' questions regarding mailing items back to the U.S. The U.S. Postal Service sends all packages to customs for examination and assessment of duty before they are delivered to the addressee. Some items are free of duty while others are dutiable. The rules have recently changed on mail imports, so do check on this before you leave the U.S.

- ***GSP and the Traveler*** itemizes goods from particular countries that can enter the U.S. duty-free. GSP regulations, designed to promote the economic development of certain Third World countries, permit many products, especially arts and handicrafts, to enter the United States duty-free. Most items purchased in Thailand will be allowed to enter duty-free. However, many items from Thailand—especially some jewelry and textiles—will be dutiable if they are not part of your US$400 exemption.

MANAGE YOUR MONEY WELL

It is best to carry traveler's checks, two or more major credit cards with sufficient credit limits, U.S. dollars, and a few personal checks. Our basic money rule is to **take enough money and sufficient credit limits so you don't run short**. How much you take is entirely up to you, but it's better to have too much than not enough when shopping in Thailand.

We increasingly find **credit cards** to be very convenient when traveling in Thailand. We prefer using credit cards to pay for hotels and restaurants and for major purchases as well as for unanticipated expenses incurred when shopping. Most major hotels and shops honor MasterCard, Visa, American Express, and Diner's cards. It is a good idea to take one or two bank cards and an American Express card. Take plenty of **traveler's checks** in U.S. denominations of $50 and $100. Smaller denominations are often more trouble than they are worth since Thailand charges a small stamp tax for each check cashed. You will receive a better exchange rate on traveler's checks than cash even though an official stamp tax is added to each check you cash. While banks and money-changers give the best exchange rates, at times you'll find hotels to be more convenient because of their close proximity and better hours. Most major banks, hotels, restaurants, and shops accept traveler's checks.

Personal checks can be used to obtain traveler's checks with an American Express card or to pay for goods to be shipped later—after the check clears your bank. Remember to keep one personal check aside to pay customs should you have dutiable goods when you return home.

Use you own judgment concerning how much **cash** you should carry with you. Contrary to some fearful ads, cash is awfully nice to have in moderate amounts—especially in smaller bills—to supplement your traveler's checks and credit cards. But of course you must be very careful where and how you carry cash. Consider carrying an "emergency cash reserve" primarily in US$50 and US$100 denominations, but also a few US$20's for small currency exchanges. These cash reserves will come in handy in many places you shop in Thailand.

USE CREDIT CARDS WISELY

Credit cards can be a shopper's blessing. They are your tickets to serendipity, convenience, good exchange rates, and a useful form of insurance. Widely accepted throughout Thailand, they enable you to draw on credit reserves for purchasing many wonderful items you did not anticipate finding when you initially planned your adventure. In addition to being convenient, you usually will get good exchange rates once the local currency amount appearing on your credit slip is converted by the bank at the official rate into your home currency. Credit cards also allow you to float your expenses into the following month or two without paying interest charges. Most important, should you have a problem with a purchase—such as buying a piece of jewelry which you later discover was misrepresented —your credit card company will sometimes assist you in recovering your money and returning the goods. Once you discover your problem, contact the credit card company with your complaint and refuse to pay the amount while the matter is in dispute. Businesses accepting these cards must maintain a certain standard of honesty and integrity.

The down-side to using credit cards is that some businesses will charge you a "commission" for using your card, or simply not go as low in the bargaining process as they would for cash or traveler's checks. Commissions will range from 2 to 6 percent. This practice is discouraged by credit card companies; nonetheless, shops do this because they must pay a 4-6 percent commission to the credit card companies. They merely pass this charge on to you. When bargaining, keep in mind that shopkeepers usually consider a final bargained price to be a "cash only" price. If you wish to use your credit card at this point, you will probably be assessed the additional 2 to 6 percent to cover the credit card commission or lose your bargained price altogether. Frequently in the bargaining process, when you near the seller's low price, you will be asked whether you intend to pay cash. It is at this point that cash and traveler's checks come in handy to avoid a slightly higher price. However, **don't be "penny wise but pound foolish."** You may still decide to use your credit card if you suspect you might have problems with your purchase.

A few other tips on the use and abuse of credit cards may be useful in planning your trip. **Use your credit cards for the things that will cost you the same amount no matter how you pay**, such as lodging and meals in the better hotels and restaurants or purchases in most department stores. Consider requesting a higher credit limit on your bank cards if you think you may wish to charge more than your current limit allows.

Be extremely careful with your credit cards. Some restaurants and shops have been known to alter credit card amounts as well as make duplicate cards. Be sure merchants write the correct amount and indicate clearly whether this is U.S. dollars or Thai baht on the credit card slip you sign. It is always a good practice to write the local currency symbol before the total amount so that additional figures cannot be added or the amount mistaken for your own currency. For example, 2500 baht are roughly equivalent to 100 U.S. dollars. It should appear as "B2500" on your credit card slip.

Forging credit cards is more difficult today given present credit card company attempts to make the perfect forge-proof card. Nonetheless, it still happens, and you could become a victim of such an attempt. Should any restaurant, hotel, or shop keep your credit card for an unduly long time, you may become suspicious. Someone could be in a back room making impressions of your card, or running it through the card machine several times in an attempt to create several blank forms with your card number to be filled out later with phony purchases and a forged signature.

And keep a good record of all charges in local currency—and at official exchange rates—so you don't have any surprises once you return home!

SECURE YOUR VALUABLES

Thailand is a relatively safe country to travel in if you take the normal precautions of not inviting potential trouble. We have never had a problem with thieves or pickpockets but neither have we encouraged such individuals to meet us. You are more likely to be cheated or charged exorbitant commissions on purchases than to encounter a simple thief. If you take a few basic precautions in securing your valuables, you should have a worry-free trip.

Be sure to keep your traveler's checks, credit cards, and cash in a safe place along with your travel documents and other valuables. While money belts do provide good security for valuables, the typical 4" x 8" nylon belts can be uncomfortable in Thailand's hot and humid weather. Our best advice is for women to carry money and documents in a leather shoulder bag that can be held firmly and which should be kept with you at all times, however inconvenient, even when passing through buffet lines. Choose a purse with a strap long enough to sling around your neck bandolier style and keep a firm grip on it. Purse snatching is not a common occurrence in Thailand, but it is best to err on the side of caution than to leave yourself open to problems that could quickly ruin your vacation.

For men, keep your money and credit cards in your wallet, but always carry your wallet in a front pocket. If you keep it in a rear pocket, as you may do at home, you invite pickpockets to demonstrate their varied talents in relieving you of your money, and possibly venting your trousers in the process. If your front pocket is an uncomfortable location, you probably need to clean out your wallet so it will fit better.

You may also want to use the free hotel safety deposit boxes for your cash and other valuables. If one is not provided in your room, ask the cashier to assign you a private box in their vault. Under no circumstances should you leave money and valuables unattended in a hotel room, at restaurant tables, or in dressing rooms. You may want to leave your expensive jewelry at home so as not to be as likely a target of theft.

If you get robbed, chances are it will be in part your own fault, because you invited someone to take advantage of you by not being more cautious in securing your valuables.

TAKE ALL NECESSARY SHOPPING INFORMATION

We recommend that you take more than just a copy of this book to Thailand. At the very least you should take:

- A prioritized "wish list" of items you think would make nice additions to your wardrobe, home decor, collections, and for gift giving.

- Measurements of floor space, walls, tables, and beds in your home in anticipation of purchasing some lovely home furnishings, tablecloths, bedspreads, or pictures.

- Photographs of particular rooms that could become candidates for home decorative items. These come in handy when you find something you think—but are not sure—may fit into your color schemes, furnishings, and decorating patterns.

- An inventory of your closets, with particular colors, fabrics, and designs you wish to acquire to complement and enlarge your present wardrobe identified.

- Pictures or models of garments you wish to have made should you decide to have tailoring done. If you have a favorite blouse or suit you wish to have copied, take it with you. It is not necessary to take a commercial pattern, because Thai tailors do not use such devices for measuring, cutting, and assembling garments.

DO COMPARATIVE SHOPPING

You should also do comparative shopping before arriving in Thailand. This is particularly important in the case of gems and jewelry which are available elsewhere in the world and which can be easily appraised for their international market value. Other Thai products tend to be unique and thus difficult to compare with shops in other countries. However, the general rule of thumb we discovered is that most unique Thai items, such as antiques and home decorative items, as well as some gems and jewelry, found in shops outside Thailand cost at least five times what they would cost in the shops of Bangkok and Chiangmai.

Within Thailand, items that originate in Chiangmai will sell for about half what they will cost in Bangkok shops. Prices among shops within cities and towns can vary as much as 500 percent!

If you are a true comparative shopper, you should first make a list of what you want to buy and then do some "window shopping" by visiting local stores at home, examining catalogs, and telephoning for price and availability information. While such comparative shopping is especially useful and easy when pricing electronic goods and cameras, these are not products you will want to purchase in Thailand because they are comparatively expensive given the duties placed on them by the Thai government.

Jewelry, one of Thailand's great shopping buys, begs comparative shopping as well as some minimal level of expertise for determining authenticity and quality. Read as much as you can on different qualities of jewelry and visit jewelry stores at home where you can learn a great deal by asking salespeople questions about craftsmanship, settings, quality, pricing, and discounts. In most of Bangkok's major bookstores and hotel sundry shops, for example, you will find a useful guide to this subject: John Hoskin's ***A Buyer's Guide to Thai Gems and Jewelry*** (Bangkok: Asia Books).

KEEP TRACK OF ALL RECEIPTS

Be sure to ask for receipts and keep them in a safe place. You will need them later for providing accurate pricing information on your customs declaration form. Take a large envelope to be used only for depositing receipts. Organize it periodically by the type of items purchased. List on a separate sheet of paper what you bought and how much you paid for each item. If you are also visiting other countries, list your purchases separately by country. When you go through customs with your purchases organized in this manner, you should sail through more quickly since you have good records of all your transactions.

PACK RIGHT AND LIGHT

Packing and unpacking are two great travel challenges. Trying to get everything you think you need into one or two bags can be frustrating. You either take too much with you, and thus transport unnecessary weight around the world, or you find you took too little.

We've learned over the years to err on the side of taking too little with us. If we start with less, we will have room for more. Your goal should be to avoid lugging an extensive wardrobe, cosmetics, household goods, and library around the world! Make this your guiding principle for deciding how and what to pack: **"When in doubt, leave it out."**

Above all, you want to return home loaded down with wonderful new purchases without paying extra weight charges. Hence, pack for the future rather than load yourself down with the past. To do this you need to wisely select the proper mix of colors, fabrics, styles, and accessories.

You should initially pack as lightly as possible. Remember, except for the winter months in the far north of the country, Thailand's climate is usually hot and humid. Take only lightweight clothes made primarily of natural fibers. Avoid garments made of polyester or wool. Since dress in Thailand is very casual, you need not take suits unless you are going on business. However, if you plan to dine in one of Thailand's top restaurants—the Oriental Hotel's Normandie Grill—men are required to wear a coat and tie. This dining experience is actually worth taking a coat and tie with you to Thailand!

Items you are likely to pack but which are readily and inexpensively available in Thailand include clothes, suitcases, bags, books, maps, stationery, and audiocassettes. You may want to take a minimum number of such items since you can always buy more along the way. But do take all the shoes, specific medications, and makeup you will need on the trip. These items may be difficult to find in the brands you desire.

Since you will do a great deal of walking in Bangkok, take at least one pair of comfortable walking shoes and one pair of dress shoes. Break these shoes in before you take them on this trip. Wearing new shoes for long can be very uncomfortable.

CHOOSE SENSIBLE LUGGAGE

Whatever you do, avoid being a slave to your luggage. Luggage should be both **expandable and expendable.** Flexibility is the key to making it work. Get ready to pack and repack, acquire new bags along the way, and replace luggage if necessary.

Your choice of luggage is very important for enjoying your shopping experience and for managing airports, airplanes, and customs. While you may normally travel with two suitcases and a carry-on, your specific choice of luggage for shopping purposes may be different. We recommend taking two large suitcases with wheels—it's best when one can fit into another; one large carry-on bag; one nylon backpack; and one collapsible nylon bag. If you decide to take hard-sided luggage, one with no middle divider will allow you to pack some of your bulkier purchases. This type of luggage may appear safer than soft-sided luggage, but it is heavier, so you must decide between the trade-off.

Your **carry-on bag** should be convenient—lightweight and with separate compartments and pockets—for taking short trips outside major cities. For example, if you visit Maesai, Chiangrai, Lampang, Lumphun, or Mae Hong Son in the North, you can leave your large luggage pieces at a hotel in Chiangmai and travel only with the carry-on bag for two or three days before returning to Chiangmai.

We also recommend taking a small nylon **backpack** in lieu of a camera bag. This is a wonderfully convenient bag, because it can be used as a comfortable shoulder bag as well as a backpack. It holds our cameras, film, travel books, windbreakers, umbrella, drinks and snacks and still has room for carrying small purchases. We take this bag with us everywhere. When we find our hands filled with purchases, our versatile backpack goes on our back so our hands are free for other items.

A collapsible **nylon bag** also is a useful item to pack. Many of these bags fold into a small 6" x 8" zippered pouch. You may wish to keep this bag in your backpack or carry-on for use when shopping.

SHIP WITH EASE

One of the worst nightmares of shopping abroad is to return home after a wonderful time to find your goods have been lost, stolen, or damaged in transit. This happens frequently to people who do not know how to ensure against such problems. Failing to pack properly or pick the right shipper, they suffer accordingly.

On the other hand, you should not pass up buying lovely items because you feel reluctant to ship them home. Indeed, some travelers confine their shopping to small items that will fit into their suitcases, because they are reluctant to ship large items or they don't know how to go about making shipping arrangements. But you can easily ship from Thailand and expect to receive your goods in excellent condition within a few weeks. We do not hesitate to make large purchases because of shipping considerations. We know we can always get our purchases home with little difficulty. For us, **shipping is one of those things that must be arranged**. We have numerous alternatives from which to choose, from hiring a professional shipping company to hand carrying our goods on board the plane. Shipping may or may not be costly, depending on how much you plan to ship and by which means. Over the years we have shipped numerous times from Thailand and seldom has it been a hassle. While we have experienced some damage, overall the shipping services have been excellent.

Before leaving home you should identify the best point of entry for goods arriving by air or sea. Once you are in Thailand, you generally have five alternatives for shipping goods home:

- Take everything with you.
- Do your own packing and shipping through the local post office (for small packages only).
- Have each shop ship your purchases.
- Arrange to have one shop consolidate all of your purchases into a single shipment.
- Hire a local shipper to make all shipping arrangements.

Taking everything with you is fine if you don't have much and you don't mind absorbing excess baggage charges. If you are overweight, ask about the difference been "Excess Baggage" and "Unaccompanied Baggage." Excess baggage is very expensive while unaccompanied baggage is less expensive, although by no means cheap.

Most major shops are skilled at shipping goods abroad for customers. They often pack the items free and only charge you for the actual postage or freight. Many of these shops use excellent shippers who are known for reasonable charges, good packing, and reliability. Other shops, such as the Elephant House, do their own packing and then arrange shipping through a reputable shipper—unquestionably the finest packing and shipping we have encountered anywhere! If you choose to have a shop ship for you, insist on a receipt specifying they will ship the item and specify that you want the shipment insured.

If you have several large purchases—at least one cubic meter—check with local shippers since it is cheaper and safer to consolidate many separate purchases into one shipment which is well packed and insured. Choose a local company which has an excellent reputation among expatriates for shipping goods. Consult the Yellow Pages under the headings "Shipping" or "Removers." Do some quick research. If you are staying at a good hotel, ask the concierge about reliable shippers. He should be able to help you. Personnel at the local embassy, consulate, or international school know which companies are best. Call a few expatriates and ask for their best recommendations. We also identify in Chapter Eleven (Bangkok) and Chapter Thirteen (Chiangmai) the names, addresses, and telephone numbers of a few shippers considered reliable by local expatriates.

Sea freight charges are usually figured by volume—either by the cubic meter or a container. **Air freight** charges are based on a combination of size and weight. For a sea shipment there is a minimum charge—usually for one cubic meter—you will pay even if your shipment is of less volume. There are also port fees to be paid, a broker fee to get the shipment through customs, and trucking fees to move your shipment from the port of entry to your home. On air freight you pay for the actual amount you ship—there is no minimum charge. You can usually have it flown to the international airport nearest your home and avoid port fees altogether. However, there will be a small customs inspection fee.

If you buy any items that are less than three feet in length and you don't wish to hand-carry them home, consider sending them by **parcel post**. This is the cheapest way to ship. Parcel post tends to be reliable, although it may take three to six months for final delivery. Most shops will take care of the packing and shipping for parcel post. Small and light weight items, such as inexpensive jewelry, can be reliably and inexpensively shipped from Thailand by **Express Mail** with the expectation of arriving within three to four days.

If you have items that are too large for parcel post, but nonetheless are small and relatively lightweight, air freight may be a viable option. Consider air freight if the package is too large to be sent parcel post, but much smaller than the minimum of one cubic meter, and does not weigh an excessive amount relative to its size. Air freight is the transportation of choice if you must have your purchase arrive right away. Sea freight is the better choice if your purchase is large and heavy and you are willing to wait several weeks for its arrival. When using air freight, contact a well established and reliable airline.

We have tried each of these shipping alternatives with various results. Indeed, we tend to use these alternatives in combination. For example, we take everything we can with us until we reach the point where the inconvenience and cost of excess baggage requires some other shipping arrangements. Sometimes we arrange to have all our large purchases consolidated with a Bangkok shipper that takes care of all packing and shipping. They pick up the items from the shops, repack, and combine them in a single sea shipment. At other times we work with one shop which agrees to consolidate all our purchases. This shop takes care of all packing and then arranges to have the items shipped in a single sea shipment. Such approaches require trusting a few key shops, making a long distance telephone call or two, and using Bangkok as the central consolidation and shipping point. While our approaches may seem complicated at first, in practice they work very well and we receive our goods with little or no problem.

When you use a shipper, be sure to examine alternative shipping arrangements and prices and play an active and critical role in the decision-making process. If you don't, you may be overcharged and literally taken for a ride. Unfortunately, shipping is not one of our more highly regarded businesses. Remember, these are very competitive businesses which sometimes want you to think they are the only game in town. For example, the type of delivery you specify at your end can make a significant difference in the overall shipping price. If you don't specify the type of delivery you want, you may be charged the all-inclusive first-class rate. If you choose door-to-door delivery, you will pay a premium to have your shipment clear customs, moved through the port, transported to your door, and unpacked by local movers. On the other hand, it is cheaper for you to have the shipment arrive at your door; you do your own unpacking and you cart away the trash. We don't recommend trying to pick up your shipment at the designated sea port. For US$75 to US$100 a local broker will save you the hassle of clearing customs and moving the shipment out of the port and onto a truck for transport to your home. However, be sure to compare prices of brokers and request that they shop around for reasonably priced truckers. Prices can vary from 100 to 200%! If you ask questions of three or four shippers, brokers, and truckers, you will learn a great deal about how to best ship your goods and save money at the same time. Please don't rely on shipping information provided by a single source.

Make sure your shipment is insured for both damage and loss. We cannot over-stress the importance of finding and establishing a personal relationship with a good shipper who will provide you with services which may go beyond your immediate shipping needs. A good local shipping contact will enable you to continue shopping in Thailand even after returning home!

4 ARRIVAL AND SURVIVAL

After preparing for your adventure, the next step is to face the realities of arrival and survival. You're going to Thailand on what will certainly become a marvelous shopping and travel adventure you will fondly recall for years.

FLYING IN

The flight into Bangkok gives you a glimpse of what lies ahead. If you are arriving from Tokyo, Hong Kong, or Taipei, your plane crosses Vietnam, Laos, and the parched plateau of Northeast Thailand. Within 40 minutes of Bangkok International Airport, the plane clears the final mountain range on the edge of the Korat Plateau and begins descending toward Bangkok.

If you arrive during daylight and on a clear day, you begin seeing Thailand's breadbasket—the flat, fertile Central Plain divided into a checkerboard of rice fields, punctuated by small villages, and outlined by country roads, rivers, canals, and highways. So far Thailand looks flat, green, wet, and sparsely populated. Within 20 minutes of landing you get a good glimpse of the muddy Chao Phya river which empties into the Gulf of Siam and the small boats and freighters working their way to and from Bangkok's busy harbor. It's as if your map has just come alive. As your plane descends onto the runway, you get a quick glimpse of Bangkok's sprawling new airport with Thai military planes at one end of the tarmac and golfers playing with their toys near the edge of the runway. Until you land, there is no hint of what lies ahead in the streets of Bangkok.

AIRPORT

The new Bangkok International Airport is located approximately 20 kilometers north of the city center, adjacent to the old Don Muang International Airport and the newly constructed domestic air terminal. Completed in 1988, this is one of Asia's busiest airports. Servicing 49 international carriers, it is an extremely modern and convenient airport handling nearly 9 million passengers a year. It has everything a modern airport terminal should and also includes some extras normally associated with Thai service—jetways, moving walkways, escalators, elevators, baggage carts, informative signs and television monitors, efficient immigration and customs officials, clean and well lighted facilities, restaurants, shops, money exchange booths, and information and reservation desks. Designed to speed visitors through entry formalities with the maximum of ease, during peak periods of the week the airport can become very congested. In general the most heavily trafficked times of the week are Friday, Saturday, and Sunday, 9am to noon and 4:30pm to 10pm. When we arrive during off-peak periods, we normally walk from our plane and complete Immigration, baggage retrieval, and customs procedures as well as exchange money and arrange for a taxi within 30 to 40 minutes—one of the fastest entry-exit systems in all of Asia.

PROCEDURES

Depending on where you deplane, the walk from the jetway to the immigration booths can be a long one. If you have much hand luggage, use one of the free push carts that are conveniently available as soon as you leave the jetway. You will walk through a long corridor and turn into another corridor which has moving walkways to ease your journey. If you deplane on the tarmac and are shuttled to the terminal building by bus, you will enter the terminal near the row of immigration booths.

The **immigration** booths are located to your left. Except during heavily trafficked periods when several international flights arrive or few immigration officials are available to man the booths, Thai immigration procedures are relatively efficient—moreso than in Hong Kong although less so than in Singapore. They merely process your paper work with the usual reading and stamping procedures.

Your next stop will be the **baggage claim** area. After completing immigration, take the escalator directly to the lower level where you will find the baggage claim area to your right. As you ride down the escalator, look ahead for the board at the front of the hall which lists the baggage carousel for your flight number. Baggage carts are conveniently located under the stairway and behind the baggage carousels.

Customs is located directly in front of the baggage retrieval area. The procedure is very simple. If you have nothing to declare, head for the green exit sign. Custom officials will take your Customs Declaration Form, look it over quickly, and probably let you proceed to the exit and service hall. If you declare anything, go to section marked in red where customs officials will inspect your declaration form and bags and determine if you need to pay any duties. In general we find Thai customs officials in Bangkok to be very accommodating and efficient.

After customs you will enter into the **arrival hall**. Here you will find several convenient services as well as many helpful airport personnel ready to assist you with all of your local arrangements. Immediately ahead of you and to your right is a row of service desks to assist you with airport to city transportation, hotel and tour arrangements, tourist information, and money exchange.

This service section of the airport is a welcome sight for many first-time and seasoned travelers to Thailand. You may wish to use several of these service desks:

- **Airport Taxi:** Stop here to get information and purchase tickets for a special taxi service that runs between the airport and hotels. You have two choices: purchase a 300 baht one-way or a 550 baht roundtrip ticket. We recommend purchasing the roundtrip ticket if you are departing Bangkok by air. You pay at this desk, receive a receipt, and take your receipt outside to queue, more or less, for an Airport Taxi. This is an excellent service offering clean, efficient, and safe taxis. These taxis, however, cost from 50 to 80 baht more than other types of taxis arranged through a nearby taxi stand or along the road adjacent to the airport terminal. We recommend paying a little more for this service because the taxis are bigger, cleaner, and more comfortable than the less expensive alternatives and the drivers tend to be more careful.

- **Thai Hotel Association:** Personnel at this desk will assist you with hotel reservations should you arrive without a booking. They will show you a list of hotels with varying price ranges from which you can select accommodations most appropriate for your budget. They will call hotels to make a reservation. This is a free service you should use if you need a hotel. Trying to phone a hotel on your own from the airport is not worth the bother given this convenient service.

- **Tour Services:** This desk is operated by one tour company which has an airport concession—Travel East Co. Ltd. It is not sponsored by the Tourism Authority of Thailand, although you may be led to believe it is. Since we know nothing about this company and we are generally suspect of companies that have monopoly concessions on tourist services, we are very hesitant to recommend their services. The personnel will show you an illustrated looseleaf notebook that outlines several popular tours. You select your tours and make reservations by paying for them in full. The tour company will then arrange to pick you up at your hotel at your designated time. However, you may or may not wish to use this service. There are many other ways to join organized tours as well as several other excellent tour companies which way be better for you than signing up at the airport. You can easily arrange for tours through your hotel or tour companies in the city. We have over the years used many excellent local tour companies, such as Tour East and Greylines, but we always arrange these tours through hotel tour information desks. If this airport desk were organized by a tour company association representing different tour companies, we would not hesitate to recommend using their services. For now, our recommendation is not to book tours through this desk immediately upon arrival. Instead, take a look at the tour options offered by this company, pick up a copy of their color brochure, and go directly to your hotel where you will be in a better position to survey additional tour options and compare prices. Should you later decide this company is the best for you, call their local number which appears on their brochure. Our experience is there is no need to be in a hurry to arrange a tour at this time. You can always arrange a tour later after you have a better idea what you want to do— in addition to shopping in Bangkok!

- **Tourist Information:** This desk is operated by the Tourism Authority of Thailand. The personnel will answer your questions and provide you with maps and tourist literature. Be sure to stop at this desk since they may have useful information you cannot find at your hotel. A stop here should save you a trip to the main office of the Tourism Authority of Thailand which is not located near the major hotels and shopping areas.

- **Left Baggage:** If you have baggage you wish to store at the airport, use this service desk. You can leave bags here for 20 baht per item per day.

- **Money Exchange:** You will find four money exchange desks in various locations in this arrival hall. Operated by major Thai banks, these exchange desks give rates offered by other banks in the city and much better rates than you will get through hotels. You may do a little better at some banks in the city, but the difference is so small that it may not be worth the bother to use valuable time trying to save a few pennies.

You may also encounter personnel in this arrival hall who will come up to you and ask if you need assistance. Most of these people work for the airport or the airlines and are genuinely helpful. Others work for the tour information desk or taxi company and attempt to steer you into buying their services. While the airport authority has done an admirable job in discouraging the presence of annoying touts and taxi middlemen that used to plague the airport arrival section, occasionally a tout will wander into this area or approach you while you queue for a taxi to offer you his "special" services. Some of these people may misrepresent their affiliation; none of them are officials with the Tourism Authority of Thailand. Some will be very helpful in easing your entry and exit from the airport. Others may want to sell you their services. Use your own judgment as to whom you should trust—but be careful.

In general, **be wary of anyone who wants to rush you into buying a service or give you something "free" such as a shopping tour.** There is no such thing as a free tour and such people invariably are working for commissions derived from your spending habits.

AIRPORT TO CITY TRANSPORTATION

Your transportation alternatives from the airport to the city include hotel car, airport taxi, regular taxi, bus, and train. Several of the major hotels have their own cars waiting for incoming guests. However, these are not free. They cost from 450 baht to 600 baht for a one-way trip from the airport to the hotel. They are usually new cars, clean and driven by sane drivers. As you move through the arrival hall, look for your hotel sign being waved in the midst of the crowd that congregates at the left end of the hall. Ask your hotel representative about their transportation service.

One of the fastest and most convenient services is the **Airport Taxi** service. This service consists of a fleet of special taxis that only operate between the hotel and city. Costing 300 baht per vehicle, these taxis are clean and roomy and their drivers are polite, courteous, and relatively safe operators. You can reserve an Airport Taxi at one of the two service desks on the right in the arrival hall.

A cheaper alternative to the limousine is to catch a **regular taxi**. While airport authorities discourage tourists from using these taxis, they are available if you know where to look for them. In fact, you may be approached inside the arrival hall by someone who offers you a ride to the city in one of these taxis which they claim are cheaper than the airport taxis. These vehicles are found to the right of the arrival hall exit as well as along the highway in front of the airport. Local residents will use the taxis because they are cheaper. You can save anywhere from 100 to 180 baht on the airport to hotel ride if you take one of these vehicles. However, be prepared for a few inconveniences and potential problems. These regular taxis tend to be much smaller and less comfortable than the airport taxis. You may have difficulty communicating with the driver who most likely does not speak English, and the ride itself may be somewhat frightening should bad luck land you a driver who is a speed demon!

If you choose this local curb-side transportation, expect to be quoted several different—and equally outrageous—prices. The first quoted price may be an attempt to see if you know better. Unless otherwise indicated, you are assumed to be new in town and thus a rich and naive tourist ready for plucking. Expect someone to ask for 500 baht, then 400, 300, and 250 baht. If you wait a little and persist, you might be able to rent the whole car for 200 baht. If it is not raining (rain is worth 50 extra baht) and if there are few other customers waiting, you may even get the ride for 150 baht. Such a price brings feigned moans and groans, exaggerated expressions of shock, and claims of poverty (*"But my family must eat!"*) from these entrepreneurs and con artists. Be good-humored about this haggling game by noting that you are a *"poor tourist who loves Thailand."*

You can also get from the airport to the city by **bus or train**. While not the most convenient ways to get to your hotel—especially if you have much luggage—and not recommended unless you are on a tight budget, since you will have to take a taxi once you get into the city, they are the cheapest ways to make the trip—costing less than 50 baht. Ask at the service desk for directions to the bus stand and the train station. You will have to walk across the main highway (take the overhead walkway) to get to the train stop. The train will eventually stop at the main railway station in downtown Bangkok—Hualampong Railway Station. From there you can take a taxi to your hotel, a ride that should not cost more than 80 baht.

If you arrive in Bangkok by **train**, you will most likely get off at the main Hualampong Railway Station. This station is centrally located within a short distance of most major Bangkok hotels and shopping areas. There are plenty of air-conditioned taxis and open-air, motorized trishaws (*rot tuk tuk*) to take you to your destination. Most rides cost 50 to 60 baht, and you should not have to pay more than 80 baht. Like the airport, some of these drivers may try to rip you off by quoting 100 and 200 baht prices. Be persistent and insist on 50 or 60 baht but be willing to give in at 80 baht. When in doubt about a fair price, walk a few hundred feet to the main street, Rama IV Road, and motion for a cab. These drivers should give you a fairer price—50 to 60 baht, depending on your destination.

Our airport to city recommendation: take the 300 baht Airport Taxi service or a car from your hotel. You will pay more, but the additional comfort, convenience, and perhaps safety are well worth the extra amount. After all, it only costs

US$12.50 which is still inexpensive for a 20 kilometer, 45 minute taxi ride.

CUSTOMS AND EXPORTS OF ANTIQUES

You must complete a customs clearance form prior to entering Thailand. It's a standard form with the usual set of questions and prohibitions. For example, you are permitted to bring into Thailand duty-free 200 cigarettes or 250 grams of tobacco, one quart of wine or liquor, and your personal effects. You are prohibited from importing narcotics, obscene materials, firearms and ammunition, and some fruits, vegetables, and plants.

You are required to observe certain rules on exporting Thai Buddha figures larger than those worn as amulets, arts, and antiques. The law prohibits the export of Buddha figures without special permits; arts and antiques need government certification for export. These documentation requirements are observed to varying degrees. During the past five years the Thai government has taken a special interest in closely scrutinizing the export of large Buddhas as well as partial Buddhas. In fact, a few antique dealers have had trouble over the illegal export of such items.

If you are interested in purchasing such items, know beforehand that you may have a potential problem with export permits. Ask your shopkeeper about potential export problems **before** making a sensitive purchase. Most shopkeepers are well aware of the changing political climate that may or may not permit the export of the Thai cultural and religious heritage. Most shopkeepers will take care of the certification requirements for you, or they will recommend how best to ship your goods trouble-free.

One important word of caution before you encounter potential export problems. If you purchase Buddha images or antiques from dealers outside Bangkok, especially in Chiangrai, hand carry those items with you to a reputable shipper in Chiangmai or Bangkok rather than rely on the shop to ship and handle the certification and export permit requirements. Some of our readers have had delivery problems with Buddha images purchased from shops in the Thai-Burmese border town of Maesai in the northern province of Chiangrai. They trusted small shops to take care of all shipping and certification. While some shops may be dishonest, others simply aren't equipped to deliver like the experienced international dealers in Chiangmai and Bangkok. When in doubt, take your purchases with you to a reputable shipper.

AIRPORT TAX AND YOUR LOOSE CHANGE

The airport departure tax on all international flights is 120 baht (US$4.40) per person. This is paid when you check in for your departure flight. Make sure you have enough baht set aside for this tax.

If you have extra baht left, consider "making merit" by dropping it in one of the charity boxes conveniently located in the departure lounge. The donations go to very worthwhile causes.

CURRENCY AND CREDIT CARDS

The baht is the currency of Thailand. It is roughly equivalent to US$.04 and is relatively stable in relation to the US dollar. The baht is divided into 100 satangs and represented by small gold 25 and 50 satang coins. Baht coins are issued in 1, 2, and 5 baht denominations. The most widely circulated baht notes are in 10, 20, 50, 100, and 500 denominations. Each bill is easily distinguished by color and Arabic numbers.

Banks will give you the best exchange rates; hotels will give the least attractive rates. Banks are in abundance and are open from 8:30am to 3:30pm, Monday through Friday. A few branches are open on Saturday. Money changers keep somewhat longer hours, especially on the weekend. Traveler's checks receive a higher exchange rate than notes, but you must pay a small government stamp fee for each transaction.

Credit cards are accepted in major hotels, restaurants, and shops of Bangkok and Chiangmai. The most widely accepted cards are Visa, MasterCard, American Express, and Diner's Club. Smaller shops may accept Visa or MasterCard, but many will attempt to pass the 4-6 percent service charge on to the customer if the bargained price is very low. This is an improper practice, but the profit margins of many small shops are so small that they cannot afford to permit customers to use a credit card on bargained prices. Expect bargained prices to be "cash prices" unless otherwise agreed. When the bargaining really gets tough, many merchants will ask whether you intend to pay cash; you'll get a slightly lower price with cash.

If you use an American Express card and a merchant attempts to add the percentage to your bill, you can either refuse to pay it or ask that it be included as a separate line item on your credit card slip. American Express will reimburse you for the amount as long as it appears as a separate line item. They, in effect, charge the amount back to the merchant since it is against their regulations to charge customers for the service charge under American Express rules.

SECURITY AND SAFETY

Thailand's airport security system is typical for most airports—hand-checks and X-rays of carry-on luggage. Compared to other airports, the Thais are more considerate in handling your personal effects. They are less likely, for example, to tear into your luggage, unwrap packages, and leave you standing with a mess on your hands as often happens in Hong Kong. The present X-ray machines appear to be safe for average speed film. High speed film may be damaged. When in doubt, ask the security personnel to hand inspect your film rather than send it through the X-ray machine. Computer diskettes should be fine when sent through the machines.

Bangkok and most of Thailand are relatively safe for visitors. The biggest problem is traffic. You must be extra cautious when crossing streets and walking along lanes and sidewalks. The buses, taxis, motorized trishaws, motorcycles, and cars can be dangerous if you don't watch them carefully. Many sidewalks are broken or uneven, so watch your step while walking. Thailand does have a crime problem, but few tourists are ever victimized. Nonetheless, use commonsense on where, when, and how you walk in Thailand. Travelers most likely to encounter crime problems are often those who stay in budget accommodations where security tends to be lax. The best hotels will have the best security. Consequently, you may find the extra cost of staying at a deluxe hotel is offset by the better security systems.

TIPPING

There is no pressure to tip in Thailand, although tips are widely accepted and appreciated. Tipping rules in Thailand are very flexible and approximate the original intent of a tip—given for good service. Major hotels and restaurants do normally add a 10 percent service charge and a 11 percent government tax to your bill. Unless service is exceptional, you need not leave an additional tip in these places.

The general Thai tipping practice in small street restaurants is to leave loose change rather than a fixed percentage of the bill. If, for example, your bill comes to 163 baht and you pay with two 100 baht bills, you may wish to leave a bill and the coins behind—17 baht. However, always leave more than one baht—a single baht tip is an insult. In small inexpensive open-air restaurants, 3, 5, or 10 baht tip on most bills is quite acceptable.

You should not tip taxi drivers since the price you pay is already negotiated. But on some occasions you may want to give an additional 10 or 20 baht because you either feel sorry for this driver (he got caught in an extra 20 minutes of traffic) or he was exceptionally helpful. If a driver takes you to one of his recommended shops, don't feel obligated to tip him for this "extra" service; he probably received a 10% commission from the shop on everything you purchased!

Hotel and airport porters should be tipped 5 baht per bag, with a 10 baht minimum. Use your own discretion in tipping all others. Keep in mind that service tends to be excellent in Thailand. It often deserves to be rewarded with a tip genuinely expressing your appreciation for a job well done.

LANGUAGE

Language does present difficulties for some visitors to Thailand. While English is widely spoken in major hotels, restaurants and tourist shops, outside these areas communication at times can present problems. Few taxi drivers, for example, speak English. Few waiters and waitresses outside major restaurants speak or understand English. On the other hand, many restaurants print their signs and menus in Thai, Chinese, and English.

The language barrier, however, should not deter you from getting around with relative ease. Many Thais, especially those in Bangkok, speak some basic English. Tours are available with English-speaking guides. You can rent a car with an English-speaking driver.

Thais generally try to be helpful and accommodating. They will usually try to understand you through a combination of sign language, writing, and a few English words. On the other hand, don't expect much help from young girls; they tend to be shy, and many will giggle and run away from you when approached.

When bargaining with taxi drivers, speak slowly in English and use your fingers to state your price—each finger representing 10 baht. Whenever possible, have someone write place names and addresses in Thai, collect name cards in Thai, and take a Thai/English map with you. Although some Thais cannot read Thai, many will ask fellow Thais for help. Some will approach you to practice their English, ask if you need any assistance, and take time to help you. In fact, half the fun in Thailand is getting lost and then finding your way to your destination. Never fear. You will seldom get lost for more than 15 minutes.

BUSINESS HOURS

Most shops are open 10 hours a day—from 10am to 8pm—seven days a week. However, some shops keep shorter hours, closing by 6pm and are closed Sunday. Check with your hotel or call ahead if you plan to visit shops in the evening.

Banks open at 8:30am and close at 3:30pm, Monday through Friday.

In Bangkok, post offices are open 8am to 6pm, Monday through Friday, and from 9am to 1pm on Saturday. Post offices outside Bangkok close at 4:30pm.

Government offices are open from 8:30am to 4:30pm, Monday through Friday, with a noon-to-1pm lunch break. The best time to conduct government business is from 9am to 11:30am.

TRANSPORTATION AND TAXIS

A fascinating variety of transportation is available for your pleasure—and displeasure—in Thailand. Indeed, the modes of transportation are often as interesting as the trips themselves, and your choices may determine how much you enjoy your travel and shopping adventure in Thailand.

In Bangkok you can choose among hotel cars, taxis, air-conditioned and regular buses, motorized trishaws, and rental cars and motorbikes. We only recommend hotel cars and taxis. They are convenient, air-conditioned, inexpensive, and plentiful—our basic requirements for decent transportation. Buses are overcrowded, uncomfortable, and extremely slow. The motorized trishaws are cute, but they are uncomfortable, unsafe, and dirty. Try them once for the novel experience, but use them often and you may get a bad case of black lung, along with a nice coating, from head to toe, of black pollutants. Renting and driving your own car or motorbike is an adventure in latent suicide; do so only if you are well insured, your children have already graduated from college, or you feel excitement is missing in your life!

The general rule for choosing transportation in Bangkok is to go with what is quick, comfortable, and reasonably priced. The most convenient way to travel is to hire a **hotel car**, with an English-speaking driver, by the hour, half-day, or full-day. If you intend to accomplish a great deal in one day, this will be your best choice. It will be more expensive than a regular taxi, but for comfort and convenience you cannot do better. You will especially appreciate a car and driver when you go shopping in the lanes and neighborhoods which are not well serviced by taxis. It's always good to know you have a car waiting, and it will be able to accommodate your purchases. And the prices of a car and driver in Thailand are very reasonable compared to other cities in the world.

One word of caution when hiring a car and driver: make sure your driver does not use your shopping time to request commissions from the shops you visit. Ask the hotel to only give you a "commission-free" driver and make sure he doesn't accompany or follow you into the shops. If he does, chances are he's requesting from the shops a 10% commission on everything you buy, which means you won't be able to bargain for as low a price as otherwise. Also, be skeptical about any driver's shopping recommendations. Drivers are not quality shoppers; many steer tourists into only those shops that give them commissions as well as avoid quality shops that do not play this game.

Taxis are available everywhere in Bangkok. They cruise the streets and lanes like an army of frantic ants. Since most drivers rent their cabs by the day and are not confined to zones, they are free to roam wherever they can find a fare. They are the ultimate example of free enterprise run amuck!

To get a cab all you need to do is wave your hand or stand near the curb looking in need of transportation. Except during rush hour, a taxi should find you within 1-2 minutes. As soon as a taxi stops, the driver will either roll down his window, or you can open the door to tell the driver where you want to go, and then negotiate the price before getting in. The price of all taxi rides must be negotiated since meters are either nonexispeanut-based sauce), and *kaeng masaman* (Indian beef curry with peanuts). For the more adventuresome, try *tom jam kung* (lemon grass soup with shrimp), *kaeng kai* (yellow chicken curry), and *bai phat krapraw* (meat and vegetable dish laced with basil leaves). Thai noodle dishes, such a *kui tiew phat see yuu*, *phat thai*, and *kui tiew nya sap*, are outstanding and not spicy hot. In fact, you will seldom go wrong ordering any of the Thai noodle dishes.

Thai restaurants are found throughout Bangkok, along its major highways and lanes. A few major hotels and restaurants sponsor Thai cultural shows which include a sampling of Thai food. Some of the best include **Baan Thai** (Soi 32 Sukhumvit Rd., Tel. 258-5403); **Pimarn** (Soi 46 Sukhumvit Rd., Tel. 258-7866); and **Sala Rim Naam** (Oriental Hotel, Tel. 234-8829). For some of the best Thai food, try the following restaurants: **Lemon Grass** (Soi 24 6/1 Sukhumvit Rd., Tel. 258-8637); **Jit Pochana** (1082 Paholyothin Rd., Tel. 279-5000 or Soi 20 Sukhumvit Rd., Tel. 258-1578); **Spice Market** (Regent Hotel, Tel. 251-6127); **Thai Pavilion** (Holiday Inn Plaza, Silom Road); **Sorn Daeng** (78/2 Rajadamneon Rd. at Democracy Monument, Tel. 224-3088); and **Busarakham** (Soi 35 Pipat 2, off Silom Rd., Tel. 235-8915).

In general the best and most expensive Western and Chinese restaurants will be found in or around major hotels. For fine Continental and French dining, try the **Normandie Grill** (Oriental Hotel, Tel. 234-0021—expensive and men must wear a coat and tie); **Fireplace Grill** (Le Meridian President Hotel, Tel. 253-0444); **Ma Maison** (Hilton Hotel, Tel. 253-0123); **Hamilton's** (Dusit Thani Hotel, Tel. 233-1130); **The Regent Grill** (Regent Hotel); **Neil's Tavern** (58/4 Soi Ruan Rudi, off Wireless Rd., Tel. 251-5644); or **Le Metropolitain** (74, Soi 63 Sukhumvit Rd., Tel. 391-3331).

One of the best ways to enjoy eating in Thailand is to try the many noon buffets. Most are served in major hotels. They are inexpensive, ranging from US$5 to US$15, and they offer a wonderful variety of international foods. For a good sampling of Thai and Chinese foods, try the extensive buffet at the **Jit Pochana Restaurant** (1082 Paholyothin Rd., Tel. 279-5000). The **Talay Thong Restaurant** (Tel. 253-0355-7) at the Siam Inter-Continental Hotel also has an excellent Thai buffets. The more traditional *dim sum* Chinese buffet is served in many restaurants in Bangkok. Our favorite Italian and Thai buffet is at **Giorgio's** (Tel. 234-5599) in the Royal Orchid Sheraton Hotel. The river view is wonderful and the widest selection of food is available Saturdays and Sundays. The relaxing **Lord Jim's**

(Tel. 234-8621) at the Oriental Hotel serves a good seafood buffet in a nice setting overlooking the river. **Le Brasserie** (Tel. 251-6127) at the Regent Hotel serves an outstanding Continental buffet.

If you are looking for a marvelous breakfast buffet, two of the best are found at the **Shangri-La Hotel** and the **Regent Hotel**.

Many Thai and Chinese restaurants are open-air restaurants in lovely water and garden settings. For a good sampling of these restaurants, try one of the numerous open-air restaurant complexes along Asoke-Dindaeng Road, such as **Kum Luang** (560 Asoke-Dindaeng, Tel. 246-3272), which are built over ponds. Be sure to apply mosquito repellant or request a mosquito coil for under your table.

Numerous food vendors are found throughout Bangkok and Chiangmai. They offer everything from a wonderful variety of sweets, such as fried bananas and *roti* (rolled Indian pancake filled with condensed milk), to numerous noodle dishes and drinks. You may want to avoid eating at these tempting establishments. While most of the foods are safe to eat, the dishes and eating utensils are usually washed in dirty, re-used water—a good breeding ground for hepatitis.

If you visit Chiangmai, you will find numerous Thai restaurants serving northern Thai dishes. For some of the more unique northern foods, try *khao soi* (curried noddle dish), *khao neow* (sticky rice), and *nam prik ong* (minced pork chili sauce eaten with fried pork skins or sticky rice). Avoid the uncooked pork delicacies, *naem* and *lap*, which can give you bad cases of trichinosis and food poisoning—not to mention a flaming digestive system if you encounter one of their small peppers! Hotel restaurants and coffee shops serve Western food as well as numerous Chinese and central Thai dishes. Chiangmai also has several good French, German, English, and Middle Eastern restaurants. For French food, try **Le Chalet** (Chaeroen Prathet Rd.). For Continental food, the **Thong Kwon** (Rincome Hotel, Tel. 221-044) is excellent. The open-air riverside **White Orchid Restaurant** and the **Nang Nual Seafood Restaurant** are also excellent for Chinese and seafood. The **Jasmine** in the Dusit Inn serves some of the best Chinese food in Chiangmai. **The Pub** (88 Huay Kaew Rd.) serves excellent and inexpensive Western food in a cozy atmosphere—one of the best buys in all of Thailand. The noon buffets at the Chiang Inn and Chiang Mai Orchid hotels are good values. Two of Chiangmai's best Thai restaurants are the **Baan Suan** (Chiangmai-Sankamphaeng Rd.) and **Kaiwan** (181 Nimmanhemin Rd.).

Thailand offers an assortment of excellent drinks. Standard international soft drinks, such as Coca Cola and Pepsi, are widely available. Thailand also produces two excellent noncarbonated orange soft drinks—Green Spot and Birelay. The local milks and ice creams, especially under the brand name Foremost, are excellent and safe to consume. Numerous noncarbonated drinks and fruit juices are available in small dairy cartons.

Coffee and tea are widely available and are often served together—tea being the chaser to a cup of strong Thai coffee laced with condensed milk. Iced Thai coffee (*olieng*) is a delightful sweet drink. But you must acquire a taste for Thai coffee since it is rather thick and strong. Thai tea is served both hot and cold, with or without cream, and is a good drink. Outside major hotels your cup of hot coffee or tea may be served in a regular drinking glass and thus difficult to handle without a pair of gloves! Let it cool before handling the glass, or wrap it in a napkin or handkerchief—if you don't mind drinking it differently from others around you.

Alcohol also is widely available. Thailand produces three excellent robust beers—Kloster, Singha, and Amarit. Mekong is a popular and cheap national liquor which looks like Scotch but tastes best when mixed with Sprite, 7-Up, Coca Cola, or Pepsi (Thais like to take it with soda water). Numerous other local liquors are produced in Bangkok and the provinces. All major international liquors are widely available in grocery stores throughout Thailand and are reasonably priced even after subjected to Thai duties. Imported wines are extremely expensive and should not be automatically ordered with dinner without first checking the price. The wine may cost you more than a dinner for four. Thailand does produce a cheap local wine, but it is not of export quality and we find it primarily useful as a cooking ingredient. Each bottle tends to come in a different color—an obvious quality control problem!

ACCOMMODATIONS

You may or may not have trouble finding accommodations in Thailand, depending on what time of year you plan to visit. Since 1988 many of Thailand's major hotels have been operating at near 100% occupancy, with the months of November to January being the hardest to find rooms in Bangkok and Chiangmai. The surge in tourism dropped somewhat in 1991—a result of both the Gulf War and continuing recession in much of the world. However, the surge in tourism is likely to be renewed. In response to the large demand for rooms, major hotels began sharply increasing prices at the beginning of 1989. Bangkok, once noted for having some of the least expensive first-class and deluxe accommodations in the world, has quickly joined the ranks of many other moderately expensive international cities. This situation may change by 1993 when several new hotels are scheduled to come on line in Bangkok. For now our advice is to make your hotel reservations well in advance and don't expect to find the great bargains of four or five years ago.

What Bangkok does offer to travelers is some of the finest hotels in the world. Indeed, you will find few other cities with such a large concentration of deluxe hotels offering the finest in service, facilities, restaurants, and shopping arcades. Two hotels—The Regent and The Oriental—have set standards of excellence that many other newer hotels have attempted to emulate. The result is some of the finest hotels in the world, outranking the best of what Hong Kong or Singapore have to offer. For travelers to Bangkok, the hotel scene itself offers a unique opportunity to sample hotel amenities and experience outstanding Thai service. You can easily and quickly become a "hotel hopper" in Bangkok as you go from one hotel restaurant and shopping arcade to another.

Bangkok boasts numerous hotels and guest houses, ranging from inexpensive (US$3 a day) to expensive (US$250 a day). Since the recent demand for first-class and deluxe hotels has outstripped the supply, hotel prices have increased sharply for the peak tourist season. You can still find inexpensive accommodations at the lower, budget end.

You may wish to treat yourself to a deluxe hotel since they offer outstanding service, facilities, restaurants, and location. One of Thailand's finest hotels is the **Regent Hotel** (155 Rajadamri Road, Tel. 251-6127). Ideally situated at the heart of Bangkok's fastest growing shopping area (World Trade Center/Amarin Plaza/Gaysorn) and adjacent to Thailand's finest shopping center (Peninsula Plaza), the Regent Hotel is an exquisite five-star hotel where you will be truly pampered. The spacious well-appointed rooms and the attention to detail put the Regent Hotel into a class of its own. The service is impeccable and the ambience is outstanding. The hotel has three of Bangkok's best restaurants—The Spice Market, The Regent Grill, and Le Braisserie. Having afternoon tea in the lobby as music wafts from a balcony across the room is a pleasurable break from a day of shopping and sightseeing. The hotel also has a small shopping arcade boasting some of Bangkok's best shops (Lotus, Elephant House, Art Resources, Khanitha, House of Handicrafts, Peninsula Gems, and Kan, Lek, and Montri). If you want to experience one of Thailand's finest hotels, and be ideally located for shopping, we highly recommend the Regent Hotel.

The **Oriental Hotel** (48 Oriental Avenue, Tel. 236-0400) is still one of the world's finest hotels—ranked in the top ten in many world lists. Overlooking the Chao Phya River, its well deserved reputation for luxury complemented by impeccable service places the Oriental in a class of its own. Although this is an expensive hotel compared to many hotels in Thailand, it is reasonably priced compared to similar class hotels elsewhere in the world. For about US$220 a night, you can treat yourself to what many seasoned travelers consider to be the best hotel in the world. The Grand Hyatt Erawan, Shangri-La, Hilton, and Royal Orchid Sheraton hotels offer excellent accommodations, service, and settings—comparable to both the Regent Hotel and Oriental Hotel.

Further from the river but located near the major shopping areas are other outstanding hotels. The **Montien Hotel,** one of the few Thai owned and operated hotels, is conveniently located just off Suriwongse Road and Patpong Road. You will find excellent restaurants, a shopping arcade, and fine service here. Its central location near major shopping areas—including the night vendor stalls lining nearby Suriwongse, Patpong, and Silom roads—makes this a convenient hotel for shoppers. The **Shangri-La, Royal Orchard Sheraton, Grand Hyatt Erawan, Hilton, Landmark, Novotel, Siam Inter-Continental, Holiday Inn Crowne Plaza, Dusit Thani, Arnonma Swissotel,** and **Le Meridian President** are also outstanding hotels located near the major shopping areas. The **Ambassador, Indra Regent, Palace, Imperial, Narai, Tawana Ramada,** and **The City** hotels are also well located.

If you plan to visit Chiangmai, we recommend making reservations ahead of time since many of the hotels are fully booked in this popular tourist destination. Chiangmai has excellent deluxe and first-class hotels and rooms are reasonably priced. Rooms in many first-class and deluxe hotels range from US$50 to US$100 a night. The city also boasts many budget hotels and guest houses ranging in price from US$3 to US$20 a night. If you want to be within walking distance of the city's major downtown shops, markets, and restaurants, your best choices of hotels are the **Mae Ping, Dusit Inn, Novotel, Chiang Inn,** and **Pornping Tower**—all located in and around

Chang Klan Road on the eastern side of the city. Lovely hotels located in less hectic and quieter areas are the **Chiang Mai Orchid**, **Rincome**, **Empress**, and **Poy Luang**. The Chiangmai Orchid is considered by many to be Chiangmai's best hotel.

The recently refurbished and reasonably priced **Rincome Hotel** (Huey Kaew Road, Tel. 053-221044) still remains one of our favorites with its excellent service and Chiangmai charm. The hotel is located across the street from Chiangmai's best quality shopping center and near numerous fine restaurants. One of its restaurants, Thong Kwon, serves a great cherries jubilee! The Rincome is conveniently located for access to outlying areas of Chiangmai.

While most of Chiangmai's hotels are fully booked during the high season (November to January), during other parts of the year when vacancy rates are lower, they offer special rates; many are known to offer 10 to 50 percent discounts for the asking.

In Chiangrai and Lampang you will find relatively inexpensive hotels which are best classified as first-class and budget up-country hotels. The hotels are comfortable but basic. You will seldom spend more than US$25 a night to stay in these cities. However, Chiangrai province also has four relatively new deluxe hotels—**Dusit Island Resort**, **Little Duck**, **Rimkok Resort**, and **Golden Triangle**—that rival the best of Chiangmai's hotels. You'll be pleasantly surprised in discovering these fine hotels in the small provincial town of Chiangrai and the Golden Triangle area (near Chiangsaen).

In the South, Phuket is a major resort destination boasting some of the finest resort hotels in Southeast Asia. Hotels such as the **Dusit Laguna**, **Phuket Acadia**, and **Amanpuri** are excellent hotels with all the amenities expected at fine beach resort hotels.

ELECTRICITY AND WATER

Electricity in Thailand is 220-volts, 50 cycle AC power. Thailand uses a two-prong electrical configuration that only accepts rounded rather than flat prongs. Most major hotels have adapters for your appliances. If you use a hairdryer, take one that works with 220 volts since most adapters won't work with hairdryers. Should you need to purchase a 220 hairdryer, local departments such as Central and Robinsons, have several excellent German, Japanese, and Taiwanese models. We also recommend taking an extension cord with you. It may come in handy since electrical outlets in many Thai hotels are often difficult to find, or they are inconveniently located in relation to the mirror you wish to use.

Tap water and ice made from tap water are not safe to consume. Ask for bottled water—Polaris is widely distributed and reliable—and ice made from bottled water. Most water and ice served in major hotels and restaurants will be from bottled water. Normally a thermos or glass bottles filled with bottled water will be in your room. Use this water for drinking and brushing your teeth. The municipal water systems treat the tap water, but they have yet to produce an acceptable product for travelers.

5 PLEASURES, PAINS, AND ENJOYING YOUR STAY

Travel is often exciting because it results in new, unexpected, and positive experiences. At the same time, travel has its downside of unpleasant and discomforting experiences.

We have experienced numerous positives and negatives in our travels to Thailand, but the positives always outweigh the negatives. Over time we have learned how to minimize the unpleasantries. You, too, will experience these pleasures and pains to varying degrees, depending on how you travel and where you stay. We share several of these with you so you can best prepare to avoid the negatives as you concentrate on the positives to more fully enjoy your Thailand adventure.

EXPERIENCING POSITIVES

Thailand is an attractive destination for many international travelers because it offers so many positive travel experiences. It is especially noted for its outstanding service, fine hotels, excellent cuisine, colorful and varied sights, warm and friendly people, and wonderful shopping opportunities. If you know where to go and how to shop in Thailand, you should have a marvelous time.

EXCEPTIONAL SERVICE

Service in Thailand is exceptional and closely tied to the polite, gentle, friendly, considerate, and deferential character of the Thai. This character is especially pronounced in northern Thailand where the northern Thai have a reputation for being the most polite, gentle, and deferential people in the country. Good hotels and restaurants will pamper you, making your visit pleasant, convenient, and comfortable. Be it laundry, haircuts, repairs, or arranging tours and shipping, you will often experience outstanding service. Indeed, you will miss such services once you return home to the drudgeries of everyday life and discover that you may indeed live in a "no-service" country!

FABULOUS HOTELS

Thailand seems to have cornered the market on some of the world's finest hotels. The Oriental Hotel continues to rank among seasoned travelers as the world's number one hotel. The Regent also frequently appears in the top five or ten on such surveys. These hotels, in turn, have set a standard of excellence that many other hotels in Bangkok attempt to emulate. As a result, such hotels as the Grand Hyatt Erawan, Royal Orchid Sheraton, Shangri-La, Hilton, Dusit Thani, Arnoma Swissotel, Landmark, Siam Inter-Continental, Montien, Holiday Inn Crowne Plaza, Ambassador, Princess, Le Meridien President, Central Plaza, and Tawana Ramada offer excellent accommodations and service.

Outside Bangkok hotels in Chiangmai, Chiangrai, Phuket, and Pattaya maintain international standards. Hotels in these areas are relatively inexpensive compared to those in Bangkok and other resort, deluxe, and first-class hotels in comparable cities elsewhere in the world.

WONDERFUL AND EXOTIC FOODS

Food in Thailand is a gourmet's delight. A truly cosmopolitan city, Bangkok's restaurants offer most of the world's major cuisines. You will find outstanding Thai, Chinese, Japanese, Indian, French, Continental, Italian, and American foods. Thai food, which ranges from spicy-hot for many visitors to simply nicely seasoned but mild, is one of the world's great cuisines with its generous use of seafoods, meats, vegetables, coconut milk, and unusual spices. Thai fruits are irresistible, from over 100 varieties of bananas to exotic and delicious mangosteens and pomelos. Sample Thai pineapples and you will forever remember how a truly great pineapple should taste!

OUTSTANDING RESTAURANTS

If one judges countries by the foods and restaurants they offer, then Thailand would rank as one of the best countries in the world. Thailand offers some of Asia's finest restaurants. This is a country where eating seems to be a national pastime, and for good reason—the food is superb. In Bangkok you will find such outstanding French and Continental restaurants as the Normandie Grill, Fireplace Grill, Ma Maison, Lord Jims, The Regent Grill, and Hamilton's. Excellent Thai restaurants abound: Lemon Grass, Busarakham, Jit Pochana, and the Spice Market. You will discover numerous fine Chinese, Japanese, seafood, and Italian restaurants in Bangkok, Chiangmai, and resort areas. Street vendors and open-air restaurants are found everywhere, offering delicious foods at very reasonable prices.

WARM, FRIENDLY, AND GRACIOUS PEOPLE

The Thai tend to be a very warm, friendly, humorous, helpful, polite, considerate, gracious, and courteous people. Many Thai love to look, smile, wave, joke, and ask innocent but sometimes shocking questions (*"How much money do you make?"*). They are particularly gracious and thoughtful, always appearing to be concerned about your well-being, and helpful. The children are delightful, usually well-mannered and curious about you. Some of your fondest memories of Thailand will be the many nice and friendly people you meet.

UNPREDICTABLE AND SERENDIPITOUS EXPERIENCES

Thailand is unpredictable, full of serendipity. Visitors are continually surprised by what they discover—the chance meeting of old acquaintances; a friendly encounter or assistance provided by a stranger; a treat or gift given by a new acquaintance; the discovery of wonderful shops, products, foods, and services; a striking view of the river or ocean; exotic sights, sounds, and nightlife; and colorful day markets and delightful night markets.

A SHOPPING PARADISE

Above all, Thailand is a shopper's paradise and Asia's best kept shopping secret. Here, you will discover excellent quality products to enhance your wardrobe and home. This is a country of talented craftspeople who excel in producing quality gems, jewelry, arts, home furnishings, clothes, and handicrafts at very reasonable prices. It's a haven for collectors of fine Thai, Burmese, Laotian, and Cambodian art, antiques, and jewelry. If you spend the time to discover Thailand's many shopping treasures, you will certainly want to return again to uncover even more exciting treasures.

ENCOUNTERING POSSIBLE NEGATIVES

Like all countries, Thailand also has its downside of negatives. Most are minor irritants, but some could possibly spoil your trip. Many of these are cultural in nature; others are based on class differences; many are basic organization and management weaknesses; some are inherent to the tourist trade; and still others are a function of social problems commonly found in Third World countries.

None of the negatives we identify should deter you from visiting Thailand. We discuss them so you will be better prepared to respond to potential problems you may encounter during your visit to Thailand.

LANGUAGE

While you should be able to get around with English, many Thai do not speak nor understand English. Few taxi drivers will be able to communicate with you except by sign language. This can be frustrating at times, but usually you will get by and after a while someone will come along who speaks English and assist you. But it is usually good to learn a few words in the Thai language, more for creating good will than for carrying on an intelligent conversation. Thais tend to be flattered and more responsive to individuals who speak a few words of Thai.

TRAFFIC PATTERNS AND HABITS

Thailand's traffic patterns and driving habits will most likely be different from those you are familiar with back home. Indeed, a visitor's first trip to Bangkok can be a frightening experience, especially if you choose to take a cheap taxi from the airport to your hotel. Most Thai taxi drivers drive fast, weaving in and out of the chaotic traffic. This is one of the world's cheapest thrills! Indeed, after checking into a hotel, some visitors venture to the curb and then decide to retreat to their comfortable hotel and room since they have no idea how to walk across a street which is clogged with overcrowded, pollution belching buses, trucks, and cars seemingly observing no rules whatsoever. At this point, it is best to confine yourself to the comfort and safety of an air-conditioned taxi or hotel car and observe the frantic lifestyle revolving around life in the streets. Within a few days, what initially appeared to be a frightening traffic environment will become a normal part of your travel experience and one of your more memorable experiences abroad!

Unless you want to repeatedly punish yourself, we do not recommend using buses in Bangkok. They are cheap, but they are terribly over-crowded, hot, slow, and occasionally serviced by your local pickpocket. Pay a little more for a relatively inexpensive air-conditioned taxi.

HEAT AND HUMIDITY

Much of Thailand can be uncomfortably hot and humid for individuals who live in temperate climates. While there are some seasonal variations, the country is primarily tropical. As such, you will encounter high humidity, high temperatures, and tropical rains during several months of the year. Bangkok, for example, becomes a virtual steam bath during March and April but is pleasant during November to February.

Yet, even the hottest seasons in Thailand are not much worse than summers in such places as Chicago, New York, Washington DC, Miami, or Los Angeles. The difference is more in how one's lifestyle relates to the climate. Back home, for example, you may confine yourself to air-conditioned places when the weather is very hot and humid. But as you shop and sightsee in Thailand, you will be outside, doing a great deal of walking, on such hot and humid days.

Assuming you will feel Thailand's heat and humidity more than back home, you can best prepare yourself for this climate by following a few of these basic rules on how to cope with Thailand's heat and humidity:

- Wear lightweight clothes made primarily from natural fibers, preferably cotton.
- Carry a collapsible hand fan and use it when necessary.
- If you visit during the rainy season, take an umbrella with you at all times.
- Wear a hat on sunny days.
- Plan to be indoors, especially in air-conditioned areas, during the heat of the day.
- Plan to do very few things that require a great deal of walking.
- Use public transportation for even short distances.
- Slow down your walking pace—shorter stride at one-half your normal walking speed.
- Bathe two to three times a day.
- Drink plenty of fluids.

By making a few of these adjustments in your lifestyle, you should be able to take the heat and humidity after a while. But if you insist on walking everywhere at a frantic pace, the heat and humidity will seem oppressive and will quickly run you down and ruin your trip.

POVERTY, SANITATION, AND POLLUTION

You will encounter some poverty and sanitation problems in Thailand, especially if you wander off the beaten tourist paths, which may at times bother you. Thailand has a very large class of poor people who live in slum and squatter settlements in and around Bangkok. One of the largest areas is Klong Toei which is located along the river in Bangkok near New Road. There is no reason you would stop here, but you may pass near this and other poor areas and notice the shabby conditions and lack of sanitation in the area.

In general, Thailand has little abject poverty that you might find in other Asian countries. The poor in Thailand are relatively better off than the poor in many other countries. You may encounter an occasional beggar—usually a young girl holding a baby—but these individuals may or may not be as poor as they look. For years some of these so-called beggars have rented children for begging purposes, and we know of at least one village in the Northeast which consists of professional beggars who regularly travel to Bangkok to make a living. The real beggars are more likely to be the ones who have some deformity, such as the blind and crippled, which you may encounter along the streets or on the overhead walkways.

While the Thais personally are a very clean people who keep themselves and their homes spotless, public areas as well as the environment do not share the same degree of cleanliness. Environmental degradation is a serious problem throughout Thailand, and it is especially pronounced in Bangkok. The sanitation problem is especially evident with some of the heavily polluted canals and the antiquated sewerage system still operating in Bangkok. While visually unattractive, the smells can at times be extremely noxious, especially in the heat of the day. In some of the beach resort areas, such as Pattaya, be careful where you swim since the municipal sewerage system has generated a great deal of off-shore pollution; it pumps raw sewerage into the bay which, in turn, creates potential health problems for surrounding beach areas.

Bangkok's air pollution is extremely bad due to the high level of auto emissions and the noxious and filthy exhaust fumes which are also being compounded by polluting industries. Chiangmai's air pollution, exacerbated by the widespread burning of hazardous charcoal in local kitchens, is also on the increase as more and more gasoline powered vehicles—especially the motorized trishaws (*rot tuk tuk*)—ply the city streets. At times the fumes are so bad that you may get headaches. While you can alleviate the worst visual effects of such pollution by riding in air-conditioned vehicles and staying indoors, the harmful pollutants are there nonetheless.

The noise pollution is also very irritating in Bangkok and Chiangmai. The traffic is so loud, from a combination of questionable muffler systems and honking horns, that you can hardly hear yourself talking, much less thinking! This, too, is a source of headaches.

Bangkok has improved its image considerably over the past few years, although its horrendous traffic and pollution problems continue to tarnish whatever incremental improvements take place in this city. The city's maverick and energetic mayor has improved this bustling city with some noticeable results that go beyond the typical Thai propensity for window-dressing measures. The traffic seems to move a little better, although first-time visitors may have difficulty believing this; the city doesn't flood as much as it once did; and the streets are relatively clean and well maintained in those areas most frequented by tourists. Bangkok has finally begun to take on "The Singapore Complex" as it tries to adopt the clean green habits of its southern neighbor. How long this will continue is anyone's guess, especially given the short staying power of local government in Thailand.

TOUTS, CHEATING, AND COMMISSIONS

Throughout Thailand, but especially in Bangkok and Chiangmai, you will encounter the universal tout who preys on tourists. These are the "10 percent men"—you are potentially worth at least 10 percent to them if you buy where they take you. They approach you ostensibly to help you get a good deal on anything from buying jewelry to satisfying your sexual fantasies. They stand on corners and hang around hotels frequented by tourists. You should always avoid these people.

Touts also come in many forms: taxi drivers, tour guides, and others who ostensibly are helping you find a "good deal" on your purchases. These people only take you to places which give them a 10 percent commission. In fact, the problem has gotten so out of hand in Chiangmai, especially among the shops along Chiangmai-Sankamphaeng Road, that these people are demanding commissions of up to 40 percent! Being taken to a shop by one of these people is no deal when you have paid their commission by purchasing an item for 10 to 40 percent more than you could have on your own had you not been accompanied by this person.

If you are approached by a street tout, do not start a conversation since you already know their game and you will merely encourage them to further pester you. Keep walking and firmly say *"No, not interested today"* or say *"mai ow"* which roughly translates as *"I don't want any."* It's not the nicest thing to say, but Thai touts will think you speak the local language and thus have no interest in trying to fool *"a local."* End the conversation there.

You should also beware of tour guides and taxi drivers who want to end your tour or journey by giving you one "extra"—an unscheduled trip to a local factory or shop where they will give you a "very special deal." Lapidaries selling gems and jewelry at inflated prices seem to be their favorite stops. The so-called "special" is most likely you getting ripped-off and the guide getting a 10 to 20 percent commission on any of your purchases. If and when this "extra" is offered to you, insist that you be returned immediately to your hotel since you do not want to take advantage of this deal. It's okay to be somewhat ugly at this point: if they persist, demand a refund or threaten to report the tour guide or taxi driver to authorities. The pattern is always the same. If you are being taken to a special shop, you are indeed being "taken." Unfortunately, this same pattern—although more subtle—occurs among guides who work for the top name tour groups operating in Thailand. Everyone in the industry knows the game, and most play it to their benefit. If a shopkeeper refuses to pay the commission, the tour guide boycotts the shop and takes the next group to another more cooperative shop. As a result, many of the so-called recommended shops given by tour guides are not necessarily the best shops you should visit—only ones that give kickbacks to the guide.

You may also encounter cheating, mostly petty, on occasion. The cheating will range from misrepresentation of goods, such as gems, jewelry, and antiques, to giving you the wrong change or over-charging you for hotels, meals, and transportation. In general we have had few problems with cheating in Thailand. However, we know others who have had such problems. It usually arises when someone is trying to buy something they know little about, they purchase it from a questionable dealer or shop, or they are trying to get something for nothing. Your best defense is to know what you are doing and don't be greedy. If, for example, you are buying gems and jewelry, know about authenticity and quality of gems and jewelry before you go to Thailand. Also, be careful in purchasing items off the street. Shops in the major hotel shopping arcades and shopping centers tend to be reputable. Remember, there is no such thing as a free lunch. If a deal sounds too good to be true, it probably is. When in doubt—but you still want to purchase the item—consider buying the item using your credit card. Even though you may pay a little more, in many cases your credit card company will help you should you become a victim of fraud when using their card. However, the credit company is not obligated to do this, so be a knowledgeable consumer.

CROWDS

Bangkok is a crowded and congested city as evidenced by its infamous traffic jams and crowded shopping centers. Crowds bother many Westerners who are used to having greater personal space and privacy. Thai crowds can become both visually and physically exhausting for many tourists. To best enjoy your shopping experience, don't spend long hours in crowds. Occasionally retreat to your hotel room or an uncongested restaurant to experience an hour or so of personal space.

Weekends are a good time to avoid shopping arcades and markets. Use the time for tours that take you outside the city. On Saturdays and Sundays sidewalks and shopping arcades tend to be very crowded with children and office workers who are shopping on their days off.

POOR LIGHTING AND FEW ELECTRICAL OUTLETS

Since many Thai hotels—especially upcountry or inexpensive hotels—use small wattage bulbs and have few lights, your room may be dark and hard to read in. Furthermore, rooms may only have one electrical outlet for plugging in your appliances. Since this electrical outlet is usually inconveniently located behind a bed or dresser, you may want to take a long extension cord with you for such occasions. You also need to carry an international electrical adapter which is configured for rounded two-prong outlets.

INSECTS, BUGS, AND MOSQUITOS

Thailand's tropical climate generates a great many flying and crawling insects you may encounter in your hotel room, restaurants, and unexpected places. Most will not harm you, but they are annoying for those who are not used to living in such a rich insect environment. You are unlikely to have these problems in the deluxe and first-class hotels. If you do have problems in your hotel room—most likely with ants, roaches, waterbugs, and mosquitos—ask the hotel to spray your room when you are out. Many hotels do so every day while others only do so upon request.

If you are particularly susceptible to mosquito bites, be sure to take with you a mosquito repellant at all times. Spray before going out at night.

While you do not need to take anti-malarial pills if you are planning to stay in the cities, you may need to if you plan to "rough it" in remote village areas. Consult a doctor, but only one who is familiar with tropical medicines; others may give you inappropriate or bad advice. Malaria pills, especially Fansidar, can kill and thus may be worse than the disease! Indeed, we have been generally surprised with the level of misinformation and ignorance among medical professionals concerning tropical diseases, medical conditions, and inoculations and medications appropriate for Thailand and the rest of Southeast Asia.

SURPRISING RESTROOMS

Should you choose inexpensive hotels or find yourself outside major cities, be prepared for the Third World toilet experience. The waterseal toilet is the standard fixture found outside most Western hotels and restaurants. Built of porcelain and nearly level with the floor, it requires squatting skills most Westerners find discomforting. Be prepared to encounter a few of these in your travels.

Also, toilet paper is usually absent in such places or comes in a grade approximating sandpaper! Be advised to always travel with an emergency supply of paper or tissues. You may also encounter restrooms which seem dirty and smelly. It is best to use your hotel room facilities before going out. If you need to use a restroom outside your hotel, try to find a deluxe hotel which should have familiar and clean public facilities.

SMOKERS

If you are a nonsmoker, many places in Thailand may bother you. Thais tend to be heavy smokers, and many smokers disregard the presence of nonsmokers as well as ignore no smoking signs. Waiting areas in airports are filled with smokers and polluted air. Many restaurants have yet to reserve nonsmoking areas, and some good restaurants have the habit of passing out free cigars to patrons at the end of the meal. If you are a nonsmoker or dislike cigar smoke, this complimentary gesture can very well ruin your evening as people at the table next to you light up to create a cloud of noxious smoke which then descends on your expensive meal! Indeed, two of our favorite restaurants—the Fireplace Grill and Normandie Grill—still persist with this tradition. One would hope they could find ways to compliment their fine cuisine with something other than a stinking cigar.

If you are a nonsmoker and encounter these problems, it is best to take preventive action or nicely complain. In public waiting areas, such as airports, which do not set aside no smoking areas, try to seat yourself as far away from crowds as possible or near a ventilated door or window. Use your hand fan for ventilation. Move somewhere else if someone begins smoking near you. If the smoke gets too oppressive, which it often does, ask airline personnel for assistance in getting relief. They usually are very helpful in satisfying your needs. In restaurants without no smoking sections, ask to be seated by a window or near a ventilated area. If you are in the middle of your meal and smoke begins to bother you—especially that complimentary cigar—ask to be moved to another table and nicely complain that *"the smoke is terrible in your restaurant."* The restaurant will usually accommodate. In fact, if more people made such requests, maybe more restaurants would have the good sense to set aside no smoking areas. Many of the restaurants in major hotels, especially the Hilton chain, have already taken the initiative to reserve no smoking sections.

QUESTIONABLE WATER, DRINKS, AND FOOD

Since tap water in Thailand is not safe to drink, it is best to drink bottled water or bottled soft drinks, fruit juices, beer, coffee, or tea. Thailand has a wide range of bottled and canned soft drinks, such as Coke, Pepsi, 7-Up, Sprite, and Green Spot as well as numerous fruit juices which make wonderful drinks and can be easily carried in your backpack. Local beers are good, rivaling the best of European beers. Local coffee tends to be very strong.

A word of caution about wines in Thailand. There is no faster way to drive up your restaurant bill than to order a bottle of imported wine. A bottle of imported wine costing US$20 in a restaurant in the United States may cost US$60 in a Thai restaurant. Unaware of this, when handed the wine list, many people routinely order a wine with dinner and then are shocked by the final bill—the wine may cost more than the dinner! Do check the price before ordering wine with dinner.

While many of the foods in Thailand are wonderful, be careful where and what you eat. Most of the foods are safe as long as they are freshly boiled, grilled, or peeled. But be especially careful of small food stalls and roadside vendors. Many set up shop with a small pushcart, folding tables, and stools. While their foods may be safe, the dishes and eating utensils may be carriers of disease since they are often washed in contaminated water. Some travelers try cleaning them again with hot tea, but this does not sterilize.

Except in top hotels and restaurants, it is usually a good idea to avoid green salads and raw vegetables. Food handling standards tend to be lax, and farmers often use human fertilizers for growing vegetables. Most important, yet little known to outsiders, farmers often improperly use dangerous pesticides, such as spraying vegetables with DDT a day or two before picking, so that the produce appears nice and green in the market.

Many of the beautiful looking dishes in Thailand are fiery hot with heavy doses of chili peppers. For the uninitiated, these dishes can wreck havoc with one's system. If you do eat something too hot, you can partially alleviate the pain by eating sugar.

Regardless of how careful you are with the local foods and drinks, you may still have stomach and intestinal problems. This usually lasts a day or two. Take some medications with you for upset stomach and diarrhea. If you eat lightly, take it easy, and use some medication, the problem should go away shortly.

PART II

SHOPPING WELL

6 SHOPPING RULES, BARGAINING SKILLS, AND TAILORING TIPS

Shopping in Thailand is as much a cultural experience as it is a set of buying and selling transactions in unique commercial settings. While many of the shops, department stores, and markets may look similar to ones you shop in back home, they do have important differences you should know about prior to starting your Thailand shopping adventure. Most of these differences relate to certain shopping and pricing traditions that constitute an important set of shopping rules and bargaining skills you can and should learn before you begin making purchases in Thailand.

Tailoring also involves special shopping rules and communication skills individuals need to know if they wish to have quality tailoring done in Thailand.

CHANGING SHOPPING SCENE

During the past seven years the shopping scene in Bangkok has changed dramatically. The quality and variety of products has improved and the number of shopping areas has expanded considerably in response to Thailand's rapidly developing economy, emerging middle class, and expanding tourist trade. Once tourists were advised to stay close to their hotels, visit the Weekend and Floating markets, frequent a few special shops catering mainly to tourists, buy Thai silk and a few trinkets normally designed for tourists, and shop for cheap prices. This has all changed today.

Surprising Bangkok is both a shopper's and a buyer's paradise. It is quickly challenging such well noted shopping cities as Hong Kong, Singapore, and Seoul. The continuing proliferation of shops throughout Bangkok is amazing. Better still, a new generation of shopkeepers, many of whom are the children of Bangkok's successful merchants who have been educated abroad, are opening quality shops offering product selections, designs, and colors that appeal to Western tourists who have an eye toward quality.

NEW SHOPPING CULTURE

Shopping in Bangkok has undergone a major transformation during the past few years. If you follow the shopping rules of five to ten years ago, you may be disappointed with your shopping adventure in Thailand. You will leave without really finding unique and exciting products for your wardrobe, home, or friends.

Bangkok has begun to transform itself into an international shopper's haven. New and exciting shopping venues are being shaped for today's and tomorrow's visitors. Indeed, this is what makes Thailand one of the best kept shopping secrets in Asia.

Today the shopping choices in Bangkok have increased tremendously as shopping is more and more concentrated around large shopping arcades, department stores, chic boutiques, and individual shops with reputations for outstanding quality products and reliability. Many shops now appeal to Thai and foreign tourists alike and carry good quality products which do not have the look of "Made in Thailand For Tourists Only." Several quality shops now maintain branch stores in two or three other shopping areas in Bangkok as well as have expanded into Singapore, Hong Kong, the United States, and Europe—complete with export offices and mail order operations. Such changes are reflected in the overall improvement in the quality of products and the increasing presence of designs more appropriate to Western tastes. The hotels are still one of the most important shopping areas, offering excellent quality goods and prices, but they are only one of many alternative areas for your shopping pleasure.

BEWARE OF UNWANTED ADVICE AND COMMISSIONS

One problem visitors to Thailand encounter is in communicating their shopping desires and standards to Thais, many of whom do not understand Western tastes nor the dramatic changes taking place in Thailand's shopping scene. Remember, Thais are a very polite and accommodating people who want you to have a good time in their country. They seek to please you, put their best foot forward, and show you where a *"good deal"* can be made. Often overly obsessed with getting a bargain, many Thais shop for the cheapest price rather than the best quality. Consequently, they frequently help you get products at a very cheap price, but the designs and quality also may look cheap.

When asked where is the best place to shop, Thais often recommend places where they shop, because they believe you must have a personal relationship with a shopkeeper in order to get the best buy. They're convinced tourists cannot get a good deal by merely walking into a shop and negotiating a price; it's best that you know someone who is a friend or relative of the shopkeeper to get the best buy. Our experience is that this belief is largely a myth on the part of many Thais who are obsessed in using personal relationships and connections in getting their way. Tourists can often do just as well —and sometimes better—on their own without the assistance of well-meaning locals who believe they are doing you a favor by loaning you their connections. Time and again we have received better buys on quality items than Thai friends because we walked unannounced into a shop by ourselves; shopkeepers were more willing to give deep discounts precisely because we were **not** from the area; they knew we would be here today and gone tomorrow. They were less likely to do so with a local Thai who would be back tomorrow expecting the same discount! Consequently, if someone tells you it is best to go shopping with a Thai who can get you better prices, it isn't necessarily so—especially if you are willing to bargain hard!

When asked where is the best place to shop, many Thais also recommend a typical tourist shop filled with trinkets—many items you neither need nor want in your wardrobe or home. But this is their idea of a "good time" for tourists. After all, you are a tourist and they feel this is what tourists want to shop for when visiting Thailand. They feel they are helping you by showing you where to buy items real cheap rather than send you to places that are *paeng mak* ("very expensive").

Their concepts of design, color, and quality will seldom be the same as yours. As a result, many visitors to Thailand leave disappointed with their shopping experience and purchases. They have difficulty finding nice things they wish to take back home, including the much-praised Thai silk.

Another shopping problem many visitors to Thailand encounter is with tour guides and drivers who take them to a particular shop near the end of a sightseeing tour. Invariably the tour guide or driver takes you to a place which gives him or her at least a 10% commission on everything you buy—the universal tout problem. The problem has gotten so out of hand in Chiangmai that some touts now demand a 40% commission from shops along Chiangmai-Sankamphaeng Road! The prices will be inflated in these shops, and the quality of goods usually will be mediocre. Most often you will be steered to a lapidary, jewelry store, or silk shop. We recommend avoiding such shops by asking the tour guide or driver to take you back to your hotel or put you in a taxi—say you feel ill. If this doesn't work, ask for your money back. There is nothing worse than wasting time in one of those shops and knowing full well you are about to be "taken." Remember, **if a tour guide or driver takes you to one of his or her recommended shops, at least 10%—and possibly as much as 40%—of the price you pay will go directly into the pocket of this "helpful" individual.** You will do everyone a favor, including yourself, if you will ditch this person as soon as possible. It is okay to be obnoxious with such human leeches.

SHOPPING BY THE RULES

The structure of shopping in Thailand is such that you should make a few adjustments to the way you normally approach shopping if you are to best enjoy your shopping adventure. The most important adjustments constitute a set of shopping rules that are applicable in most shopping situations:

- **The most important shopping areas are concentrated in the central business districts and a few outlying suburban areas.**

  The best products in terms of quality, designs, and colors are found in shopping centers, hotel shopping arcades, department stores, and shophouses concentrated along one or two major streets in the central business districts of most major cities and towns. However, don't expect to find much shopping in rural areas other than at factory shops and cottage industry houses on the outskirts of Chiangmai, Chiangrai, Lamphun, and Lampang. Knowing these shopping patterns, it's a good idea to stay at a hotel in close proximity to the main shopping streets in the center of town. Except for Bangkok and Chiangmai, where you should visit factories and shops outside the central business district, expect to do 90 percent of your shopping along a few downtown streets.

- **Concentrate your shopping on a few shopping areas within close proximity of each other each day.**

  While it is relatively easy to get around in Bangkok, Chiangmai, and other towns, it's best to focus your shopping in particular shopping areas rather than continuously travel from one shop to another between areas. Compile a list of shops or areas you wish to visit, locate them on a map, and each day try to visit those close to one another.

- **Prepare to walk a great deal within each shopping area, but use transportation to go from one shopping area to another.**

  While most shops, shopping centers, and department stores are located along a few streets in the central business district, these are often very long streets requiring a considerable amount of walking. Take a good pair of walking shoes, slow your pace of walking, and take taxis whenever possible.

- **Use taxis or hotel cars when going between shopping areas or even within some shopping areas.**

  Public transportation, such as buses and trishaws, are inexpensive but often inconvenient for shoppers. Given the high heat and humidity as well as the long walking distances involved in shopping, avoid extensive walking. Our rule of thumb: if we must walk more than one kilometer, we take a taxi or rent a hotel car and driver by the hour, half-day, or day. However, in the case of Chiangmai, Chiangrai, Maesai, Lampang, Lamphun, and

Phuket, you may want to rent a car and drive yourself to the major shopping areas.

- **Take your rain and sun gear whenever you go out.**

  Unless you know for certain the weather forecast for the day, it's always a good idea to take an umbrella—a small collapsible one is perfect—sunglasses, and hat when you go out during the day and an umbrella at night. Thailand's hot and humid climate can be unpredictable at times. The umbrella keeps both the rain and sun off our heads. When we forget to take our umbrella, invariably it rains!

- **Expect to shop in two very different shopping cultures.**

  The first world is the most familiar one for visitors—shopping centers, department stores, and hotel shopping arcades. Shops in this culture tend to have window displays, well organized interiors, and fixed prices which may or may not be all that fixed, depending on your ability to get discounts. The second shopping culture consists of the traditional shophouses, markets, and hawkers which tend to be somewhat disorganized and involve price uncertainty and bargaining skills. You will most likely be able to directly transfer your shopping skills to the first culture, but you may have difficulty navigating in the second shopping culture.

- **The day and night markets can be fun places to shop, but only if you are open to new sights, sounds, and smells not normally found in other shopping sites.**

  Many of the markets combine fresh fruits, vegetables, and meats with hawker food stalls and shop stalls selling household goods. Somewhat chaotic, these markets can be very interesting and colorful places to visit. They tend to cater to a different class of local residents—lower to lower-middle—than the department stores and shopping centers. Many locals prefer shopping in the markets because prices appear cheap compared to other shopping alternatives. While these markets offer few items of interest to visitors, they do provide a cultural experience and are good places for exotic photo opportunities. Other markets primarily offer inexpensive clothes, household goods, electronics, handicrafts, jewelry, and antiques. These, too, are great places to experience the more traditional buying and selling culture. Depending on the market, you may or may not find good quality products in these places. In most markets the emphasis is on buying cheap goods. You may find inexpensive clothes, handicrafts, souvenirs, and fake products to make the trip to these markets worthwhile. Bargaining, with discounts ranging from 20 to 60 percent, is the only way to buy in these markets. You will be foolish to pay the first price. In Bangkok the Weekend Market is most popular on Saturdays and Sundays while the night markets along Patpong and Silom roads are favorite destinations for tourists in search of inexpensive clothes, copy watches, and imitation leather goods. Chiangmai's Night Bazaar is the center for most market shopping of interest to tourists.

- **Most department stores and some shopping centers primarily cater to the shopping preferences of local residents rather than to foreign tourists.**

  Don't expect to find a great deal of quality local products in department stores and shopping centers. Most of these places orient their product lines to the local middle-class with numerous average quality consumer products and imported goods. However, you will find a few exceptional shopping centers in Bangkok that are primarily oriented to foreign visitors and Thailand's upper class—River City Shopping Complex, Oriental Plaza, Peninsula Plaza, Amarin Plaza, and New World Trade Center. These are "must visit" places for most visitors.

- **The best quality products are invariably found in the major hotel shopping arcades and a few shopping centers with reputations for quality.**

  There is nothing surprising to discover that the best quality shops tend to congregate near the best quality hotels which cater to the more affluent business travelers and tourists. The shops in these places will offer a mix of expensive imported products—designer label clothes, jewelry, luggage, shoes, and accessories—as well as excellent quality local products, especially antiques, jewelry, textiles, and tailored clothes. The prices in such shops can seem high, but they offer good quality products. The "best buys" will be on high quality local products rather than the usual mix of upscale imported goods that are available in many other cities and duty-free shops around the world.

- **Expect to get the best prices on locally produced items that use inexpensive labor.**

  Imported goods will be expensive regardless of their duty-free status. But any products that use inexpensive local labor—textiles, woodcarvings, woven handicrafts, handcrafted jewelry—are excellent buys because the cost of labor is going up and many of the handcrafting skills are quickly disappearing with the onslaught of inexpensive plastic materials and machine labor.

- **Don't expect to get something for nothing.**

  If a price seems too good to be true, it probably is. Good quality products, especially jewelry, antiques, and art, may not seem cheap in Thailand. But they are bargains if you compare prices to similar items found in the shops of Tokyo, Sydney, Paris, London, or New York City.

- **Ask for assistance whenever you feel you need it.**

  At times you may feel lost and have difficulty finding particular shops or products. Whenever this happens, just ask for assistance from your hotel, shopkeepers, and people you meet on the street. The Thai are friendly and will assist you if they can.

- **Don't be surprised if some shopkeepers take a great deal of your time in developing a personal and long-term relationship with you.**

  Business in Thailand is still a personal set of relations, regardless of all the symbols of impersonal efficiency. While some merchants may initially appear distant and suspicious, most are generally inquisitive if you will initiate a conversation that involves their family, work, or country. Many merchants in Thailand are extremely friendly, enjoy learning more about visitors, are willing to share their knowledge about their country and products, and prefer cementing personal relationships with their customers. The lines between buyer and seller may quickly fade as you develop a friendship with the shopkeeper. You may even find some shopkeepers inviting you to lunch, dinner, or their home as well as giving you special gifts. You may even feel you are being adopted by the family! This is usually a genuine expression of interest, concern, and friendship rather than a sales tactic. Such personal encounters may well become the highlights of your shopping adventure in Thailand and they may lead to lasting friendships with these individuals.

You will also discover other shopping rules as you proceed through the many shophouses, shopping centers, hotel shopping arcades, department stores, and markets in Thailand. Many of these relate to pricing policies and bargaining practices that you can and should learn if you want to become an effective shopper in Thailand.

PRICING PRACTICES AND BARGAINING

Bargaining still remains the way of shopping life in most parts of Thailand. Therefore, if you want to become an effective shopper in Thailand, you need to know something about the basics of bargaining.

Most North American and European tourists come from fixed-price cultures where prices are nicely displayed on items. The only price uncertainty may be a sales tax added to the total amount at the cash register. Only on very large-ticket items, such as automobiles, boats, houses, furniture, carpets, and jewelry, can you expect to negotiate the price. If you want to get the best deal, you must do comparative shopping as well as wait for special discounts and sales. Bargain shopping in such a culture centers on comparative pricing of items. Shopping becomes a relatively passive activity involving the examination of advertisements in newspapers and catalogs.

Expert shoppers in fixed-price cultures tend to be those skilled in carefully observing and comparing prices in the print advertising media. They clip coupons and know when the best sales are being held for particular items on certain days. They need not be concerned with cultivating personal relationships with merchants or salespeople in order to get good buys.

Like a fish out of water, expert shoppers from fixed-price cultures may feel lost when shopping in Thailand. Few of their fixed-price shopping skills are directly transferable to Thailand's shopping environments. Except for department stores and some ads in the monthly tourist literature as well as local newspapers announcing special sales, few shops advertise in the print media or on TV and radio.

COPING WITH PRICE UNCERTAINTY

Goods in Thailand fall into three pricing categories: **fixed, negotiable**, or **discounted**. The general trend in Bangkok is toward fixed prices on more and more goods. In the meantime, **price uncertainty**—negotiable or discounted prices—is the standard way to sell most goods and services in Thailand. The general pricing guideline is this: **Unless you see a sign stating otherwise, you can expect prices of most goods in small shops to be negotiable.** You can safely assume that all stated prices are the starting point from which you should receive anything from a 10 to 60 percent discount, depending upon your haggling skills and level of commitment to obtain reduced prices.

Discount percentages in Thailand will vary for different items and from one shop to another. In general, however, expect to receive at least a 10 to 20 percent discount on most items in shops willing to discount. Some will discount as much as 50 or 60 percent.

The structure of prices on certain goods and services varies. The prices on items in department stores are fixed, although the jewelry section may discount up to 20 percent. Prices for tailors, hairdressers, airport limousines, and medical personnel are fixed. Hotel prices are subject to a variety of discounts for different categories of travelers—VIP, business, government, weekend, and tourist.

When in doubt if a price is fixed, negotiable, or subject to discounts, **always ask for a special discount**. After the salesperson indicates the price, ask one of two questions:

"What kind of discount can you give me on this item?"

"What is your best price?"

If the person indicates a discount, you can either accept it or attempt to negotiate the price through a bargaining process.

While skilled shoppers in fixed-price cultures primarily compare prices by reading ads and listening to special announcements, skilled shoppers in bargaining cultures primarily engage in face-to-face encounters with sellers. To be successful, the shopper must use various interpersonal skills. Once you know these and practice bargaining, you should become a very effective shopper in Thailand—as well as elsewhere in Asia.

ESTABLISH VALUE AND PRICE

Not knowing the price of an item, many shoppers from fixed-price cultures face a problem. *"What is the actual value of the item? How much should I pay? At what point do I know I'm getting a fair price?"* These questions can be answered in several ways. First, you should have some idea of the **value** of the item, because you already did comparative shopping at home by examining catalogs and visiting discount houses, department stores, and specialty shops. If you are interested in a ruby or sapphire ring, for example, you should know what comparable quality jewelry sells for back home.

Second, you have done comparative shopping among the various shops you've encountered in Thailand in order to **establish a price range** for positioning yourself in the bargaining process. You've visited a department store in Bangkok to research how much a similar item is selling for at a fixed price. You've checked with a shop in your hotel and compared prices there. In your hotel you might ask *"How much is this item?"* and then act a little surprised that it appears so expensive. Tell them that you are a hotel guest and thus you want their *"very best price."* At this point the price usually decreases by 10 to 20 percent as you are told this is *"our very special price," "our first-customer-of-the-day price,"* or *"our special hotel guest price."*

Once you initially receive a special price from your first price inquiry, you may get another 10 to 20 percent through further negotiation. But at this point do not negotiate any more. Take the shop's business card and record on the back the item, the original price, and the first discount price; thank the shopkeeper, and tell him or her that you may return. Repeat this same scenario in a few other shops. After doing three or four comparisons, you will **establish a price range** for particular items. This range will give you a fairly accurate idea of the going discount price. At this point you should be prepared to do some serious haggling, playing one shop off against another.

Effective shoppers in Thailand quickly learn how to comparative shop and negotiate the best deal. In learning to be effective, you don't need to be timid, aggressive, or obnoxious —extreme behaviors frequently exhibited by first-time practitioners of the Asian art of bargaining. Although you may feel bargaining is a defensive measure to avoid being ripped-off by unscrupulous merchants, it is an acceptable way of doing business in many Asian cultures. Merchants merely adjust their profit margins to the customer, depending on how they feel about the situation as well as their current cash flow needs. It is up to you to adapt to such a pricing culture. Some shopkeepers also adjust their prices depending on the nationality of the customer: highest prices for the Japanese because they are likely to think they are still getting a good deal compared to the high prices back home; higher starting prices for Italians because Italians want to bargain hard; and lower starting prices for Americans because they don't like to bargain and thus are likely to walk away after hearing the first price if it seems too high!

One problem you may soon discover is that every situation seems to differ somewhat, and differences between items and shops can be significant. You can expect to receive larger discounts on jewelry than on home furnishings. For example, discounts on jewelry may be as great as 50 to 60 percent whereas discounts on home furnishings may only be 10 to 20 percent.

The one major exception to bargaining concerns tailors. Tailors normally quote you a fixed-price subject to little or no negotiation; you merely trust that you are getting a fair price and, after all, it is not a good idea to make your tailor unhappy by bargaining when he doesn't want to. He may "get even" by cheapening the quality of your clothes. Only in tailor shops do we avoid forcing the price issue by bargaining. At best ask for *"your best price,"* use a common friend's name as reference, or ask for an extra shirt, but don't risk being short-changed on quality just to save a few dollars. If you comparative shop among a few tailor shops, you will quickly identify what should be the "fair market rate" for tailoring services assuming the use of comparable quality materials.

Our general rule on what items to bargain for is this: **bargain on ready-made items you can carry out of the shop**. If you must have an item custom-made, be very careful how you arrive at the final price. In most cases you should not bargain other than responding to the first price by asking *"Is this your best price?"* Better still, drop a few names, agree on a mutually satisfactory price, and then insist that you want top quality for that price.

Except for custom-made items, department stores, and shops displaying a "fixed prices" sign, **never accept the first price offered.** Rather, spend some time going through our bargaining scenario. And in some cases so-called "fixed price" shops will also bargain—at least it doesn't hurt to try!

Once you have accepted a price and purchased the item, be sure to **get a receipt** as well as **observe the packing process.** While few merchants will try to cheat you, some tourists have had unpleasant experiences which could have been avoided by following some simple rules of shopping in unfamiliar places.

GET THE BEST DEAL POSSIBLE

Chances are you will deal with a Thai-Chinese merchant who is a relatively seasoned businessman; he or she is a family entrepreneur who thrives on status and personal relationships. As soon as you walk through the door, most merchants will want to sell you items then and there.

The best deal you will get is when you have a personal relationship with the merchant. Contrary to what others may tell you about bargains for tourists, you often can get as good a deal—sometimes even better—than someone from the local community. It is simply a myth that tourists can't do as well on prices as the locals. Indeed, we often do better than the locals because we have done our comparative shopping and we know well the art of bargaining—something locals are often lax in doing. In addition, some merchants may give you a better price than the locals because you are "here today and gone tomorrow." After all, you won't be around to tell their regular customers about your very special price.

More often than not, the Thai pricing system operates like this: **If the shopkeeper likes you, or you are a friend of a friend or relative, you can expect to get a good price.** Whenever possible, drop names of individuals who referred you to the shop; the shopkeeper may think you are a friend and thus you are entitled to a special discount. But if you do not have such a relationship and you present yourself as a typical tourist who is here today and gone tomorrow, you need to bargain hard.

PRACTICE THE 12 RULES OF BARGAINING

The art of bargaining in Thailand can take on several different forms. In general, you want to achieve two goals in this haggling process: **establish the value of an item** and **get the best possible price**. The following bargaining rules work well.

- **Do your research before initiating the process.**

  Compare the prices among various shops, starting with the fixed-price items in department stores. Spot-check price ranges among shops in and around your hotel. Also, refer to your research done with catalogs and discount houses back home to determine if the discount is sufficient to warrant purchasing the item abroad rather than at home.

- **Determine the exact item you want.**

  Select the particular item you want and then focus your bargaining around that one item without expressing excessive interest and commitment. Even though you may be excited by the item and want it very badly, once the merchant knows you are committed to buying this one item, you weaken your bargaining position. Express a passing interest; indicate through eye contact with other items in the shop that you are not necessarily committed to the one item. As you ask about the other items, you should get some sense concerning the willingness of the merchant to discount prices.

- **Set a ceiling price you are willing to pay—and buy now!**

  Before engaging in serious negotiations, set in your mind the maximum amount you are willing to pay, which may be 20 percent more than you figured the item should sell for based on your research. However, if you find something you love that is really unique, be prepared to pay more if you can afford it. In many situations you will find unique items not available anywhere else. Consider buying **now** since the item may be gone when you return. Bargain as hard as you can and then pay what you have to—even though it may seem painful—for the privilege of owning a unique item. Remember, it's only money and it only hurts once. You can always make more money, and after returning home you will most likely enjoy your wonderful purchase and forget how painful it seemed at the time to buy it at less than your expected discount. Above all, do not pass up an item you really love just because the bargaining process does not fall in your favor. It is very easy to be "penny wise but pound foolish" in Thailand simply because the bargaining process is such an ego-involved activity. You may return home forever regretting that you didn't buy a lovely item just because you were too cheap to "give" on the last US$5 of haggling. In the end, put your ego aside, give in, and buy what you really want. Only you and the merchant will know who really won, and once you return home the US$5 will seem to be such an insignificant amount. Chances are you still got a good bargain compared to what you would pay elsewhere if, indeed, you could even find a similar item!

- **Play a role.**

Shopping in Thailand involves playing the roles of buyer and seller. While Thais do prize individualism in certain areas of their life, they are also terrific role players, moreso than Westerners. In contrast to many Western societies, where being a unique individual is emphasized, in Thailand individualism is not as highly valued. Thais learn specific sets of behaviors appropriate for the role of father, son, daughter, husband, wife, blood friend, classmate, superior, subordinate, buyer, seller. They easily shift from one role to another, undergoing major personality and behavioral changes without experiencing mental conflicts. When you encounter a Thai businessperson, you are often meeting a very refined and sophisticated role player. Therefore, it is to your advantage to play complementary roles by carefully structuring your personality and behavior to play the role of buyer. If you approach sellers by just "being yourself"—open, honest, somewhat naive, and with your own unique personality—you may be quickly walked over by a seasoned seller. Once you enter a shop, think of yourself as an actor walking on stage to play the lead role as a shrewd buyer, bargainer, and trader. But at the same time, you may encounter a very individualistic shopkeeper who unpredictably decides to give you a special gift or invite you home for dinner just because he or she likes you.

- **Establish good will and a personal relationship.**

A shrewd buyer also is charming, polite, personable, and friendly. You should have a sense of humor, smile, and be light-hearted during the bargaining process. But be careful about eye contact which can be threatening to Thais. Keep it to a minimum. Thai sellers prefer to establish a personal relationship so that the bargaining process can take place on a friendly, face-saving basis. In the end, both the buyer and seller should come out as winners. This can not be done if you approach the buyer in very serious and harsh terms. You should start by exchanging pleasantries concerning the weather, your trip, the city, or the nice items in the shop. After exchanging business cards or determining your status, the shopkeeper will know what roles should be played in the coming transaction.

- **Let the seller make the first offer.**

If the merchant starts by asking you *"How much do you want to pay?"*, avoid answering; immediately turn the question around: *"How much are you asking?"* Remember, many merchants try to get you to pay as much as you are willing and able to pay—not what the value of the item is or what he or she is willing to take. You should never reveal your ability or willingness to pay a certain price. Keep the seller guessing, thinking that you may lose interest or not buy the item because it appears too expensive. Always get the merchant to initiate the bargaining process. In so doing, the merchant must take the defensive as you shift to the offensive.

- **Take your time, being deliberately slow in order to get the merchant to invest his or her time in you.**

The more you indicate that you are impatient and in a hurry, the more you are likely to pay. When negotiating a price, **time** is usually in your favor. Many shopkeepers also see time as a positive force in the bargaining process. Some try to keep you in their shop by serving you tea, coffee, soft drinks, or liquor while negotiating the price. Be careful; this nice little ritual may soften you somewhat on the bargaining process as you begin establishing a more personal relationship with the merchant. The longer you stay in control prolonging the negotiation, the better the price should be. Although some merchants may deserve it, **never** insult them. Merchants need to "keep face" as much as you do in the process of giving and getting the very best price.

- **Use odd numbers in offering the merchant at least 40 percent less than what he or she initially offers.**

Avoid stating round numbers, such as 700, 1800, or 10,000. Instead, offer 620, 1735, or 8100 baht. Such numbers impress upon others that you may be a seasoned haggler who knows value and expects to do well in this negotiation. Your offer will probably be 15 percent less than the value you determined for the item. For example, if the merchant asks 2500 baht, offer 1530 baht, knowing the final price should probably be 1800. The merchant will probably counter with only a 10 percent discount—2250 baht. At this point you will need to go back and forth with another two or three offers and counter-offers.

- **Appear a little disappointed and take your time again.**

Never appear upset or angry with the seller. Keep your cool at all times by slowly sitting down and carefully examining the item. Shake your head a little and say, *"Gee, that's too bad. That's much more than I had planned to spend. I like it, but I really can't go that high."* Appear to be a sympathetic listener as the seller attempts to explain why he or she cannot budge more on the price. Make sure you do not accuse the merchant of being a thief! Use a little charm, if you can, for the way you conduct the bargaining process will affect the final price. This should be a civil negotiation in which you nicely bring the price down, the seller "saves face," and everyone goes away feeling good about the deal.

- **Counter with a new offer at a 35 percent discount.**

  Punch several keys on your calculator, which indicates that you are doing some serious thinking. Then say something like *"This is really the best I can do. It's a lovely item, but 1625 baht is really all I can pay."* At this point the merchant will probably counter with a 20 percent discount—2000.

- **Be patient, persistent, and take your time again by carefully examining the item.**

  Respond by saying *"That's a little better, but it's still too much. I want to look around a little more."* Then start to get up and look toward the door. At this point the merchant has invested some time in this exchange, and he or she is getting close to a possible sale. The merchant will either let you walk out the door or try to stop you with another counter-offer. If you walk out the door, you can always return to get the 2000 baht price. But most likely the merchant will try to stop you, especially if there is still some bargaining room. The merchant is likely to say: *"You don't want to waste your time looking elsewhere. I'll give you the best price anywhere—just for you. Okay, 1900 baht. That's my final price."*

- **Be creative for the final negotiation.**

  You could try for 1800 baht, but chances are 1900 baht will be the final price with this merchant. Yet, there may still be some room for negotiating "extras." At this point get up and walk around the shop and examine other items; try to appear as if you are losing interest in the item you were bargaining for. While walking around, identify a 100 baht item you like which might make a nice gift for a friend or relative, which you could possibly include in the final deal. Wander back to the 100 baht item and look as if your interest is waning and perhaps you need to leave. Then start to probe the possibility of including extras while agreeing on the 1900 baht: *"Okay, I might go 1900 baht, but only if you include this with it."* The "this" is the 100 baht item you eyed. You also might negotiate with your credit card. Chances are the merchant is expecting cash on the 1900 baht discounted price and will add a 2-5 percent "commission" if you want to use your credit card. In this case, you might respond to the 1900 baht by saying, *"Okay, I'll go with the 1900, but only if I can use my credit card."* You may get your way, your bank will float you a loan in the meantime, and your credit card company may help you resolve the problem in case you later learn your purchase was mispresented. Finally, you may want to negotiate packing and delivery processes. If it is a fragile item, insist that it be packed well so you can take it with you on the airplane or have it shipped. If your purchase is large, insist that the shop deliver it to your hotel or to your shipper. If the shop is shipping it by air or sea, try to get them to agree to absorb some of the freight and insurance costs.

This slow, civil, methodical, and sometimes charming approach to bargaining works well in most cases. However, Thai merchants do differ in how they respond to situations and many of them are unpredictable, depending on whether or not they like you. In some cases, your timing may be right: the merchant is in need of cash flow that day and thus he or she is willing to give you the price you want, with little or no bargaining. Others will not give more than a 10 to 20 percent discount unless you are a friend of a friend who is then eligible for the special "family discount." And others are not good businessmen, are unpredictable, lack motivation, or are just moody; they refuse to budge on their prices even though your offer is fair compared to the going prices in other shops. In these situations it is best to leave the shop and find one which is more receptive to the traditional haggling process.

BARGAIN FOR NEEDS, NOT GREED

One word of caution for those who are just starting to learn the fine art of Thai bargaining. **Be sure you really want an item before you initiate the bargaining process**. Many tourists learn to bargain effectively, and then get carried away with their new-found skill. Rather than use this skill to get what they want, they enjoy the process of bargaining so much that they buy many unnecessary items. After all, they got such "a good deal" and thus could not resist buying the item. You do not need to fill your suitcases with junk in demonstrating this ego-gratifying skill. If used properly, your new bargaining skills will lead to some excellent buys on items you really need and want.

EXAMINE YOUR GOODS CAREFULLY

Before you commence the bargaining process, carefully examine the item, being sure that you understand the quality of the item for which you are negotiating. Then, after you settle on a final price, make sure you are getting the goods you agreed upon. You should carefully observe the handling of items, including the actual packing process. If at all possible, take the items with you when you leave the shop. If you later discover you were victimized by a switch or misrepresentation, contact the Tourism Authority of Thailand as well as your credit card company if you charged your purchase. You should be able to resolve the problem through these channels. However, the responsibility is on you, the buyer, to know what you are buying.

BEWARE OF SCAMS

Although one hopes this will never happen, you may be unfortunate in encountering unscrupulous merchants who take advantage of you. This is more likely to happen if you wander away from recommended shops in discovering your own "very special" bargains or enter the *"Hey, you mister"* shops. While we have never had these problems happen to us, we do know others who have had such misfortunes. The most frequent scams to watch out for include:

- **Switching the goods.**

  You negotiate for a particular item, such as a piece of jewelry or a blouse, but in the process of packing it, the merchant substitutes an inferior product.

- **Misrepresenting quality goods.**

  Be especially cautious in jewelry, leather, and antique shops. Sometimes so-called expensive watches are excellent imitations and worth no more than US$15—or have cheap mechanisms inside expensive cases. Leather briefcases, purses, and belts are often fake leathers or leather of very poor quality. Precious stones, such as rubies, may not be as precious as they appear. Synthetic stones, garnets, or spinels are sometimes substituted for high quality rubies. Some substitutes are so good that experts even have difficulty identifying the difference. Accordingly, you may pay US$2,000 for what appears to be a ruby worth US$10,000 back home, but in fact you just bought a US$25 red spinel. Pearls come in many different qualities, so know your pearls before negotiating a price. Real jade and ivory are beautiful, but many buyers unwittingly end up with green plastic, soapstone, or bone at jade and ivory prices. In fact, since it is now illegal to bring ivory into the U.S., you are really better off with carved bone—but at bone prices! The antique business is relatively unregulated. Some merchants try to sell "new antiques" at "old antique" prices. Many of the fakes are outstanding reproductions, often fooling even the experts. Better still, there is a reputable business in fakes. You may want to just shop for fakes!

- **Goods not shipped.**

  The shop may agree to ship your goods home, but once you leave they conveniently forget to do so. You wait and wait, write letters of inquiry, and receive no replies. Unless you insured the item and have all proper receipts, you may not receive the goods you paid for.

Your best line of defense against these and other possible scams is to be very careful wherever you go and whatever you do in relation to handling money. A few simple precautions will help avoid some of these problems:

- **Do not trust anyone with your money** unless you have proper assurances they are giving you exactly what you agreed upon. Be especially careful with your credit cards. Keep them within your sight during the transaction process.

- **Do your homework** so you can determine quality and value as well as anticipate certain types of scams.

- **Examine the goods carefully**, assuming something may be or will go wrong.

- **Watch very carefully how the merchant handles items** from the moment they leave your hands until they get wrapped and into a bag.

- **Request receipts** that list specific items and the prices you paid. Although most shops are willing to *"give you a receipt"* specifying whatever price you want them to write for purposes of deceiving customs, avoid such pettiness because customs know better, and you may need a receipt with the real price to claim your goods or a refund. If the shop is to ship, be sure you have a shipping receipt which also includes insurance against both loss and damage.

- **Patronize shops which are affiliated with the Tourism Authority of Thailand.** They are more likely to treat you honestly since the parent organization does somewhat police its members.

- **Protect yourself against scams by using credit cards** for payment, especially for big ticket items which could present problems, even though using them may cost you a little more. Many credit card companies will try to assist you to resolve problems.

If you are victimized, all is not necessarily lost. You should report the problem immediately to the Tourism Authority of Thailand, the police, your credit card company, or insurance company. While inconvenient and time consuming, nonetheless, in many cases you will eventually get satisfactory results.

DISAPPOINTING TAILORED GARMENTS

Time and again visitors to Thailand—like their brethren in Hong Kong, South Korea, and Singapore—come away with disappointing tailored clothes. Invariably tourists are disappointed with their tailored garments: they don't fit properly, they weren't delivered on time, or the final product was not what the buyer expected.

We know the many pitfalls that can trap the unwary shopper who, used to buying clothing off-the-rack at home, decides to indulge in this unique experience and have clothing custom tailored. Having heard from acquaintances who traveled to this part of the world years ago about the great values in custom tailored goods, our traveler is easy prey for unbelievable deals on tailored garments. How does US$89 sound for a suit, 3 extra pairs of slacks, 3 custom-made shirts, 1 bathrobe, and a few other extras? Unbelievable! Indeed, if it sounds too good to be true, it probably is. In the end you get what you pay for. In fact, this experience could cost you plenty if the garments you pay for are so shoddily made that you seldom or never wear them.

First, consider whether you really want to have custom tailoring done. If you are hard to fit and can never find anything to fit properly at home, you may be a candidate for tailoring in Thailand. But if you have no trouble buying garments that fit well "off-the-rack," ask yourself if you really want to go through the hassle and risk of custom tailoring. The hassle involves effectively communicating your wishes to the tailor, returning to the shop for several fittings (don't even hope for a good fit without this), and possibly having to arrange for shipment of the garments to your home if the tailor fails to finish them on time. The risk is that you will have to pay for goods that are not satisfactory and that you would never have selected if you had found them hanging on the rack. In general, you may find that ready-made clothes back home are a better value in terms of quality, design, fit, and cost.

TAILORING CONSIDERATIONS

If you do decide to go ahead with custom tailoring after our warnings, follow these guidelines:

- **Don't expect to get something for nothing.** Quality fabrics and good workmanship cost money anywhere in the world. Go to a good tailor and be willing to pay for quality. The best tailors tend to be located in and around the shopping arcades of Bangkok's deluxe hotels. We identify several of these tailors by name, address, and phone number in Chapter Ten.

- **Look at fabrics and examples of finished work carefully.** Are the fabrics of good quality? Are they soft and supple so they will lay smoothly in the finished garment? Go to the racks of completed sample garments. Check the general appearance of garments including topstitching, buttonholes, and button quality, smoothness of darts and pocket application. Hand sewing is one mark of quality custom tailoring. Turn up the collar and examine the underside for the slightly uneven hand stitches which indicate that it was partly hand sewn. Check the way hems are finished. Check women's jackets and coats to see that the chest area is not excessively form fitted with darts which create a fitted look not popular in the West—especially if you plan to wear the jacket unbuttoned and loose.

- **Check garments waiting for first or second fittings.** Next, go to the rack where other customers' unfinished garments are waiting for first or second fittings. Examine the inside construction of several garments to see how well each is constructed. Firm interfacing should be used inside the upper part of jackets and coats and inside the lapels and collar to give support and shape to the garment. Many tailors now use fusible (iron-on) interfacing to save time instead of the more supple woven interfacing which needs to be sewn into place. Fusible interfacing is fine when used in a limited way, but the exclusive use of fusible rather than woven interfacing results in stiff garments. If fabrics have a pattern check to see how well the pattern matches wherever seams meet.

- **Specify the right style for you.** Be prepared with photos showing the style or combination of styles you want. (Remember, Thai tailors do not work from prepackaged patterns. You can select a collar from one photo to be combined with a jacket front from another). Men's suits, for example, can be fashioned in three different styles or silhouettes:

  The American Silhouette: Derived from the Brooks Brothers "sack" suite of the '50s. Cut straight and full with lightly padded natural shoulders, a center rear vent, and medium armholes, it is body concealing and conservative.

  The European Cut Silhouette: This is sleeker and features a more dramatic fit around the chest and hips with padded shoulders, high armholes, narrow lapels, and a generally slim line which looks best on smaller men.

The British Silhouette: Often called the Updated American model, this suit has slightly padded shoulders, nipped in the waist, two deep rear side vents, and cuffed and pleated trousers. The jacket pockets are angled and flapped.

You can, of course, specify other styles. But know before you enter a tailor shop what looks best on you. Avoid being swayed by the salesperson to go with the "latest fashion" if it won't fit your lifestyle back home or your shape.

- **Communicate every detail.** Don't assume your image is similar to the salesperson's image of the finished product. For example, if the fabric you've selected has stripes, specify the direction—horizontal, vertical or diagonal—for the stripes in the finished garment. The rule here is to: **assume nothing and explain everything.**

- **Give the tailor enough time to do a quality job.** Expect to have a minimum of two fittings —three is better—for garments in which fit is critical such as suits or slacks. One fitting might be acceptable for a loosely constructed garment such as a blouse. Expect a suit to take at least four days while a blouse might be completed in one or two days. Good work is not done overnight, and usually only *"Hey, you mister"* shops will make such rash promises.

- **Arrange to take delivery of your finished garments no later than the day before you leave.** Leave yourself a little extra time in case the tailor fails to make the scheduled deadline or time is needed to rectify problems you discover when picking up the completed garments and trying them on for the first time.

If you will be wary of potential pitfalls of custom tailoring and follow these guidelines, you will be a smart shopper for tailored garments. Like many other people, you may be pleased with the outcome of having tailoring completed during your stay in Thailand.

We address custom tailoring at some length, including a separate chapter on how to ensure proper tailoring in our ***Shopping and Traveling in Exotic Hong Kong*** and ***Shopping and Traveling in Exotic Asia*** volumes. You might want to refer to one of these books for more detailed "how-to" information on tailoring if you believe you need more specifics than outlined here.

7 MAJOR SHOPPING CHOICES

Thailand offers a wonderful array of products and services for discriminating shoppers. While Hong Kong and Singapore are excellent destinations for buying electronic goods, tailored clothes, and jewelry, Thailand's strengths are in the areas of arts, crafts, and gems. Thailand's long and proud traditions in the arts and crafts continue today in the numerous factories and shops of Bangkok and Chiangmai. The Royal Court continues to promote many of the arts and crafts as do the many families that produce quality products for the growing tourist and export markets.

SHOPPING STRENGTHS

Thai product markets are constantly changing. Quality, selection, and styles are being continually upgraded, and new shops and shopping arcades offering unique quality items regularly spring up and expand in many different areas of Bangkok. The shopping scene seems to transform itself every five years with new offerings and services. While only a few years ago Thailand was well known for several typical tourist items—lacquerware, silk, bronzeware, hilltribe handicrafts, woodcarved elephants, precious and semiprecious stones, and temple rubbings—today Thailand offers a dazzling array of additional goods ranging from gorgeous Burmese tapestries and antiques to stylish woodcarvings and designer jewelry, clothes, and accessories. Thailand is well on its way to becoming a major world shopping center.

Thailand's major shopping strengths for uniqueness, quality, and value include the following products:

- silk and cotton fabrics
- tailored and ready-made clothes
- gems and jewelry
- silver and nielloware
- bronzeware, brassware, and pewterware
- celadon, ceramics, and pottery
- leather goods
- handmade wood and rattan furniture
- paintings, sculptures, and framing
- antiques
- woodcarvings
- handicraft items
- arts and antiques from Burma and Cambodia
- fake designer clothes, watches, and carvings

For discriminating shoppers, Thailand's major strengths are in the areas of **decorative items**, **home furnishings**, and **gems**. Handmade items from copies of originals are especially good values in Thailand. Thai clothes are plentiful and inexpensive, but they are often disappointing in terms of quality and style, particularly if you have already seen the wonderful selections in Hong Kong and Singapore. Thailand has yet to adequately respond to Western shopping tastes for clothes with talented designers who understand current Western preferences for particular colors, designs, and quality. While this situation is improving, Thailand will have to make some major changes before becoming a major international market for these goods. Although Thai silk, cotton, tailored clothes, ready-made clothes, and shoes may be good buys and look lovely on many Thai women, they are no bargain if they are inappropriate for your wardrobe back home.

THAI SILK AND COTTON

Thai silk and cotton are world famous, at least according to what you hear in Bangkok. But there is much more to this story if you are particular about your clothes. Thai silk has a rough quality and is heavier than silks found in many other countries. The colors are often very bright and patterns are somewhat traditional—often a floral or flame pattern. The unique *mutmee* silk produced in Northeast Thailand is a rough material with a particular geometric design and is normally produced in muted colors. Most Thai silk is purchased by the meter or yard from which to make tailored dresses, blouses, shirts, suits, and ties.

When worn by Thai women on festive occasions, the Thai silk looks gorgeous. And for one very good reason. The bright colors contrast nicely with the dark hair and skins of the Thai who generally tend to have coloring enhanced by these powerful, bright colors. However, less than one-third of Western tourists have coloring complimented by very bright colors. Thai silks and cottons offered by many shops continue to overpower the coloring of many Western tourists.

Many tourists purchase Thai silks and cottons, because they look so beautiful in Thailand. But once they return home, some become disappointed with their clothing purchases. Many of the colors and patterns are not stylish for Western countries nor one's personal coloring scheme. The fabrics tend to be too heavy for many clothing styles. Indeed, blouses and shirts tend to be very stiff, lacking the grace and elegance associated with the lighter weight Chinese silks. But Thai silks do work well for evening dresses as long as the skirt is not too full. They also are great for caftans and robes, and are far superior to the lighter weight Chinese silk for home decorating items, such as bedspreads, pillow covers, and frame mats for paintings and carved pieces. As with any silk, Thai silks can be difficult to care for. The colors may run and they may require dry cleaning.

Thai silks and cottons are excellent for decorative items and home furnishings. They are beautiful when used for upholstering sofas and chairs or when made into draperies, pillow covers, napkins, placemats, wall hangings, jewelry boxes, picture frames, and a variety of custom-made handicrafts. If you purchase paintings, antiques, or other items you wish to have framed, the very rough quality Thai silk makes an inexpensive and beautiful framing mat. Many art and framing shops will do this custom work to your specifications. Ironically, standard paper mat selections are very limited in Thailand because they must be imported. Duties on such imports discourage shops from carrying large selections and inventories. But the shops can make gorgeous mats using your choice of silk fabric for very reasonable cost. For art connoisseurs, this is one of the best buys found anywhere in the world. In fact, we often take our purchases from the United States, Hong Kong, Burma, Indonesia, and other countries to have them uniquely framed in Bangkok using the Thai silk.

If you wish to purchase stylish Thai silk clothes or fabric for tailor-made clothes, you need only visit one shop in Bangkok—**Jim Thompson Silk Company** at 9 Suriwongse Road. This is Thailand's premier silk shop. They sell silk by the meter as well as have a large selection of lovely ready-made clothes for both men and women, pillow covers, matching placemats and napkins, jewelry boxes, picture frames, bags, scarves, neckties, and a variety of other silk items. Their silk prices are some of the highest in Thailand, but you get outstanding quality products for your money. We strongly recommend this shop, because it offers high quality silk. Its talented designers have developed very creative and elegant designs, and their selection of colors are more appropriate for Westerners than what is found in many silk shops. Jim Thompson's also has an excellent selection of Thai cottons, upholstery materials, and neckpiece accessories for coordinating your wardrobe. There are also branch shops at the Oriental Hotel and in the new Grand Hyatt Erawan Hotel. A few other shops, such as **Design Thai** (304 Silom Rd.), **Anita Thai Silk** (294/4-5 Silom Rd.), **Khanitha** (Oriental Plaza, Regent Hotel, River City Shopping Complex, and Siam Shopping Centre), **Jagtar** (37 Soi 11 Sukhumvit Rd.), and **Shinawatra** (94 Soi 23 Sukhumvit Rd.) also offer good quality silk and cotton.

Even if you are not interested in Thai silk, you should visit the Jim Thompson Silk Company just to observe their exquisite materials and designs, experience professional Thai service, and make at least a small purchase just to get one of their gorgeous shopping bags or boxes!

TAILOR-MADE CLOTHES

If you purchase Thai silk or cotton for tailor-made clothes, you should be very selective in who makes your clothes. A great deal of the tailoring in Thailand lacks the smooth clean lines and fits associated with quality tailoring found in Hong Kong. The cuts and pressing tend to produce clothes that lack a first-class look. Some look old-fashioned and rumpled. If you plan to visit Hong Kong after Thailand, you may want to take your material with you to have your clothes made there.

If you want to have clothes made in Thailand, stay near the hotel tailor shops and be sure to take with you a picture, or an example, of what you want made. Thai tailors are very good at copying styles from pictures, although they may not get all the details right. If you have a suit made, insist on three fittings and be sure the item fits right before accepting it. If you have a man's suit made, check to be sure the tailor specializes in men's suits. Some tailors primarily work with women's clothes and occasionally will do a man's suit. The tailoring skills are not the same. As you quickly discover, you get what you pay for.

Some of Bangkok's best men's tailors include **Perry's** (60/2 Silom Rd., Tel. 233-9236—does both men's and women's clothes), **Adam's Tailor** (23/3 Thaniya Rd., Tel. 233-7857 and Charn Issara Tower), and **C. Fillipo** (Shangri-La and Hilton hotels). Bangkok's best seamstress is probably **Penny's Boutique** (Peninsula Plaza). They have an excellent selection of Thai, Chinese, French, and Italian silks and do quality work.

If you are looking for some truly unique clothes, you may want to examine hilltribe clothes which are being made into popular designs and sold in boutiques. Stop at the **Golden Triangle** (3rd floor, River City Shopping Complex, Tel. 234-9365, ext. 301), **Anong Gallery** (second floor, Oriental Plaza, Tel. 235-7991 and Peninsula Plaza, Tel. 252-3070), **Babthai** (2nd floor, Oriental Plaza, Tel. 234-1320-9, ext. 44), **Prayer** (197 Phyathai Road at Siam Center), and **John Fowler** (Silom Road at the corner of Convent Road, Tel. 234-3778).

READY-MADE CLOTHES

The Thai garment industry has been growing by leaps and bounds during the past decade. You will find Thai ready-made clothes in small shops, department stores, markets, and sidewalk stalls and tables, especially in the **Indra Arcade** and the **Pratunam Market** adjacent to the Indra Hotel on Rajaparop Road. Many of the ready-made clothes in the markets and sold by street vendors, such as polo shirts, are fakes placed under designer labels. These are inexpensive imitations, but the quality is poor. Many tourists like to buy these as gifts, similar to imitation Rolex and Cartier watches and Gucci bags. However, many of these garments quickly deteriorate after a few washings.

Except for ready-made clothes found at Jim Thompson Silk Company and a few other quality shops (Design Thai, Khanitha, Choisy, Jagtar, Ajai Zecha/A Cha) we have not been attracted to Thai ready-made clothes. The designs and colors are unusual and inappropriate for our wardrobes. These clothes are primarily designed for local consumption and do not fit most Westerners. Indeed, Thais in general do not have the same sense of color and design as Westerners. Although neat and pretty as separate pieces, few pieces seem to go together. Expect to find ready-made clothes with a decided adolescent look and which are either too bright or too muted in color.

GEMS AND SEMI-PRECIOUS STONES

Thailand offers some of the world's best values on precious and semi-precious stones. The best buys are found on Thai sapphires—available predominately in blue or black in either star or plain cabochon—or various shades of blue in faceted cuts. Zircons, garnets, cat's eye, jadeite, nephrite, tiger eye, and turquoise are also widely available. Another excellent buy are rubies from Burma and Cambodia, but make sure you do not buy an inexpensive spinel at ruby prices! Many visitors to Thailand report being cheated on gem purchases. Most, however, create their own self-fulfilling prophesy: they don't know what they are doing; they try to get something for nothing; or they frequent fast-talking and questionable dealers. Sadly, some write to us asking us to warn other visitors about this "problem with Thailand." The problem is **not** Thailand. Rather, the problem is the naive shopper who should "known better" than to shop in such questionable places and entrust large sums of money to strangers!

Thailand is also doing a great deal of diamond cutting. More and more diamonds at good prices should be appearing on the Thai market as Thailand attempts to become one of the world's largest diamond cutters.

Many visitors prefer to buy loose cut stones and have them set in Hong Kong or at home. Others prefer to have the stones set in Bangkok according to their own designs. Most buyers report savings of 75 percent on Thai stones compared to similar ones back home. The quality of the stones, cuts, and settings will vary from excellent to poor, so be sure you know your stones and examine them carefully. Several lapidaries in Bangkok provide tours of their factories. The Tourist Authority of Thailand lists several recommended establishments which are supposed to adhere to fair business practices. Some of the most reliable include **Thai Lapidary** (277/122 Rama I Road, Tel. 214-2641), **Uthai Gems** (23/7 Soi Ruam Rudee, Tel. 252-4365), and **New Universal** (1144-46 New Road, Tel. 234-

3514). Make sure you bargain for all of these purchases. Avoid the touts, tour guides, and taxi drivers who steer you to particular shops. In 99 percent of the cases they will receive a commission on everything you purchase, and they will not take you to the most reputable shops.

We cannot over-stress the importance of knowing what you are doing when you purchase gems and jewelry in Thailand. Always patronize reputable shops, many of which are located in the major deluxe hotels. If you don't, you may join the growing list of individuals who report getting swindled on such purchases.

GOLD AND SILVER

Thailand offers excellent buys on gold and silver. If you wish to buy pure gold, visit a Chinese gold shop and ask for the near pure 24-carat gold "Baht Bracelet" or rings. These are convenient ways to buy gold. The gold is sold at the market rate, and you pay primarily for the gold content—not the craftsmanship that goes into making the bracelets or rings. A small mark-up over the price of the gold is normally equivalent to what you would pay over the daily gold price for a new U.S. gold coin.

Gold jewelry can be purchased in different karats. Thais tend to prefer 18-karat (785), although they can make jewelry any karat you want, and some willingly stamp any karat designation you wish to appear on your jewelry.

Since Thai craft labor is so inexpensive, one of the best values is to have your gold jewelry made or repaired in Thailand. If you need to have a wedding ring or bracelet rebuilt, for example, take it to Thailand. You're be pleased with the price and the workmanship. Thai craftsmen are excellent in copying designs, and the quality of workmanship can be outstanding. Make sure you take pictures of your preferred designs with you so the craftsmen have a model from which to work.

Lovely yellow and white gold-dipped flowers are widely available in both Bangkok and Chiangmai. The **Royal Orchid Company** of Chiangmai, as well as several imitators, produce and distribute these flowers as pins, earrings, and neckpieces. Made from a fascinating nickel, copper, and gold dipping and plating process, this jewelry is relatively inexpensive and it makes lovely trip gifts.

Silver is also widely available in Thailand. The silver is produced in traditional and modern designs as rings, bracelets, earrings, necklaces, accessories, cups, bowls, and a variety of handicraft forms. The workmanship is relatively good, and the intricate traditional designs are truly unique. In Chiangmai you will find thinly hammered silver bowls with raised Buddhist figures as well as a wide selection of silver hilltribe jewelry. Silver is also used in making Thai nielloware—decorative items produced by a unique Thai silver inlaid process.

JEWELRY AND ACCESSORIES

Thai jewelry shops are not as dazzling as those in Hong Kong, but they offer as good, if not better, value. Many pearls, for example, come from the southern Thai province of Phuket. Other pearls must be imported into Thailand and are subject to duties.

We have been surprised to find comparable quality pearls to be better priced in Bangkok than in Hong Kong. But you must shop around in Bangkok to find such pearls. We have purchased quality pearls at excellent prices and with fine service from **Joli Jewelery** (Amarin Plaza). **Tok Kwang** (224-6 Silom Road, next to the Narai Hotel) is also highly recommended for pearls, especially pearl clasps. If you buy loose pearls in Hong Kong, you may want to have them strung in Bangkok. Again, take a picture of what design you want. If you want a fancy clasp, you may wish to take a clasp with you since selections in Bangkok are limited. Alternatively, you may wish to have the pearls strung at home where you also will find a better selection of clasps. In the case of the United States, loose or temporarily strung natural pearls without a clasp enter duty free. If permanently or temporarily strung with an attached or separate clasp, you must pay a 6.5 to 11% duty.

Jewelry shops in Bangkok offer a wide variety of quality jewelry. There are excellent shops, however, many stores offer mediocre jewelry. The designs look old-fashioned and the stones and settings are often poor quality. Part of the problem is that many shops are largely patronized by local Chinese and Thai who are satisfied with the traditional styles and workmanship, and who purchase jewelry, in part, as an investment. This is particularly true of the numerous jewelry shops found in the Chinatown area in and around Yaowarat and Charoen Krung roads.

The best quality jewelry, with styles appropriate for Westerners, will be found in shops around the major hotels. The **Dusit Thani Hotel**, for example, has a very large concentration of high quality jewelry shops. The **Peninsula Plaza, Oriental Plaza, Charn Issara Tower**, and **Amarin Plaza** have several jewelry shops offering exquisite designs and outstanding quality. Many of these shops are patronized by very wealthy Thai and Chinese and foreign tourists who seek international quality jewelry. For examples of some of the best quality jewelry available in Thailand, visit **Franks, Bualaad,** and **Paa** at the Peninsula Plaza; **Yves Joaillier** and **Valda Jewelry** at the Charn Issara Tower; **Alex & Co.** along Oriental Lane; **Sincere Jewelry** at the Dusit Thani Hotel and on Silom Road and Sukhumvit Road; **Joli Jewelry** and **D. Diamonds** in the Amarin Plaza; **Peninsula Gems** and **Ken, Lek, and Montri** at the Regent Hotel; **J.P. Jewelry** in the Hilton Hotel; and **Cosmos Jewelry** in the Royal Orchid Sheraton Hotel. **Uthai's Gems** (28/7 Soi Ruam Rudee, Tel. 253-8582) has been popular among expatriates for over two decades. Numerous other shops in or near the Shangri-La, Oriental, Royal Orchid Sheraton, Narai, Dusit Thani, Regent, Grand Hyatt Erawan, Le Meridian President, Siam Inter-Continental, Montien, Indra, and Ambassador hotels offer good quality jewelry. Be sure to bargain in all of these shops.

Several Thai shops are beginning to develop accessories in the form of neckpieces and belts using gold, silver, semi-precious stones, and leather. The designs and varieties are still limited, but the prices are relatively reasonable. Some of the best selections and designs are found at **Jim Thompson Silk Company** (second floor display case) and **Bee Bejour** (second floor of the Peninsula Plaza).

The **Royal Orchid Company** produces inexpensive neckpieces which include yellow or white gold dipped flowers with a variety of semi-precious stones. If you visit Chiangmai, you can stop at their factory (9 Charoen Muang Road) and buy from their selection or arrange to have pieces custom-designed to your specifications. Be sure to take pictures or designs with you as well as clasps. Since most clasps must be imported into Thailand and are thus subject to heavy duties, the clasp selection is very limited and some styles are difficult to open and close. We also recommend taking your own stringing materials, especially if you require a color other than white. The quality and color selection of stringing material is very limited in Thailand.

You should watch the local English-language newspaper or ask at your hotel if any gem shows are scheduled in Bangkok during your stay. These shows provide a wonderful overview of good quality gems, jewelry, and accessories available in shops throughout Thailand. You can make purchases at these shows. Again, be sure to bargain.

COPY WATCHES

Bangkok is one of the best places to buy copies of name brand watches. These watches become many tourists' favorite and most memorable purchases. You'll have fun meeting some local entrepreneurs, shopping in a festive setting, practicing your bargaining skills, and feeling you got a real deal without spending much money. This may well become your favorite form of cheap street evening entertainment in Bangkok! After all, where else can you buy a good copy of a $10,000 Rolex for only $25, find that it actually runs better than your $300 watch? And where else can you shop on the black market with relative ease, safety, and confidence of getting a good deal? These purchases are as much fun to make as the products are to wear!

Most of the copy watches in Bangkok are produced in Taiwan, Hong Kong, or Japan, but they often cost less in Bangkok than in the countries of origin. A wide selection of well-known brand name traditional and designer men's and women's styles are available: Rolex, Cartier, Gucci, Patek Philippe, and many more. Many of the watches have excellent Seiko mechanisms. They are good copies that may fool all but the experts or connoisseurs who know that Rolex Oyster watches do not have quartz mechanisms! Most of these watches cost between $12 and $30 and they make fun gifts for friends and relatives. The leather bands—though often fake—on some watches alone are worth the price of the watch.

But before you buy one of these watches, you should be aware of certain potential problems:

- **Not all copy watches are the same quality.** The ones made in Taiwan are reputed to be better than those from Hong Kong or Japan. The best you can do is to ask before buying if the watch is from Taiwan, Hong Kong, or Japan.

- **The gold casing on some watches wears badly or will turn green after repeated wearings.** The facings may be crooked or the hands bent incorrectly. Examine your purchases carefully for obvious flaws. But keep in mind these are cheap copies which will not always be perfect.

- **Some of the watches stop working after a day or two.** Test them before leaving Thailand. Set the time as soon as you buy one and check it regularly to see if it runs fast, slow, or not at all. If it stops, take it back to the vendor who will usually exchange it. Try to remember from whom you purchased it.

- **It is not illegal to buy these watches, but it may be illegal to bring them into some countries.** Manufacturers of the real name brand watches, as well as some governments, do not believe "imitation is the highest form of flattery." They consider imitation to be first of all an illegal activity. Indeed, U.S. Customs may seize them as a trademark violation should they find them in your possession. A few other countries may have similar restrictions. But for the most part you will probably travel without any trouble. The Thai police are their usual tolerant selves by occasionally making half-hearted attempts to stop this trade. Buying these watches is indeed a "black market" adventure which is relatively safe to play. If you like these watches, you may decide to buy now and worry later about how they will pass through customs. You'll probably be successful if you are discrete. Copy watches are most widely available along Patpong Road (off Silom and Suriwongse Roads) just adjacent to The Bookseller bookstore and across from the Queen's Castle (Bangkok's raunchiest nightclub which is also next to a Christian bookstore!) and along Silom Road in and around Silom Village shopping center. Along **Patpong Road** this watch trade is most lively in the evenings, especially beginning around 7pm, when several vendors set up small tables to display their wares. Along Silom Road vendors operate during the day. Be sure to bargain vigorously. The asking price for Rolex watches may be 900 baht, but you should be able to buy it for 600 baht. Cartier and Gucci watches can be purchased for

230 to 400 baht. However, many of the watches sold along Patpong Road have problems—don't work after a few days, turn color, have bent hands. Other areas for buying these watches are found around the **major hotels**, such as the Oriental and Royal Orchid Sheraton, and a few **temple complexes**, especially the Marble Temple. Watches sold near the temples have extremely inflated prices—a 600 baht Rolex may cost 1400 baht—and vendors do not like to bargain. Avoid making purchases in these areas unless you find a particular style you must have regardless of the inflated price.

BRONZE, BRASS, AND PEWTER

The Thais are very skilled in working with bronze, brass, and pewter. They produce a variety of items which make lovely utensils, gifts, and decorative items, such as letter openers, bells, candle holders, cups, plates, bowls, vases, and flatware.

The bronze flatware is very popular and widely available in shops throughout Bangkok. The flatware comes in several styles and designs, from traditional to modern, and is available with teakwood storage boxes. Chopstick style and black-burnished bronzeware is also available. You can buy the flatware in any number of pieces desired or purchase sets in boxes ready to go.

Before buying Thai bronzeware, you should be forewarned of the different qualities of bronzeware. The beautiful Thai bronzeware you see in shops has been meticulously polished to attract your eye. But in reality, some of this bronzeware tarnishes, is not dishwasher approved, and is a constant headache to keep clean and spotless. If you buy the bronzeware, ask for the "nickel bronze" version. Nickel bronze tarnishes less and can be run through a dishwasher.

You will find bronzeware in many jewelry shops throughout Bangkok. The bronze letter openers are inexpensive (25 to 35 baht) and make nice little gifts for friends, relatives, and colleagues. You may want to buy 30 or more of these for trip gifts. The bells, key chains, shoe horns, bottle openers, and candle holders also make nice gifts.

Thailand makes some pewterware, but not nearly as much as you will find in Malaysia. Most of the pewter items are similar to the bronze and brass items—vases, cups, plates, candle holders. Many shops that carry bronze and brass items also sell pewter.

For the bronze, brass, and pewter, check with shops in and around your hotel. The major areas with the largest concentrations of shops specializing in such items is found along **Phetburi Road** (between Rama IV and Phyathai roads) and along **Suriwongse Road** (between the Manohra and Trocadero hotels), **New Road**, and **Oriental Lane** leading up to the Oriental Hotel. **Lin Plaza Gems & Thai Silk LP** (2nd floor, 1-7 Chartered Bank Lane, across from the Oriental Plaza) has a good selection of bronze, brass, and pewterware as well as jewelry and tailored clothes—our all-in-one shop. If you want to go beyond the typical tourist styles and are looking for some truly unique patterns and fine quality craftsmanship in bronze flatware, visit **Thai Home Industries** (35 Oriental Lane, Tel. 234-1736) near the Oriental Hotel. Their unique handmade, black-burnished handle flatware is lovely and looks terrific on Western dining tables. Other unique bronze flatware patterns are found at **Design Thai** (Silom Road). When buying bronze or brass decorative items, ask that they be coated with silicon. This prevents them from tarnishing. Many shops will do this upon request. They will not use silicon on flatware or other utensils which are used for eating. Even the nickel bronze will spot and tarnish, but not as bad as other types of bronze. Even the nickel bronze will spot and tarnish, but not as bad as other types of bronze.

WOODCARVINGS AND ANTIQUES

Thailand is a virtual treasure chest for fabulous woodcarvings and antiques—both old and new. Major department stores in the U.S.—such as Neiman Marcus, Saks Fifth Avenue, and Bloomingdales—are regular importers of these items. They buy everything from wood salad bowls and serving trays to carved decorative animals. You can buy these in Thailand at a fraction of the U.S. prices.

Thai woodcarvings and antiques have moved into a whole new stage of development during the past seven years. Given the stagnating economy and separatist rebellions in Burma, coupled with enterprising Thai importers, numerous shops in Bangkok and Chiangmai are literally museums for some of the most lovely and exotic Burmese antiques and art works. Temple woodcarvings and panels, lacquerware, and tapestries—both old and new—abound in Bangkok's many shops.

Thailand is particularly well noted for both its old and new antiques. Old antiques mainly come from Burma, Cambodia, Laos, China, and Vietnam. Bronze drums, ceramics, silver figures, wood panels, bronze bells, baskets, chests, sculptures, puppets, and tapestries are only a few of the fabulous items you will find digging through Bangkok's many antique shops. Similar items can be found in the antique shops of Hong Kong and Singapore, but prices will be at least double those found in Bangkok.

But it is the reproductions which are of particular interest to many tourists. Thailand has a well deserved reputation for making excellent copies of art and antiques. In fact, Thailand might best be described as a **copycat culture** rather than a creative culture. From very early ages, Thais learn to copy models from all aspects of life. Copies of old Burmese tapestries—the *kalagas*—are now mass produced and available at very reasonable prices in numerous shops throughout Bangkok.

If you are not an expert judge of Asian arts and antiques but nonetheless wish to purchase some lovely home decorative items, you should shop for new antiques and woodcarvings. You will find a vast selection of woodcarved animals, temple panels, mirror frames, doors, windows, and mythical scenes which integrate nicely into many contemporary Western homes. However, large woodcarvings often crack when introduced into dry, temperate climates. Because of the large demand for these carvings and the limited amount of dried wood available, many are made with wood that has not properly aged. Newer wood pieces may crack after a few months. While you can minimize such problems by purchasing older pieces and shopping at reputable stores, even many of the old pieces will crack in temperate climates. Cracking may occur as wood is subjected to heating systems in much drier climates. If this happens to a prized piece, we recommend contacting a conservator who can both restore and conserve the piece. Contact a museum for information on a conservator nearest you. In addition, consider installing a home humidifier system to help preserve your arts and antiques during the dry winter months.

For examples of Thailand's finest old and new antiques and woodcarvings, you should visit **NeOld** (main shop at 149/2-3 Suriwongse Rd., Tel. 235-8352 and small shops in the Hilton Hotel, Tel. 253-0123, and River City Shopping Complex); **Elephant House** (67/12 Soi Phra Phinit, Soi Suan Phlu, Sathorn Tai Road, Tel. 286-5280; and branch shops at the Regent Hotel, River City Shopping Complex, and across the street from the Shangri-La Hotel); **Peng Seng** (942/1-3 Rama IV Road, on corner of Suriwongse and Rama IV Road and next to the Jim Thompson Silk Company, Tel. 233-1891 or 234-3836); **Monogram** (Menam Mall and the Author's Lounge at the Oriental Hotel, Tel. 235-1875); **Lek Galleries' Art** (1310 New Rd., Tel. 234-4184); **The Fine Arts** (Oriental Plaza, Tel. 234-1320, ext. 03, and River City Shopping Complex, Tel. 235-2972, ext. 452-454); **Santi's** (174/4-6 Silom Road, Tel. 235-8071, 178 Sukhumvit Road, Tel. 253-3391, and River City Shopping Complex); **Oriental Commercial House Co., Ltd.** (3rd floor, River City Shopping Complex); **Rama Antique** (Oriental Plaza, Tel. 237-5826); **Artisan's** (Silom Village, Tel. 234-4447, ext. 32); and several shops on the third and fourth floor (Art and Antique Centre) of the **River City Shopping Complex** next to the Royal Orchid Sheraton Hotel.

Many of the woodcarvings in Bangkok are actually made in **Chiangmai**. If you plan to visit Chiangmai, be sure to stop at **Borisoothi Antiques** (15/2 Chiangmai-Sankhampaeng Rd.) and **Amaravadee Antiques** (31/3-4 Nantaram Rd.)—Chiangmai's two major antique dealers. Several small shops on the third and fourth floors of the **Chiangmai Night Bazaar** in downtown Chiangmai offer good selections of antiques, woodcarvings, and handcrafted items. We especially like **Siam Gallery** and **Chofah Antiques**. The factories in **Hang Dong**, approximately 12 kilometers south of Chiangmai, and along **Chiangmai-Sankhampaeng Road**, just east of the city, are filled with woodcarvings of all shapes, sizes, and motifs. **Chiangmai Banyen**, located adjacent to Jaifah Chiangmai Lacquerware Co. at 209/3 Super Highway (near the airport intersection and the road to Hang Dong), is one of Chiangmai's most famous and reliable factories supplying numerous shops in Bangkok as well as department stores and shops abroad with quality woodcarvings.

ART AND FRAMING

Thailand is not well noted for its paintings. However, you may find some lovely oil paintings, watercolors, or sketches for your home or for gifts. Indeed, some of our favorite purchases in Asia have been Thai paintings. They are available in a variety of styles from traditional Buddhist art to portrait, landscape, and abstract paintings. Thai artists also produce beautiful modern bronze and brass sculptures as well as wood blocks and temple rubbings. Art work in Bangkok is relatively inexpensive and framing is ridiculously cheap.

You will need to shop in several locations for this art. Many shops sell paintings, but much of what you find is mass produced for tourists and looks cheap and gaudy. If you look enough you will find some lovely works in traditional Thai style, depicting Hindu epics and Buddhist scenes, landscapes, portraits, and modern art. We have been particularly drawn to the watercolors of Kit (now deceased former art professor at Silapakorn University in Bangkok) depicting rural scenes in Thailand; they are now hard to find. The value of his paintings has increased tremendously during the past few years.

If you buy art in Thailand you may want to have it framed there too. You should consider framing different types of art purchases, such as wood panels, carvings, lacquer pieces, tapestries, or anything that would look attractive hung on a wall. Many Thai art shops do nice work with silk mattings and frames. Indeed, the mats and frames are often as much a creative work of art as the piece being framed!

The quality of framing is often good and prices are inexpensive. Thai craftsmen can design any type of frame you wish for paintings, carvings, textiles, and lacquer pieces. For example, a framing job that would normally cost you $200 back home may only cost $30 in Bangkok.

While Thai art shops can custom-make frames for you, their selections of stock frames and mattings are limited. Most matting materials must be imported and thus are limited in width size, color selection, and texture. The frame selections also are limited. But you should not focus only on the stock materials. Focus instead on creating some unique custom-made mats and frames. The real strength of these shops is their ability to custom-design mattings and frames—something few shops may do back home. Thai shops can make mattings by using any silk material you desire. You may, for example, want to visit Jim Thompson Silk Company to select your favorite silk material to be used as a frame matting which might also match upholstery material or pillows you selected for a particular room. In the other hand, most framing shops have silk samples from which you can choose a matting material. As for frames, the present stock design, size, and color selections are limited. Most shops can make frames to your exact specifications.

For examples of quality Thai art and framing, visit **Art Resources** (142/20 Soi Sueksavitaya, off of Silom Rd., Tel. 235-4846 and The Regent Hotel, Tel. 250-0723; see Promote

Bonyarungsrit who does some of the finest framing in Thailand); **Surawongse Gallery** (287/25-6 Suriwongse Road, Tel. 233-5333, and on the third floor of River City Shopping Complex); **C.V.N. Exotic Ltd.** (131-3/4 Sukhumvit Road, between Sois 7 and 9, Tel. 235-1860); **Petchburi Gallery** (1807-17 New Petchburi Rd., Tel. 251-2426); **Sombat Gallery** (Dusit Thani Hotel, Royal Orchid Sheraton Hotel, and River City Shopping Complex, Tel. 233-3611); and **Amarin Art Gallery** (3rd floor, Amarin Plaza). Several other shops, such as **"A" Framer** (160/12 Soi 55, Sukhumvit Rd.), **Sathon Framing** (Soi St. Louis, South Sathorn Rd.), and **Uthai and Sons** (58/5 Soi 21, Sukhumvit Rd., Tel. 258-3660), specialize in good quality framing. Most of these art shops will arrange for packing and shipping.

One word of caution is in order. If you are buying very valuable art work which should be mounted on acid-free paper, do not have it framed in Thailand. Acid-free mounts are not available there. In addition, framing shops use plywood for frame backings. This tends to make the picture heavy, and large pieces may warp. Hence, you need to consider whether the monetary savings and custom-design capabilities are worth the additional costs of shipping and possible problems with warping and acid damage. Nonetheless, Thai shops enable you to create some very unique frames and art displays unavailable back home. We have been very pleased with all of our art and framing purchases in Bangkok.

LEATHER GOODS

You will find many goods made from crocodile, lizard, snake, buffalo, and cow hides. The most widely available items are belts, purses, handbags, wallets, key chains, briefcases, jackets, shoes, and boots. We cannot strongly recommend purchasing such items in Thailand, even though some shops are attempting to become fashionable. The quality is at best mediocre, and you may have problems getting some leather through Customs back home.

One chain of stores sells some of Thailand's better quality leather goods—**Ragazze**. Found in the Amarin Plaza, Rajdamri Arcade, Central Plaza, and Siam Center, these shops offer locally designed "Italian style" leather bags, briefcases, shoes, and golf bags. You may or may not find their designs fashionable for your wardrobe.

Ready-made shoes in Thailand are generally of poor quality. The selection of large sizes is limited, many do not fit well, and they quickly deteriorate on Bangkok's sidewalks and streets. You can have your shoes and boots handmade. The prices are reasonable, but again the quality is not exceptional. Shops such as **Chao Phya Bootery** (266-268 Sukhumvit Rd., Tel. 251-3498), **Siam Bootery** (294-4 Sukhumvit Rd., Tel. 251-6862), and **Tony Leather** (300-302 Sukhumvit Rd., Tel. 251-6861) produce made-to-order shoes and other leather goods. These are reputed to be the best shops for such custom work. On the other hand, you may want to save your money and buy your letter goods in Hong Kong or watch for sales back home. Our advice: you may be pleased with your leather purchases, but don't expect a great deal or excellent quality. Like much of Thai tailoring, Thai leather work still lacks a clean "finished" look which is apparent when comparing with Italian leather products.

If you have problems with any leather goods you bring with you, such as a suitcase or a shoe, Bangkok is a good place to get repairs done inexpensively. You can have your shoes resoled and reheeled for under US$6. Department stores, such as Central, usually have a shoe repair booth ("Mr. Minit") which does excellent quality work while you wait. Repairs can be completed within 30 minutes. We do not recommend using the repairmen populating the sidewalks and street corners throughout Bangkok. Their makeshift workmanship is very crude; they may do more damage in the process of repairing your leather goods and shoes. Use them only for emergencies (your heel fell off while walking in front of them or you need something glued!).

NIELLOWARE AND BENJARONG

Two truly unique and lovely Thai art forms are Nielloware and Benjarong. The Nielloware is a special silver inlaid process available in a variety of colors in addition to the traditional black and white. The traditional designs are in the delicate and graceful Thai flame and floral patterns. Nielloware is made into jewelry, small boxes, ashtrays, cigarette lighters, cuff links, and a variety of other items. It is available in some shops in Bangkok. The best quality Nielloware is produced in the southern province of Nakorn Si Thammarat.

The less known Benjarong is a special Thai pottery made with intricate designs painted in five colors. Its origin is both

Thai and Chinese—pottery made in China but colors applied in Thailand. The shapes, designs, and colors of this pottery are so beautiful and delicate that you may quickly become a Benjarong collector. The five-color Benjarong comes in many different color combinations, several of which may work well with your home decor.

You can find individual pieces of Benjarong in many jewelry and handicraft shops as well as in department stores. **Lotus Ceramics** (Soi 3/1 Sukhumvit Road, Tel. 253-004 or 253-2890) has a large selection of Benjarong ware. For uniquely pottery which combines Benjarong and celadon processes, visit **Prempracha's** large factory-shop in Chiangmai (224 Chiangmai-Sankamphaeng Rd., Tel. 331-540).

CELADON AND LACQUERWARE

In recent years the ancient art of Thai celadon has been revived. The celadon has a crackled appearance. It is covered by a thick clear coating. Fired in kilns, Thai celadon is produced in different green, blue, or tan shades. It is made into pottery, cups, plates, bowls, ashtrays, and an assortment of other small decorative items. It is most widely available directly at the factories in Chiangmai (one of the best being Mengrai Kilns, 31/1 Ratuthit Rd., Tel. 241-802) or you can see it in Bangkok at the **Celadon House** (278 Silom Rd., Tel. 234-3767) and in several small shops selling jewelry and handicrafts.

Thai lacquerware in the distinctive **black and gold** colors makes lovely decorative pieces or trip gifts. It is made into a variety of goods, from serving trays, plates, and boxes to coasters. The Thai designs are traditional flame, floral, and portrait patterns.

Other Thai lacquerware is produced in a distinctive **red** color. Many shops sell lovely baskets, small tables, figures, and a variety of furniture items in the red lacquer. You may find the red lacquer pieces will work much better in your home than the more traditional black and gold lacquerware.

Many shops in Bangkok and Chiangmai also stock unique **Burmese** lacquerware pieces. This lacquerware is produced in distinctive rust and green colors with intricate designs etched in different colors. If you don't have a chance to visit even more exotic Burma, Thailand is a good place to pick up some lovely Burmese lacquer bowls, plates, boxes, trays, coasters, tables, and room dividers.

One of the largest collections of antique Thai and Burmese lacquerware is found at the **Elephant House** (67/12 Soi Phra Phinit, Soi Suan Phlu, Sathorn Tai Rd., Tel. 286-5280) in Bangkok. For excellent quality lacquerware in Chiangmai, be sure to visit **Maneesinn** (289 Thapae Rd., Tel. 236-586). Several shops in the **Chiangmai Night Bazaar** (3rd and 4th floors) also offer good quality lacquerware.

HANDICRAFTS

Thai handicrafts are well represented in the shops of Bangkok and Chiangmai. They include a large variety of lovely and unique items: baskets, spirit houses, dolls, hilltribe jewelry, quilts, pottery, picture frames, carvings, placemats, Christmas decorations, embroidered items, hats, etc. For a good selection of quality handicrafts, visit **Thai Home Industries** (35 Oriental Lane), **Chitralada Shop** (top floor, Oriental Plaza and Thaniya Plaza), **Local House Co.** (7/1-2 Captain Bush Lane, near Royal Orchid Hotel, Tel. 234-2919), and **House of Handicrafts** (Regent House). Thailand's largest handicraft emporium is the government-run **Narayana Phand** (The Mall, Rajadamri Rd.). Most major department stores, such as **Central, Soho,** or **Robinson,** have a handicraft section with fixed prices. It's worth browsing in these department stores to get a good overview of selections, prices, and quality.

Two relatively new shops specializing in uniquely designed quality handicrafts are **Rasi Sayam** (32 Sukhumvit Soi 23, Tel. 258-4195) and **The Legend** (3rd floor, Amarin Plaza, Tel. 256-9929). Both shops offer some wonderful pottery, baskets, carvings, and boxes that make nice home decorative items and gifts. Serious collectors of quality handicrafts are well advised to visit both shops, especially Rasi Sayam.

Three very interesting shops specialize in handcrafted dolls, Christmas ornaments, and related items: **Bangkok Dolls** (80 Soi Rajatapan, Rajaprarop Rd., Tel. 245-3008; and the Peninsula Plaza); **Lao Song Handicrafts** (69 Soi Watana or Soi 19, Sukhumvit Rd., Tel. 253-2948); and the **Fatima Self Help Center** (Good Shepherd Sisters, 17/65 Asoke Din Daeng Rd., Tel. 245-0458).

Outside Bangkok, near the city of Ayuthaya, is the **Royal Folk Arts and Crafts Center** at Bansai. Sponsored by Her Majesty the Queen, this is a training center where young people learn the traditional arts and crafts. They produce furniture, baskets, leather goods, glass figures, woven items, and paintings as well as numerous small display items. In addition to observing the production of arts and crafts in various workshops, you can also purchase the finished products from the main arts and crafts shop. If you plan to travel to Ayuthaya on your own, you may want to stop here along the way. However, few if any tours to Ayuthaya schedule stops at this center.

In Chiangmai you will find handicraft shops in the **Night Bazaar** (go to second and third floor for good quality) and along **Chiangmai-Sankhampaeng Road** (Siam Gifts has a good selection). Two good Hilltribe handicraft shops are found across the street from one another on Bumrung Rat Road—**Thai Tribal Crafts** (208 Bumrung Rat Rd., Tel. 243-493) and **Northern Tribal Crafts** (121 Bumrung Rat Rd., Tel. 245-079). The **Hilltribe Products Foundation** on Suthep Road also has a very nice selection of hilltribe handicrafts. **Sarapee Silk Lace** at 2 Rajwithi Road, one of Chiangmai's and Thailand's most unique shops, produces fine handsewn lace.

TAPESTRIES

In recent years Bangkok has been flooded with the unique, lovely, and exotic Burmese tapestries, known as ***kalagas***. A stunning and mysterious art form originating in Burma more than 200 years ago, it disappeared during the 20th century. It has recently been revived, partly in response to tourism.

These tapestries come in numerous sizes, designs, and color combinations. Most are intricately designed with Buddhist scenes and floral patterns, sewn with gold and silver sequins, and stitched with different colored raised cotton, silk, and velvet materials. The fine designs and labor-intensive work is fascinating. Every time you look at a *kalaga* it tends to yield new details.

You can still find some antique Burmese tapestries in the shops of Bangkok and Chiangmai, but these rare pieces are very expensive, costing $1,500 on up. Most of the new pieces are very attractive and extremely inexpensive. For example, a nice 2' x 2' tapestry may only cost about $15 and can be framed for less than $20. A 3' x 7' tapestry might cost $150 and can be framed for $80. But be sure to bargain hard; expect to receive at least a 20 percent discount, and maybe as much as 50 percent from the initial price.

The Burmese tapestries make interesting trip gifts, or you may want to purchase one as a wall hanging or center piece for a special room. They may appear somewhat gaudy at first, but if you look hard enough you should be able to find one with the right design and colors to work in your home.

Most tapestries in Bangkok are imitations of the old Burmese tapestries or are newly commissioned designs. The new pieces are very well done. One of the best places to see a wide selection of these tapestries is among the many art and antique shops on the third and fourth floors (Art and Antique Centre) of the **River City Shopping Complex** next to the Royal Orchid Hotel.

FURNITURE

Thailand is an excellent place to buy handmade wood and rattan furniture. Several reliable quality factories in Bangkok will make pieces to your specification in a variety of woods and finishes, especially teakwood. The shops will pack and ship for you. All you need to do is bring your designs with you. They can copy from catalog pictures, but the more details you can provide, the better. Many visitors to Thailand have tables, chairs, beds, chests, cupboards, and other items made according to their designs. After you leave Thailand, you can continue to order furniture through the mail by sending the factory detailed designs. The prices are reasonable, even considering the extra costs of shipping, and the craftsmanship is very good. A rosewood dining room set costing $4,000 in the United States, for example, can be copied for $1,500 in Thailand. With shipping costs, you can still save money.

We regularly use furniture makers in Bangkok to add pieces to our household furniture, many of which have been discontinued by manufacturers. These Thai factories also can make wood display bases and small tables for pottery and other artifacts. Some of the best furniture factories in Bangkok with display rooms are: **Sweet Home** (Soi 21 Sukhumvit Road or 33 Sukhumvit Road Soi 27, Tel. 258-3419), **Gersons** (287 Silom Road), **Peter's Furniture** (157/6 Mahadlek 2 Rajadamri Road, behind the Regent Hotel, Tel. 252-6727), **Pong Sin** (109 Suthisan, Tel. 277-0355), and **Prinya Decoration LP** (3106-8 New Phetburi Road, Tel. 318-1824).

A few shops also make unique furniture. One of our favorite items and designs are tables made from dark brown antique opium mats with legs and sides finished in red or brown lacquer. Examples of this furniture are found at the **Elephant House** at 67/12 Soi Phra Phinit, Soi Suan Phlu,

Sathorn Tai Road (Tel. 286-5280, and ask for Cherie who is the owner and designer) or the branch shops at 409-410 River City Shopping Complex (Tel. 234-9365 or 235-2976 thru 9), The Regent Hotel, and across the street from the Shangri-La Hotel. Similar opium mat furniture is found at **NeOld** at 149-2-3 Suriwongse Road (Tel. 235-8352).

If you are looking for something very special, be sure to visit **Pure Design** at 30 Ruam Rudee Road (Tel. 253-1719). This is one of Thailand's premiere home decorative and designer shops. They make very unique pieces of furniture. If you are serious about decorating your home with furniture that expresses Thai design and style, some of which has been seen on the pages of *Architectural Digest,* be sure to consult with the designer—Mr. Chantaka Puranananda. His work is well represented in many of Thailand's major hotels and the homes of Thailand's wealthy.

If you are interested in wicker furniture, concentrate your shopping efforts on several shops along **Sukhumvit Road** between Soi 39 and 43. We especially like the designs at **Corner 43 Co., Ltd.** 769 Sukhumvit Rd., Tel. 260-1124) and **Pacific Design** (779-781 Sukhumvit Rd., Tel. 258-4726). These shops also will make furniture to your specifications.

Individuals interested in collecting antique or old furniture should visit **Yesterday Once Again** on Soi Asoke. This rather cluttered shop collects and refinishes old Thai furniture, especially period furniture. This is a favorite shop for many expatriates.

If you visit Chiangmai, be sure to stop at the furniture factories and showrooms that tend to be concentrated along Chiangmai-Sankamphaeng Road. Most of the furniture produced in Chiangmai is in traditional Thai designs—somewhat gaudy and too ethnic for many foreign visitors. To view a large variety of such furniture, stop at **Tusnaporn** on the Chiangmai-Sankamphaeng Road (Route 1006 directly east of Chiangmai city). Several other furniture factories also are found along this same road. However, try to visit these places on your own. Many, including Tusnaporn, are notorious for paying drivers and guides 10-30 percent commissions for bringing clients to their shops. The commissions, of course, are hidden in your "special" price. The quality of this furniture varies, and it seems to get worse each year. Good teakwood furniture is hard to find given the present government bans on forestry. You may end up with inferior quality woods which tend to crack in more temperate climates.

THE MORE YOU LOOK

The Thai produce numerous other arts and crafts many travelers find attractive. The more you poke around the many shops of Bangkok and Chiangmai, the more you discover interesting and unique items. Indeed, the more you look, the more you may get hooked on this shopping paradise. In addition to the major products just discussed, you will find beautiful lamps, wood and stone statues, sculptures, ancient Ban Chiang pottery, textiles, batik, costumes, head dresses, ivory carvings, handmade Oriental carpets, luggage, dolls, stuffed animals, spirit houses, bells, bronze drums, Chinese and Thai ceramics, porcelain, exotic birds, and much, much more. The list simply goes on and on. You will quickly find there is no substitute for wandering around from one shop to another discovering the infinite variety of Thai shopping treasures.

Thailand may not have the glitter and sheer volume of shops found in Hong Kong and Singapore. But these other famous shopping cities have little to compare to the lovely decorative arts and crafts you can only find by going to Thailand and searching on your own.

PART III

SURPRISING BANGKOK

8 WELCOME TO BANGKOK

Bangkok is a chaotic and ugly city in the eyes of many first-time visitors who expect major cities to have attractive architecture and skylines. Except for newer hotels, condominiums, shopping malls, high-rise office buildings, and temple complexes, by any standard Bangkok is not a visually attractive city. It's beauty lies elsewhere, off the main streets and beneath surface appearances.

CHAOS AND CONTRASTS

Bangkok is one of Asia's most exotic destinations. Row after row of architecturally unexciting two and three-story Chinese commercial shops—worn by a mixture of tropical climate, air pollution, and cheap construction materials—dominate the ever changing and dynamic landscape of this bustling and sprawling city of nearly 7 million people who muddle-through in a typical Thai fashion of seeming disorganization and chaos which somehow works.

Bangkok and the Thai have a certain charm not found in other Asian cities. Amongst the chaos, pollution, congestion, heat, poverty, and ugliness of this city stand nearly 400 glittering, colorful, and serene Buddhist temples which punctuate Bangkok's newly developing skyline of modern high-rise office buildings, hotels, and condominiums. The ever

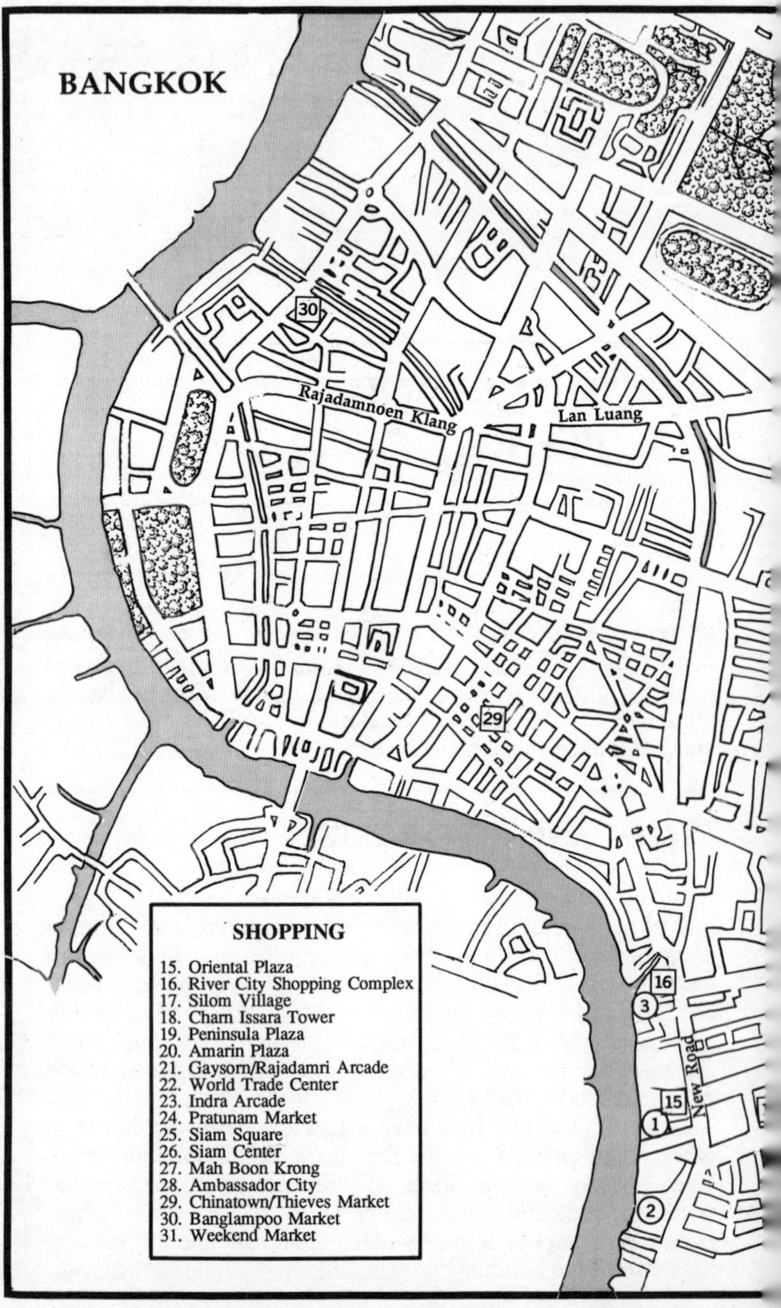
BANGKOK
30
Rajadamnoen Klang
Lan Luang
29
16
3
New Road
15
1
2
SHOPPING
15. Oriental Plaza
16. River City Shopping Complex
17. Silom Village
18. Charn Issara Tower
19. Peninsula Plaza
20. Amarin Plaza
21. Gaysorn/Rajadamri Arcade
22. World Trade Center
23. Indra Arcade
24. Pratunam Market
25. Siam Square
26. Siam Center
27. Mah Boon Krong
28. Ambassador City
29. Chinatown/Thieves Market
30. Banglampoo Market
31. Weekend Market

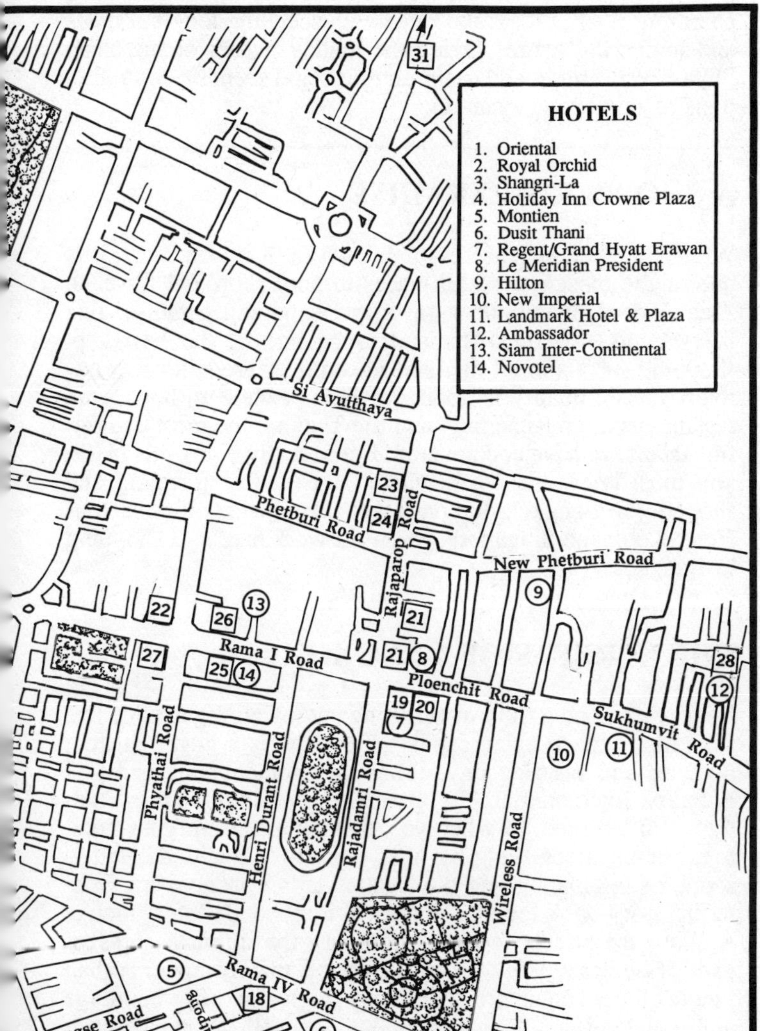
HOTELS
1. Oriental
2. Royal Orchid
3. Shangri-La
4. Holiday Inn Crowne Plaza
5. Montien
6. Dusit Thani
7. Regent/Grand Hyatt Erawan
8. Le Meridian President
9. Hilton
10. New Imperial
11. Landmark Hotel & Plaza
12. Ambassador
13. Siam Inter-Continental
14. Novotel
31
Si Ayutthaya
23
24
Phetburi Road
Rajaparop Road
New Phetburi Road
9
22
26
13
21
Rama I Road
21
8
27
25
14
28
12
Ploenchit Road
19
20
7
Sukhumvit Road
10
11
Phyathai Road
Henri Durant Road
Rajadamri Road
Wireless Road
5
Rama IV Road
18
Patpong
6
Suriwongse Road
Silom Road
North Sathorn

charming river and canals, filled with speeding long-tail boats and lumbering barges plying the muddy waters of the Chao Phya River, further add to the contrasts and seeming contradictions of this exotic Asian city.

A SHOPPER'S PARADISE

While Bangkok is relatively unknown to many travelers, it is one of the most wonderful places to both shop and travel in Asia. Indeed, it is both a travel and shopping paradise. Just between us, we find Thailand to be one of the best kept shopping secrets in all of Asia. Most prices are still comparatively cheap, quality is good, service is excellent, hotels and restaurants are outstanding, and the Thai are the most delightful Asians we have encountered. But to really enjoy this place, you must know the what, where, and how of traveling and shopping in Bangkok. In contrast to other Asian cities such as Hong Kong and Singapore, you must work harder at shopping in Bangkok.

THE STREETS OF BANGKOK

Bangkok can be a truly disorienting yet rewarding experience. Like many other Asian capitals, Bangkok is a large, chaotic, hustling and bustling city. From the moment you arrive at Bangkok International Airport and descend into the crowds at the main terminal, to when you first venture from your hotel to cross the street, Bangkok hits you full force with a kaleidoscope of fascinating and often intimidating phenomena. Glittering story-book temples and saffron-robed Buddhist monks walking the streets in early morning—the ultimate signs of exotic Southeast Asia—co-exist amongst an ugly modern urban jungle of worn commercial buildings, high-rise office buildings and condominiums, and fabulous as well as nondescript shopping centers, plazas, hotels, and restaurants. Noisy, overcrowded, and polluting buses lumber down the streets alongside rickety tuk-tuks, taxis, and chauffeur-driven Mercedes-Benz and BMWs. The mass of humanity trying to ply the streets of Bangkok is so fascinating that one should spend an hour just observing the phenomena and contemplating what makes this city tick.

OVERCOMING STREET SHOCK

Tucked away in the midst of this urban jungle is a truly exciting shopping adventure with numerous shops offering a dazzling array of products and bargains. But this shopping experience becomes most rewarding once you overcome what for many visitors is the initial visual shock of a chaotic and intimidating Bangkok. The best ways to do this are to:

- **Develop a very tolerant attitude toward everything going on around you**—view Bangkok as a unique, challenging, and humorous experience rather than as a set of insurmountable problems you must cope with. To really enjoy Bangkok you must get out into its streets and happily muddle-along with its masses. This is not the place for neat and tidy minds wedded to plans, schedules, and predictable behavior. It's the place for the adventuresome traveler who is open to new experiences and enjoys serendipitous and makeshift situations.

- **Hire an air-conditioned hotel car with an English-speaking driver or take air-conditioned taxis to various shopping areas and city sights.** Unless you are poor, very adventuresome, seek novel experiences, or foolish, do not take buses, *tuk tuks*, or non-air-conditioned taxis, except for very short distances. You will be "pennywise but pound foolish" as you suffer the worst effects of Bangkok's hot and polluted streets.

- **Concentrate your shopping on a few shopping areas within close proximity of each other each day.** Avoid making long trips between shopping areas since you will waste a great deal of time in Bangkok's gridlock of slowly moving traffic.

- **Minimize the hassles of traffic by avoiding rush hour traffic which is normally at its peak during 7:30-8:30am and 4:30-6:30pm.** Spend these hours in your hotel, at shops and restaurants, or sightseeing at a particular location, such as along the river or in temples.

- **Ask for assistance whenever you feel you need it.** Thais are a warm and hospitable people who tend to be very helpful and accommodating. If they don't know the answer, or can't understand you, many will try to find someone who can assist you.

- **If you get exhausted, tired, or frustrated with your day on the streets, escape to the peace and quiet of a temple, or the luxury, ambiance, and service of a deluxe hotel lobby, restaurant, or coffee shop.** Bangkok offers many wonderful places to escape to for reorganizing your schedule and contemplation. For those moments, we highly recommend staying close to the Regent, Oriental, Royal Orchid Sheraton, Shangri-La, Dusit Thani, Grand Hyatt Erawan, Siam Inter-Continental, Arnoma Swissotel, Novotel, Le Meridian President, Hilton, or Landmark hotels.

GETTING ORIENTED

Bangkok is one of the few truly Asian cities—spontaneous and largely unplanned—overlaid with traffic arteries and a set of street rules most appropriate for Western cities designed around city plans, zoning regulations, and automobiles.

The **streets** of Bangkok do have a certain logic. Bangkok's main traffic arteries consist of superhighways/toll roads, streets, lanes, and canals. Lacking any semblance of urban zoning, commercial and residential areas are mixed together along the streets and lanes. No central city exists—only different government and commercial areas best identified by the names of particular streets, hotels, department stores, government buildings, and temples.

The **lanes**, or *soi*, are similar to small one-lane streets or alleys found in other countries. They lead into the major streets and are often linked together in a maze of interconnecting lanes. Many of the best shops, restaurants, hotels, and sights in Bangkok—such as the Elephant House, Thai Heritage Antiques, Rasi Sayam, Fatima Self Help Center, Bangkok Dolls, Royal Orchid Sheraton Hotel, Jim Thompson House, and Shinawatra silk company—are found along these lanes. Therefore, you need to look beyond the major hotels, shopping centers, and shops which are most evident along Bangkok's major streets: Sukhumvit, Ploenchit, Phetburi, New Phetburi, Rajaprarop, Rajadamri, Silom, Suriwongse, and New Road. The interior lanes leading from these major traffic arteries yield some of the best quality shops in Thailand.

Canals, or *klong*, used to be the major traffic arteries in Bangkok. Today most canals have been filled with dirt, concrete, or asphalt and are now streets and lanes. The remaining canals are extremely polluted or are charming commercial and residential waterways which many tourists enjoy exploring. But don't expect to do much shopping along these canals. What shopping exists is limited to fruits and vegetables, basic Thai consumer goods, and a few tourist trinkets. You primarily travel the canals to view the exotic lifestyles or to get somewhere quicker than by road.

Most of the canals are found across the river from Bangkok, in the sister city of Thonburi. If you want to enjoy the unique canal experience, buy a copy of Geo-Ch Veran's ***50 Trips through Siam's Canals***, which is available at a few major bookstores in Bangkok, or hire your own boat at the dock just adjacent to the Oriental Hotel off New Road, or at the dock next to the Pingklao Bridge near the National Museum. Comfortable 10-passenger boats can be hired for about 200 baht per hour. But be careful. Some of the middlemen and boatmen may try to take advantage of you by overcharging. Agree on the price **before** getting into the boat and starting the trip; make sure the person repeats the price at least three times; and write the price on a piece of paper in full view of the boatman. If he tries to overcharge you, just leave or say you need to see a policeman (*tamruat*). These actions usually result in getting you what you want. During your trip into the canals, you will see a great deal of commercial and residential activity and maybe do some limited shopping.

NAVIGATING STREETS AND LANES

Bangkok is divided into a series of administrative districts, but these are relatively meaningless to taxi drivers and shopkeepers. The major locations are identified by particular street names, hotels, government buildings, temples, department stores, shopping centers, or names of tourist sights. If a particular shop is located on a lane, be sure you have the complete address. This includes the name of the main street and the number of the establishment on the particular lane off the main street. For example, "131/7 Soi 9, Sukhumvit Road" means the place is located at number 131/7, which is on Soi 9, and Soi 9 connects with Sukhumvit Road. The driver will then go to Sukhumvit Road and turn into Soi 9 to find number 131/7.

As you navigate the streets of Bangkok, going from one shopping area to another, we caution you to be sensitive to certain aspects of these streets. Most important of all, be sure you:

- **Watch where you walk.** In some areas sidewalks are broken or uneven. Sometimes trees suddenly appear in the middle of the sidewalk or tree branches hang low—examples of periodic municipal beautification campaigns that forgot pedestrians must also use the sidewalks along with the greenery! If you don't watch your feet, you can easily stumble, twist an ankle, walk into puddles, or, worst of all, fall into an open sewer trench—a fate worse than death! If you don't look ahead, you may wrap your body around a tree or bang your head on the branches. And water constantly drips from the roofs of commercial buildings onto the sidewalks, and onto your head—if you don't watch above you. If you are in the Silom-Patpong-Suriwongse Road area at night, beware of the army of feathered creatures that line the overhead wires. Stay clear of the sidewalks or you may be in for an unpleasant volley from Bangkok's bombardier birds—the ultimate sign you have been carousing through Bangkok's sleazy bars at night!

- **Keep your valuables close to you wherever you go.** Like other big cities, Bangkok has its share of thieves and pick-pockets who prey on tourists. This is not a major problem, but it does exist. So don't make it easy for them. Men should keep their wallets in their front pockets, however uncomfortable. Women should hold their handbags securely; never leave them unattended, even when passing through a luncheon buffet line.

- **Use taxis even for short distances of a mile or less if the traffic is not too heavy and slow.** Walking in Bangkok's heat, humidity, and air pollution is not good exercise nor a convenient way to get around. It is debilitating and will ruin your day, and your stay.

- **Walk only in safe places at night.** Streets and lanes are not well lit at night for your safety against either speeding vehicles or thieves. Use taxis at night whenever and wherever possible.

- **Have taxis wait for you in the lanes.** If you take a taxi very far into a lane, you may want to pay the driver to wait. Sometimes it is very difficult to find another taxi to take you out of the maze of lanes. You can easily get lost and spend a confusing and hot 30 minutes or more trying to walk your way out to the main street.

- **Take a small umbrella with you and head for high ground during the rainy season.** When it rains in Bangkok, it really pours and the city temporarily comes to a halt. Unfortunately, Bangkok's rains come at you from above and below as streets and sidewalks quickly flood during heavy downpours. Deluxe hotels and shopping centers outside the New Road area are good places to seek high ground.

- **Use overhead crosswalks, cross streets at intersections, observe the stop lights, and always look to your right as well as to your left.** While Thais are a very polite and considerate people in face-to-face situations, many seem to take on a totally different personality when sitting behind the wheel of a car. Assume you have no rights as a pedestrian, and it is foolhardy to test the traffic with your body. You must walk defensively. It is very dangerous to jaywalk. Use the many overhead crosswalks or cross only at intersections, but always keep an eye on the traffic even though you ostensibly have the right-of-way. Drivers often run stop lights and seldom slow down or stop for pedestrians. Since Thais drive on the left and bus lanes often run against the traffic, make a habit of always looking to your right and then to your left. Many people, including tourists, have been killed or seriously injured by buses, cars, trucks, *tuk tuks*, and motorbikes because they failed to regularly make these cautious observations.

- **Avoid the Silom-Rama IV Road intersection at the Lumpini Park and Dusit Thani Hotel area whenever possible.** This is the longest stop light in Thailand and it is the most congested intersection. Expect to spend 7 to 15 minutes to get across this key intersection. More than one trip through this intersection in a single day will indeed ruin your day. Sometimes it is best to walk across the intersection and then catch a taxi on the other side. Taxis may charge you an additional 10 to 20 baht if they must take you through this intersection—a justifiable sum once you see the gridlock of traffic impatiently waiting to speed through this light.

If you follow some of these basic rules for navigating Bangkok's streets and handling its shopping, you should be able to get around Bangkok with relative ease. Since you want to best use your time for shopping and sightseeing rather than hassle the traffic and discomforts of Bangkok, try to approach Bangkok with a sense of humor and tolerance. Better still, use your time wisely in shopping centers and shops rather than in buses, taxis, and on the streets of Bangkok.

9 WHERE TO SHOP

If you are looking for unique items and quality goods, you must go beyond the typical tourist paths and find the shops that deliver uniqueness and quality. Fortunately, more and more shops are opening in Bangkok in response to the tastes of sophisticated Thai and Western visitors. If you seek these other shops, your shopping experience in Thailand will be one of the best of any trip.

Before venturing into Bangkok's shopping areas, do what we recommended earlier—purchase a copy of Nancy Chandler's ***Map of Bangkok*** which is available in most major hotels and bookstores, as well as found in the back pocket of the ***Bangkok Guide*** (published by the Australian-New Zealand Women's Group). This map will take you to all the major shopping areas as well as point you to some of the best restaurants and sights. The Chinatown, Weekend Market, and Siam Centre insert maps are nicely detailed for a do-it-yourself walking tour of these areas.

Shopping in Bangkok is best approached in terms of different types of locations for directing your shopping energies. These include shopping areas, arcades, centers, department stores, markets, and stalls. Each offers a certain mix of products in varying qualities. Moreover, they offer different styles of shopping.

SHOPPING AREAS

Most of the quality shopping in Bangkok is concentrated along a few major streets and centered around hotels, shopping arcades, and department stores. Major shopping is found in and around:

- **Silom-Suriwongse-New Road area:**

  This is Bangkok's major business and financial district. It runs east and west off of Rama IV Road. **Major hotels**, such as the Dusit Thani, Montien, Tawana Ramada, and Plaza, as well as two of Bangkok's most up-market shopping centers—**Charn Issara Tower** and **Thaniya Plaza**—are found at the eastern end of this area. The infamous Patpong Road area, with its numerous straight, gay, and transvestite bars and lively night market of vendor stalls, is located at the upper end of this district. Excellent shopping is found in and around the hotels, especially the Dusit Thani and Montien hotels. At the upper end of Suriwongse Road, near Rama IV Road, are two of Thailand's finest shops—**Peng Seng** for antiques and **Jim Thompson Silk Company** for quality fabrics, clothing, and decorative items. Next door to Jim Thompson is **Choisy** (9/25 Suriwongse Rd.), one of Bangkok's well established French operated boutiques catering to Western designs. Nearby you will find the **Charn Issara Tower** building (Rama IV Road) which houses several major airline offices as well as three levels of up-scale shops. Except for **Yves Joaillier**, **Valda Jewelry**, **Living Extra** (unique modern unisex jewelry), and **Adams Tailor**, most other shops here are local boutiques catering to Bangkok's upper class. The designs, fabrics, and colors appeal to few visitors. The new **Thaniya Plaza** (off Silom Road) has quickly become a popular center for restaurants, clothing and textile stores, jewelry shops, art galleries, and antique shops. Some shops at the Oriental Plaza and River City Shopping Complex may soon relocate to Thaniya Plaza.

  Returning back to Suriwongse Road, other good shops, such as **NeOld** (149/2-3 Suriwongse Rd.) and **Erawan Antiques** (149/8 Suriwongse Rd.) for antiques and home decorative items, and **Thaipan** (35/6 Suriwongse Rd.), **Khomapastr** (Suriwongse Rd. at Montien Hotel), **Khanitha** (Thanom Surawong Center), **Orano**

(149/4-6 Suriwongse Rd.), and **Designer's Showcase** (115/1 Suriwongse Rd.) for fashionable women's clothes, are found in the area between Jim Thompson Silk Company and a block past the Tawana Ramada Hotel. Many of the shops in and around the nearby Montien Hotel are also good. For example, **Tiphayabun** in the Montien Hotel Shopping Arcade has a small but very exclusive collection of antiques.

Toward the lower end of Suriwongse Road (across from the second Toyota dealer sign) you will find **Surawongse Gallery** which has beautiful art work and does nice framing. Also included in this area are numerous tourist shops in and around the New Peninsula, New Fuji, Monohra, and New Trocadero Hotel. Look for **Asian Galleries** (460), **Tai Fah Antiques** (406), and **Ma Peng Seng Antiques** (404) in this area.

Once you reach **New Road**, turn left and explore the numerous jewelry, art, antique, and knickknack shops lining both sides of this street. Half way down this street, on the right, you come to **Oriental Lane** which leads to the Oriental Hotel, Oriental Plaza, Menam Plaza, and the river. Many of the shops in this area offer good quality products, such as **Alex & Co.** for jewelry, **Thai Home Industries** for bronzeware and handicrafts, **Pagoda Thai Handicrafts**, and **Lin Plaza Gems and Thai Silk LP** for everything from tailored clothes to jewelry and bronzeware.

Oriental Plaza is well worth an hour or two of browsing for jewelry, clothes, antiques, woodcarvings, handicrafts, and paintings. Some of the best shops here include **The Fine Arts**, **Rama Antique**, and **Wimaan** for antiques; **Anong Gallery** and **Babthai** for fashionable hilltribe and silk mutmee clothes and accessories; **Kim** for jewelry; **Khanitha** and **Darlene** for fashionable silk and cotton clothes; and **Chitralada Shop** for handicrafts.

Many of the adjacent hotel shops, found in the **Menam Mall**, **Author's Lounge** building, and the **Oriental Hotel** are excellent. **Monogram**, with three shops in both the Menam Mall and the Author's Lounge building, offers some of Bangkok's best antiques and home decorative items. Also look in the Author's Lounge building for the **Pink Poodle** for haute couture, **Sartorial** for tailoring, **de l'Oriental** for nice gift items, and **Cabochon Jewellers** for exclusive jewelry. Just off the lobby of the Oriental Hotel, adjacent to the Bamboo Bar, is **Royal Thai Gems** with its beautiful and unique gold designs. The street vendors selling leather goods, watches, polo shirts, paintings, and toys near the Oriental Hotel on Oriental Lane may pester you. They also sell a great deal of tourist junk. Unless you want to be pestered, keep moving and tell them *"I already bought too many."*

At this point you have a choice of returning to New Road or taking a 15-minute hotel ferry to the Royal Orchid Sheraton Hotel and the adjacent **River City Shopping Complex**. We recommend the ferry. It's free and a very pleasant ride. Catch it at the Oriental Hotel's dock at the end of the outdoor dining area and in front of the Author's Lounge. Once you arrive at the **River City Shopping Complex**, you will find the first and second floor have several clothing, jewelry tailor, handicraft, and shoe stores. Two of our favorite shops on second floor are **January** (2nd floor) for childrens' smocked dresses, stuffed toys, and silk, and **River Mark** for tailoring. Be sure to visit the third and fourth floor art and antique shops. This area, also known as the "Art and Antique Centre," has the largest concentration of such shops in Thailand. Some of our favorite shops in this area include **The Golden Triangle**, **Oriental Commercial House**, **Santi's**, **Elephant House**, **The Height**, **Saowthai**, and **T.K. Art & Antiques**. From River City's second level you can walk directly into the Royal Orchid Sheraton Hotel. You'll be on the second floor to survey their jewelry and art shops. **Royal Jewelry**, **Cosmos Jewelry**, and **Orchid Gems** offer exclusively designed jewelry. **Sombat Gallery** has a good collection of oil and watercolor paintings done by noted local artists. From the River City's second level you can walk directly into the **River City Shopping Complex**.

After visiting this area, you can either walk to the Oriental Hotel or take another ferry to the Shangri-La Hotel. If you decide to walk, we recommend taking the less congested **Captain Bush Lane**. Here you will find a few new shops offering excellent quality arts, antiques, and clothing. **Local House Co.** at 7/1-2 Captain Bush Lane offers excellent quality handicrafts, textiles, pottery, baskets, and kites. **Ben Antiques** at the corner of New Road and Captain Bush Lane has an interesting collection of antiques and home decorative items. Just around the corner, to your right along New Road, is **Betel Nut**, a small shop specializing in unique silver items and beads.

If you take the ferry back to the Oriental Hotel or wish to go to the Shangri-La Hotel board, at the River City Shopping Complex. Unfortunately you cannot go directly from the Oriental Hotel to the Shangri-La Hotel, or visa versa, on one of the free hotel shuttle ferries. You must transit at the River City Shopping Complex docks.

If you go to the **Shangri-La Hotel**, you will find several shops in and around this hotel. The hotel's small shopping arcade has several quality shops: **C. Fillipo** for men's tailoring; **Cotton Corner** and **C.S. Thai Silk** for stylish silk and cotton clothes; **S.S. Gems** for jewelry; and **Pat's Arts & Crafts** for gift items. A new branch of the **Elephant House** is located across the street from the hotel near the dock.

If you return to the Oriental Hotel, walk down Oriental Lane and take a right onto New Road. The remainder of this shopping area primarily consists of shops along Silom Road. As you walk down **New Road**, you will see more jewelry, antique, art, and clothing shops. One of Thailand's best art and antique shops, now converted into a gallery, is located here—**Lek Galleries' Art** (1310 New Road, Tel. 2344184). Also look for **Yong Antiques, Somboon Enterprises, From Siam With Love, Maison des Arts, Thai Thong Gallery Art, U-Thong Antiques, Petchburi Gallery, Majestic Art, Artcraft Exports, Alexandra Thai Silk**, and **A. Gallery**.

When you come to **Silom Road**, take a left at the corner antique shop, pass by the small flower market, and begin walking up Silom Road. Many small tourist shops line this street. Within a few minutes you will see the **Holiday Inn Crowne Plaza** on your right. It has a shopping arcade with several jewelry, clothing, and handicraft shops. Within another 5 minutes you should come to the **Central Department Store, Design Thai, Motif, Anita Thai Silk**, and **Santi's Arts and Antiques**—all worth a stop. Next comes **Silom Village**, a small but nice shopping and restaurant center. The front section is filled with small shops and vendors selling leather goods and souvenirs. A few small home decorative, antique, jewelry, and handicraft shops are found in this shopping area. **Artisan's**, small but good quality and reasonably priced, is one of our favorite art, antique, and home decorative shops. Also look for **Hill Tribe Products** and **Old Times**. You may want to stay at Silom Village a while to sample some of the Thai food and enjoy the lovely outdoor atmosphere. Directly across the street is **Chai Ma Antiques**.

Further along Silom Road you will see numerous jewelry, clothing, and antique shops catering to tourists, especially around the **Narai Hotel**. Keep an eye on both sides of the street. A few excellent shops, such as **Galerie D'Art**, stand alone across from the Narai Hotel. If you don't look carefully, you will miss some good shops in this area. **Tok Kwang** (224-226 Silom Rd.), for example, offers some of the best pearls and jewelry designs in all of Thailand.

From the Narai Hotel you may want to explore two nearby streets that offer out-of-the-way art shops. The **Artists Gallery and Savoury Restaurant** (60 Pan Road, Silom, Tel. 236-4830) has a nice collection of local art produced by some of Thailand's top young artists. The restaurant is excellent for lunch or dinner. Also look for **Art Resources** at 142-20 Soi Sueksavitaya, North Sathorn Rd. (Tel. 235-4846) for traditional Thai paintings, art deco bronze decorative pieces, and framing. You may need to take a taxi from Silom Road to locate these two excellent shops.

Returning to the Narai Hotel, it's a long walk up the remainder of Silom Road. At this point you may want to take a taxi to Patpong Road, Thaniya Plaza, or the Dusit Thani Hotel. Across from Patpong Road—on the corner of Silom Road and Convent Road—is **John Fowler** for causal ready-made clothes, many using hilltribe designs. During the day **Patpong Road** has little to offer shoppers other than two bookstores and a supermarket. Save Patpong for the evening when this area become a huge open air market with vendors selling all kinds of fake watches, clothes, leather goods, audiocassettes, and videos—one of Thailand's most interesting shopping experiences. At the end of Silom is the **Dusit Thani Hotel** with its numerous fine jewelry and antique shops, such as **Sombat Gallery**, **La-one**, **K.C. Gem Centre**, **Sincere Jewelry**, **Sky Light Thai Silk**, **Gems Warehouse**, **Cabochon Jewelry**, **Fortuna**, **P.R. Gem Center**, and **Boutique Dusit**. On the opposite corner is **Robinson's Department Store**. Just down this side of Silom Road you will see **Perry's**, one of Bangkok's best tailors for both men and women. At this point you have completed this shopping area and are situated at Thailand's busiest intersection. From here you can cross to Lumpini Park and then head up Rajadamri Road to the **Regent Hotel** and the **Peninsula Plaza**.

- **Sukhumvit, Ploenchit, Rama I, Rajadamri, and Phyathai Road area:**

This is one of the largest and most diverse shopping areas in Bangkok. Sukhumvit Road runs east and west. The confusing aspects of this area are the street names—Sukhumvit Road changes to Ploenchit Road at Soi 1, and then Ploenchit Road changes to Rama I Road at the Rajadamri Road intersection. This shopping area is one long street about 9 kilometers in length, starting with Soi Ekamai (Soi 63) at the far eastern boundary and ending with Phyathai Road at the far western boundary. Sukhumvit, Ploenchit, and Rama I roads are actually one continuous street linking these two boundaries.

Sukhumvit Road and its network of lanes is the major home for many of Bangkok's expatriates. As a result, several stores cater to this group—bookstores, grocery stores, stationery shops, restaurants, furniture stores, shoe stores, etc. In addition, you will find many shops catering primarily to Western and Middle Eastern tourists. Many visitors to Thailand are interested in the wicker furniture shops between Soi 39 and 43 and the shops in and around the huge **Ambassador Hotel complex** at Soi 11. Between the furniture shops and the Ambassador Hotel are several stores worth noting: **Taptim Antiques** (second floor Villa Supermarket, 591/1 Sukhumvit Road), **Corner 43 Co.** and **Rugs Corner Co.** (769 Sukhumvit Rd.—wicker furniture and rugs), **Pacific Design** (779-781 Sukhumvit—wicker furniture), **Santi's Art & Antiques** (178 Sukhumvit Road), and **Asia Books** (221 Sukhumvit Road, between Soi 15 and 17). The Ambassador Hotel has numerous jewelry, antique, silk, and clothing shops along with several restaurants and an interesting collection of exotic caged birds. One of Bangkok's top seamstresses is found here —**Penny's Boutique** (also located at the Peninsula

Hotel). Several other good shops are located a ways off of Sukhumvit Road, along the lanes, and require taxis to reach them: **Asian Heritage** (57 Soi 23—quality arts and antiques), **Rasi Sayam** (32 Soi 23—unique handicrafts), **Nandakwang** (108/3 Soi 23—lovely cotton products), **Shinawatra** (94 Soi 23—two huge shops with silk and cotton yardage, clothes, handicrafts), **Golden Bo Tree East** (41 Soi 13—wonderful papier mache products), and **Lao Song Handicrafts** (Soi 19—for hilltribe handicrafts). However difficult to find, be sure to visit these shops—they are some of the best in Thailand!

From the Ambassador Hotel complex until the end of Sukhumvit Road at Soi 1, you pass by several small shops selling jewelry, leather goods, celadon, handicrafts, and a variety of items for tourists. For women's dresses, look for **Koody** and **Infini. C.V.N. Exotic Ltd.** at 131 3/4 Sukhumvit Road has a nice gallery of Thai paintings as well as does inexpensive framing. At Soi 4 you will see the Narai Hotel. Directly across the street are two very good art and jewelry stores, **Galleria D'Art** and **Sincere Jewelry**. Near Soi 3 numerous shop signs are in Arabic as you enter into Bangkok's Arab district. Tailors and tourist trinket shops abound here. You will also come to the **Landmark Hotel and Plaza** with its five levels of shops. Here you will find tailors, leather, gift, souvenir, jewelry, silk, and home decorative shops along with a branch of **Asia Books**.

At Soi 1, Sukhumvit Road becomes Ploenchit Road. Just after crossing the railroad tracks, you come to the **Bangkok Night Bazaar** and **The Tourist Shopping Plaza and Night Market** which are filled with small stalls selling inexpensive clothes and tourist items.

As you go further beyond the railroad tracks, you come to the **TAT Duty Free** shop, Thailand's first and only duty-free shop. This classy shop primarily caters to Japanese and Taiwanese tourists who wish to purchase imported "duty-free" items just before leaving Thailand. It's well stocked with the typical duty-free items these tourists expect—European perfumes, candies, leather goods, bags, scarves, jewelry, and nicely packaged gift items. The shop also has a Thai handicraft section. As expected, the service is exceptional. If you buy duty-free items here, they will be delivered to the airport where you pick them up when you depart. You need to stop here at least four hours before departure. Nearby TAT

Duty-Free is **Royal Porcelain** (117 Sinthorn Bldg., Wireless Road), a popular shop offering Thai made porcelain at good prices.

At the intersection of Ploenchit and Wireless roads you can go left and walk a few hundred yards until you come to the **New Imperial Hotel complex** which has several good shops and restaurants. Behind this hotel is Ruam Rudi Road which has a few good shops, such as **Uthai Gems** and **Pure Design** (antiques, furniture, home decorative items). At the corner of Ruam Rudi Road and Ploenchit Road is **Norika**, a fashionable boutique. If you turn right at the same Ploenchit-Wireless Road intersection, walk north to the **Hilton International Hotel** at Nailert Park. The hotel has a few nice jewelry, antique, and tailor shops. A branch of the famous **NeOld** art, antique, and home decorative shop is found here. The hotel's nearby shopping plaza was torn down in 1990. It may soon be replaced by some new shops.

If you go straight along Ploenchit Road, you will next come to the **Central Department Store.** This is the largest branch of Bangkok's first department store. It has a handicraft section on the second floor as well as a small bookstore.

After crossing Chitlom Road you next come to one of Bangkok's major shopping complexes—**Le Meridian President Hotel-Gaysorn-Amarin Plaza** area. The Le Meridian President Hotel has a shopping arcade with several tourist shops offering clothing, jewelry, and knickknacks. The adjacent Gaysorn shopping area has a few nice antique, art, woodcarving, jewelry, and gift shops. We especially like **Wandee Antiques** for antiques and home decorative items, **Jada** for inexpensive gift items, and **New Charming Souvenir** for souvenirs and gifts. You also will find a food arcade and restaurants in this area.

If you walk through Gaysorn and turn right at Rajadamri Road, you will head north to another major shopping area—**Rajadamri Arcade, Phetburi/New Phetburi Road, Pratunam**, and the **Indra Arcade**. We'll return to this area shortly.

Amarin Plaza is located directly across from the Le Meridian President Hotel and Gaysorn. Take the escalator and overhead walkway to enter this plaza. Anchored by Sogo Department Store and attached to the new Grand Hyatt Erawan Hotel, Amarin Plaza has many jewelry, art, clothing, leather goods, and gift shops as well as Bangkok's first McDonald's. More and more of Bangkok's quality jewelry shops are locating here. Some of the best quality shops include **Joli Jewelry, The Legend** (unique handicrafts), **Ragazze** (local leather designs), **Pure Thai Silk, Tisa Gems, Chavana Jewelry, D. Diamonds, Vogue Jewelry, Pitcha Thai Silk, Kako Boutique, Michelle 2, Amarin Art Gallery, House of Handicrafts**, and **Gemsmond**.

At the intersection with Rajadamri Road, Ploenchit Road becomes Rama I Road. If you take a left at the colorful Erawan Shrine on this corner, you will immediately come to **Sogo** which offers the most up-scale imported and locally-produced licensed designer products in Thailand. Here you will find such famous designer labels as Gucci, Salvatore Ferragamo, Chanel, Christian Dior, Givenchy, Bruno Magli, Elle, Calvin Klein, Guy Laroche, and Pierre Cardin. This store primarily caters to Bangkok's growing middle and upper classes. The Japanese and Taiwanese tourists can purchase similar items at the TAT Duty Free shop on Ploenchit Road. You'll find a good food court—"Restaurant Avenue"—on the lower level. Adjacent to Sogo is the new Grand Hyatt Erawan Hotel.

Just a short walk south of the Grand Hyatt Erawan Hotel is the elegant Peninsula Plaza and Regent Hotel, Bangkok's best quality shopping area. **The Peninsula Plaza** has one of the best collections of quality shops selling everything from arts and antiques to jewelry and accessories. It is anchored by the Galeries Lafayette Department Store. Some of the best quality shops in the Peninsula Plaza include **Anong Gallery, Bangkok Dolls Arts and Crafts, Blue River Diamond, Frank's Jewelry, Paa, Bualaad Joaillier, Penny's Boutique, Chailai, Bee Bejour, Prasert Collection, Peninsula Thai Silk, Kai Boutique**, and **Asia Books**. The **Regent Hotel** also has some of Thailand's finest antique, handicrafts, clothing, art, jewelry, and home decorative shops: **Elephant House, Art Resources, Lotus, Peninsula Gems, House of Handicrafts, La-One Thai Silk, Khanitha, Tiew**, and **Kan, Lek, and Montri**.

If you cross the Rajadamri Road intersection at Rama I Road, you will come to the huge new **World Trade Center**. It's four floors of up-scale shops have made this one of Bangkok's most popular shopping centers.

Combined with several other adjacent shopping centers and hotels, such as the Arnoma Swissotel Bangkok, Gaysorn, Le Meridian President Hotel, Amarin Plaza, Sogo Department Store, Grand Hyatt Erawan Hotel, Peninsula Plaza, Regent Hotel, Rajadamri Arcade, The Mall, Robinson's Department Store, Thai Daimaru Department Store, and Narayan Phand, the World Trade Center has virtually transformed this busy intersection into Bangkok's major shopping center. The emphasis here is on upscale shops offering clothes, accessories, jewelry, home decorative items, sporting goods, electronics, toys, and food. The shopping center is anchored by **Zen** (Central) **Department Store**. On the first floor, you will find a very nice boutique, **Sonja**, a branch of Penny's Boutique which is also found at the Peninsula Plaza and the Ambassador Hotel shopping arcade. Other clothing and accessory shops include **Nina Ricci**, **Calvin Klein**, **Bernini**, **Charles Jourdan**, and **Noriko**. However, not everything is imported. Many of the name brand items, such as the Charles Jourdan shoes, are actually produced in Thailand under licensing arrangements. Also look for **Asian Mystique**, **International Gems**, **K.R. Jewels**, and **P&P Jewelry**.

If you walk 10 minutes directly west of this intersection along Rama I Road, you will first come to the beautiful Siam Inter-Continental Hotel and then to the huge Siam Centre, Siam Square, and Mah Boon Krong shopping complex. **Siam Inter-Continental Hotel** has several good jewelry, home decorative, and art shops located in an arcade to the left as you face the hotel. Look for a branch of **Pink Poodle**, one of Bangkok's leading haute couture shops. Next door is the four-story **Siam Centre**. While this center appears to be in decline—increasingly dominated by loud and trendy clothing shops for the local youth—it does house a few nice clothing and jewelry shops, such as **Khanitha** silk shops and **Florentina** jewelers. Banks, travel agents, restaurants, clothing stores, and gift shops are found throughout this building. Directly across the street from Siam Centre is **Siam Square**. This large shopping center consists of hundreds of small shops, restaurants, theaters, and fast food establishments lining several crowded lanes with the imposing **Novotel Hotel** at its center. Here you will find travel agents, tour companies, antique shops, shoe stores, boutiques, bookstores, sporting goods shops, electronic stores, appliance shops, and a host of other businesses appealing to both Thais and tourists. At the Novotel look for one of Bangkok's best jewelers—**Merlin et Delaunay**—with its exquisite French designs. If you are interested in unique hilltribe clothes and fashions, look for **Prayer** which is located at the corner of Phyathai Road and Rama I Road (very hard to find since it is a small shop—197 Patumwan Circle, Siam Square, Tel. 251-7549). For fashionable name brand clothes and accessories, visit the new fashion square in Siam Square, **Marui 0101** (Siam Square S012).

At the end of Siam Centre and directly across Phyathai Road (and Prayer) stands one of Southeast Asia's largest shopping centers—**Mah Boon Krong**. Connected to Siam Centre by an automated overhead walkway, this center is anchored by **Tokyu Department Store**. It houses hundreds of small shops selling clothes, jewelry, electronic goods, and numerous other specialty items.

- **Rajaparop-Rajadamri-Phetburi-New Phetburi Road area:**

This shopping area parallels the Sukhumvit and Ploenchit shopping area and intersects with it near Gaysorn on Rajadamri Road. Indeed, as new shopping centers open, this area appears to be merging with the World Trade Center, Amarin Plaza, and Peninsula Plaza to create a new mega-shopping area—the closest Bangkok has to a city shopping center. The lines between this area and other shopping areas are no longer as clear as they were three years ago. This is a very mixed shopping area in terms of types of shops, quality of goods, and variety of products. An extremely crowded, congested, and chaotic area, here you will encounter traditional street vendors, markets, shopping arcades, and department stores. The streets are somewhat confusing because street names change once again: Phetburi Road becomes New Phetburi Road and Rajaparop Road becomes Rajadamri Road at an intersection called Pratunam. To the north of this intersection is Rajaparop Road. It is lined with numerous small shops selling all types of consumer goods. However, it is the **Indra Hotel** and the adjacent **Indra Arcade** that is of most interest to shoppers. The arcade is filled with all types of small shops catering to both locals and tourists: tailors, jewelers, silk stores, gift shops, electronic stores, etc. As you go south on Rajaprarob you come to **Pratunam Market**, an enclosed market area consisting of small consumer goods stalls and surrounded on the outside by numerous street vendors selling food, consumer goods, and tourist trinkets. Also known as the **Indra Garment Export Center**, here you will enter into a maze of over 500 small clothing stalls selling inexpensive ready-made garments. This is actually Bangkok's major factory outlet market where you can buy clothes directly from the manufacturers at wholesale prices. However, don't expect to find many clothes that fit (if you are large) since sizes tend to be small and styles and colors may not integrate well with your wardrobe and tastes. Turning right at Pratunam, you head west on Phetburi Road. Immediately next to Pratunam on Phetburi Road is the **City Plaza Department Store**. Across the street is **Pantip Plaza**. The small shops which line both sides of Phetburi Road are largely consumer goods shops or they sell a few tourist items—bronze, leather, dolls, woodcarvings, etc. If you go further west on the left side of Phetburi Road for about one kilometer, or where Rama VI Road meets Phetburi Road, you will come to several bronze factory shops, such as **Samron Thailand** (302-308 Phetburi Road) selling a large variety of bronze items.

If you return to the Pratunam intersection and go east one-half kilometer on New Phetburi Road and then turn left, you will come to a shopping area next to the Bangkok Palace Hotel: **Metro Department Store** and **City Square**. You can also enter this area by taking Makkasan Road off of Rajaparob Road. Shopping along the remainder of New Phetburi Road is very limited given the impact of on street parking restrictions. Many businesses have declined or moved to other areas of the city since they are no longer easily accessible by car. Near Soi Asoke on New Phetburi Road is **Petchburi Gallery** (1807-17 New Phetburi Rd.), Bangkok's largest art gallery.

If you return again to Pratunam intersection and go south along Rajadamri Road toward the Ploenchit-Rama I intersection, you will come to a very crowded and congested shopping area that eventually flows into the huge Sukhumvit-Ploenchit-Rama I-Phyathai-Rajadamri Roads shopping area where the World Trade Center, Amarin Plaza, and Peninsula Plaza dominate at the intersection of Ploenchit, Rama I, and Rajadamri Roads. To your left you will find **Rajadamri Arcade** and **The Mall. Robinson's Department Store** and **Thai Daimaru Department Store** serve as the anchors to these two congested shopping centers, selling food, audiocassettes, leather goods, clothes, and a host of consumer and tourist items. Don't miss the huge **Narayana Phand** handicraft emporium that dominates the first two floors of The Mall. Here you will find just about every type of Thai handicraft and gift item available. While the first floor is somewhat disappointing, the second floor is crammed with a good range of varying quality handicrafts. If you walk a little further, you will come to the Gaysorn area which joins with the Sukhumvit-Phyathai Road shopping area.

Other noteworthy shopping areas—older and of less appeal to tourists—are **Chinatown** and **Thieves Market** (along Charoen Krung and Yaowarat roads) and **Banglampoo** (Pra Sumen and Chakrapong roads) in the older western part of the city. You can normally walk along these streets and discover hundreds of shops selling all types of goods for local residents and tourists. However, numerous other quality shops are tucked away on side streets and along the lanes. You need names and addresses and a driver to get to these establishments. Be sure you have a copy of Nancy Chandler's ***Map of Bangkok*** to explore these areas. The map provides numerous details on products and shops in these areas.

SHOPPING ARCADES AND COMPLEXES

Most shopping arcades and complexes are air-conditioned shopping malls anchored to major hotels or they function as free-standing shopping centers which may or may not be found in air-conditioned enclosures. Since they offer some of the best quality products and prices anywhere, we recommend confining at least 70 percent of your shopping to these areas. Many shops that used to be difficult to find have moved to these arcades for your shopping convenience. The major arcades and complexes are:

- **Oriental Plaza:** Located just off New Road and near the Oriental Hotel. Filled with excellent quality jewelry stores, antique and home decorative shops, boutiques, handicraft shops, art galleries, tailor shops, and silk stores. Many other excellent shops are found within a one-half kilometer radius of this plaza. However, within the past year this shopping plaza has come under new ownership and several quality shops have moved out to relocate in the new Thaniya Plaza, World Trade Center, and Amarin Plaza.

- **Oriental Hotel Shops:** You will find a few exclusive jewelry, antique, art, and clothing shops in three areas surrounding the Oriental Hotel: the **Author's Lounge Building**, **Menam Mall**, and the area adjacent to the rear of the **hotel lobby**. Visit these shops while shopping in the nearby Oriental Plaza.

- **River City Shopping Complex:** Adjacent to the Royal Orchid Sheraton Hotel on the Chao Phya River and connected to the Oriental Hotel by ferry. One of the best quality shopping arcades. Pleasant setting along the river. Third and fourth floor "Art and Antique Centre" offers a dazzling array of Thailand's finest quality art and antique shops. Other shops offer good quality handicrafts, clothes, and a host of other items appealing to tourists.

- **Shangri-La Hotel Shops:** Located off of New Road along the Chao Phya River, the Shangri-La Hotel has a small shopping arcade with shops offering tailored garments, ready-made clothes, gifts, and souvenirs. Numerous clothing, jewelry, antique, and souvenir shops line the road leading to the Shangri-La Hotel and extending to the ferry dock.

- **Holiday Inn Crowne Plaza Shops:** This newly opened hotel along Silom Road (at Surasak/Mahesak roads) recently completed a shopping arcade with more than 50 shops offering everything from clothes and jewelry to souvenirs. A pleasant arcade offering a wide range of products for the tourist budget.

- **Silom Village:** Located near the western end of Silom Road between the Narai Hotel and Central Department Store. Small shopping complex with a mix of vendors selling leather goods, tourist knickknacks, jewelry, home decorative items, antiques, and handicrafts. Pleasant open-air restaurants in a water and garden setting. Thai dinner-cultural show presented here at night.

- **Thaniya Plaza:** Bangkok's newest upscale shopping center located in the heart of the financial and shopping district just off Silom Road near Patpong Road and the Dusit Thani Hotel. It's four floors of shops offer quality jewelry, clothes, accessories, silk, textiles, antiques, art, and handicrafts as well as several Japanese, Chinese, and Western restaurants. Includes a branch of Asia Books. Many of Bangkok's best quality shops are moving here from the Oriental Plaza and River City Shopping Complex.

- **Charn Issara Tower:** A shopping arcade located in one of Bangkok's major commercial buildings on Rama IV Road, between Silom and Suriwongse Road. This is one of Bangkok's most exclusive shopping centers frequented by many of Bangkok's wealthy residents and airline employees who yearn for European styles and quality. The four floors of this shopping center have numerous jewelry and clothing stores. A popular place for Japanese tourists who seek name brand items and exclusive jewelry. While some clothing stores position themselves as haute couture, they have a long ways to go before they achieve the stylish and finished looks associated with haute couture found in European capitals, or even Australia. An up-market shopping center of disappointing boutiques with pretensions of being "the best."

- **Montien Hotel Shops:** Located opposite Patpong Road and just off Suriwongse Road, the Montien Hotel has a small but good quality shopping arcade with shops offering antiques, jewelry, clothes, and gift items. Numerous shops surround the hotel just outside the front door and along Suriwongse Road. This is one of the best shopping areas in Bangkok, especially for fashionable clothes, antiques, and home decorative items. You will find such shops as Jim Thompson Silk, NeOld, and Peng Seng as well as several shops in the Charn Issara Tower and Thaniya Plaza within easy walking distance of the Montien Hotel. This area becomes another type of shopper's paradise from 6:30pm to 11pm every night as over 100 vendors set up tables and stalls among Patpong, Suriwongse, and Silom roads to sell inexpensive clothes, accessories, watches, briefcases, cassettes, videos, souvenirs, and toys in what has become known as the Night Market. Consequently, the Montien is literally a center for non-stop shopping in Bangkok.

- **Peninsula Plaza:** Situated next to the Regent Hotel on Rajadamri Road, this is Bangkok's most upscale shopping center. Anchored by Galeries Lafayette Department Store. Filled with excellent quality boutiques, art and antique shops, jewelry and accessories stores, a large bookstore, and restaurants. This is where Elizabeth Taylor buys her jewelry when visiting Bangkok (Franks). Many shops are branches of other shops found at the Oriental Plaza, River City Shopping Complex, or belong to main shops that are tucked away along Bangkok's many lanes. Nice ambiance. A wonderful place to escape from the heat, pollution, and rains.

- **Regent Hotel Shops:** Located next to the Peninsula Plaza on Rajadamri Road, this is one of Thailand's best hotels. Although very small, its shopping arcade is one of the best with several exclusive jewelry, art, clothing, antique, home decorative, and handicraft shops. Don't miss this one!

- **The Landmark Hotel and Plaza:** Found at the lower end of Sukhumvit Road, across from Soi 3 and just near the railroad tracks, this is one of Bangkok's largest hotel shopping arcades. Its five levels of shops offer clothes, souvenirs, gifts, antiques, home decorative items, leather goods, silk, and books. Often has special art exhibits in the center of the plaza. Well worth stopping in this pleasant air-conditioned plaza if you have been pounding the pavement for a few hours looking for street shops along Sukhumvit Road.

- **Siam Square/Siam Centre:** Found near the Siam Inter-Continental Hotel on Rama I and Phyathai roads. The tall Novotel Hotel stands in the center of Siam Square. Now somewhat worn and extremely crowded with young people, theater goers, and diners, this is one of Bangkok's first major shopping centers. Siam Square consists of hundreds of two and three-story commercial shops spread over several blocks just north of Chulalongkorn University. Shops offer everything from sporting goods to antiques. Major travel agents, theaters, bookstores, electronic shops, shoe stores, restaurants, coffee shops, and fast food establishments crowded with young people are clustered in this area. Popular middle class shopping area for Thais and tourists offering a wide range of varying quality goods and services. Connected to the huge Mah Boon Krong Centre by an overhead walkway crossing Phyathai Road. The newer Siam Centre is one large four-story air-conditioned shopping arcade housing over 150 shops which offer a large variety of goods: clothes, jewelry, antiques, handicrafts, silk, electronics, records, audiocassettes, and much more. Includes banks, travel agents, and restaurants. Tends to be overcrowded with Bangkok's youth cruising the arcade in search of something to do or those shopping for the latest youth fashions. Filled with loud rock 'n roll music. A mixed shopping area with a few good shops (try the Novotel Hotel). We consider this area to be more of a cultural experience than a destination for quality shopping.

- **Mah Boon Krong Centre:** Located across from Siam Center at the intersection of Rama I and Phyathai roads, this is one of the largest shopping centers in Southeast Asia. Anchored by the Tokyu Department Store and filled with small shops typical of such shopping centers as Rajadamri Arcade and Amarin Plaza. A popular shopping center for local residents and a favorite hang-out for Bangkok youth in search of local action. Another cultural experience offering few items of interest to tourists.

- **Gaysorn/Le Meridian President Hotel:** Gaysorn is an older shopping area located next to the Le Meridian President Hotel on the corner of Ploenchit and Rajadamri roads. An outdoor shopping complex of two and three-story commercial buildings. Includes several jewelry, antique, clothing, souvenir, home decorative, and art shops. The Le Meridian President Hotel has an expansive shopping arcade that extends into the Gaysorn shopping area. You will find several tailors, gift, and souvenir shops. These are good places to browse before or after visiting the shops in the Amarin Plaza.

- **Amarin Plaza:** Located on Ploenchit Road opposite the Le Meridian President Hotel and Gaysorn shopping area and behind the Grand Hyatt Erawan Hotel. Anchored by Sogo Department Store and filled with all types of small shops—jewelry, clothing, shoe, leather goods, gift, art, and electronic goods—and restaurants. During the past two years this plaza has become a center for some of Bangkok's best jewelry stores. If you are interested in jewelry, be sure to stop here. Popular among middle-class Thai and tourists. Boasts Thailand's first McDonalds.

- **Sogo:** Adjacent to both the Amarin Plaza and the Grand Hyatt Erawan Hotel at the corner of Ploenchit and Rajadamri roads, this is Bangkok's first attempt to primarily offer under one roof exclusive designer label men's and women's clothes and accessories (Gucci, Salvatore Ferragamo, Chanel, Christian Dior, Givenchy Bruno Magli, Pierre Cardin, Elle, Calvin Klein, Guy Larouche). Four shopping levels also include a Thai silk section (2nd floor), and home decorative, audio-visual, and art gallery sections on the fourth floor. Lower level is a "Restaurant Avenue" food court consisting of several nice cafes and restaurants. Primarily caters to wealthy Thai and Asian tourists.

- **World Trade Center:** Opposite Gaysorn and Sogo on the corner of Rama I and Rajadamri roads, this imposing commercial center includes one of Bangkok's largest and most upscale shopping arcades. Anchored by Zen (Central) Department Store, the first six floors of this massive complex are filled with shops offering clothes, shoes, handbags, jewelry, gold, home decorative items, silk, music, electronics, sporting goods, rugs, and optical goods as well as several restaurants. A pleasant place to escape from the heat and humidity of the congested streets and sidewalks outside.

- **Rajadamri Arcade/The Mall:** Located on Rajadamri Road across the street from the World Trade Center and near the Le Meridian President Hotel and Grand Hyatt Erawan hotels and the Gaysorn shopping area. Consists of several department stores and small shops clustered in a highly congested area. Offers all types of products, but especially geared toward middle-class Thai consumers.

Another popular area with Bangkok's youth who cruise for the latest fashions and eat, eat, and eat. Good place to buy pirated audiocassettes. Rather disorienting shopping arcade but interesting to explore. Vendors lining Rajadamri Road and the lane in front of Robinson's Department Store sell leather goods, audiocassettes, clothes, and a variety of other items. Be sure to bargain with these vendors. Also, be sure to visit the huge Narayana Phand handicraft emporium on the first two levels of The Mall.

- **Indra Arcade:** Attached to the Indra Hotel on Rajadamri Road just north of Pratunam Market. Houses over 100 small shops offering everything from clothes and jewelry to knickknacks. Similar in many respects to the Siam Square/Siam Centre and Rajadamri Arcade shopping areas. Crowded with young people and filled with loud music. A mixed shopping area trying to appeal to both local Thais and tourists with consumer goods, theaters, tailors, coffee shops, restaurants, a grocery store, and numerous other middle-class shops. Includes a few quality shops, but tends to have a large number of nondescript tourist shops. Not high on our list of "must visit" places, unless you are staying at the Indra Hotel.

- **New Imperial Hotel Shops:** Located on Wireless Road, the New Imperial Hotel has a small shopping arcade with shops offering clothes, jewelry, gifts, and souvenirs. This pleasant hotel shopping complex boasts a good variety of restaurants which make it an excellent place to shop during noon time.

- **Ambassador City**: Part of the Ambassador Hotel complex on Sukhumvit Road, between Soi 11 and 13. Includes numerous jewelry, clothing, fabric, antique, and handicraft shops along with several specialty restaurants. Exotic birds caged outside and inside this complex make it one of the more unique shopping arcades in Thailand. Hundreds of additional shops offering jewelry, clothes, art, antiques, handicrafts, furniture, and leather goods line Sukhumvit Road just adjacent to Ambassador City. This is an excellent area to roam up and down the street and into a few of the lanes—especially Soi 19, 21, and 23.

- **Central Plaza:** Located next to the Central Plaza Hotel on Paholyothin Road and near the Weekend Market—a long distance (30-35 minutes) from the other major shopping areas in Bangkok. Large enclosed air-conditioned shopping center similar to many malls in the United States. Anchored by Central Department Store. Very popular with Thais on weekends. Shops sell a full range of consumer goods, from microwave ovens to toys for children. Pleasant place to explore if you have just come from the nearby Weekend Market.

Shops in and around many other hotels in Bangkok, such as the Palace and Imperial, have small shopping arcades offering similar goods. However, **Oriental Plaza, River City Shopping Complex, Thaniya Plaza, Charn Issara Tower, Peninsula Plaza, Sogo, Amarin Plaza, World Trade Center** and shops in Bangkok's top hotels are the premier shopping areas for the best quality products. Many shops in these arcades are branches of shops in other arcades. When you visit these areas, be sure to look for additional shops within a radius of one-half kilometer. You will discover many interesting shops offering a wide range of quality goods.

DEPARTMENT STORES

Bangkok has gone through a department store building craze during the last five years. Indeed, during one weekend in November 1984, six new department stores and shopping centers opened on the same day and nearly immobilized traffic in Bangkok! The department stores primarily cater to the growing local middle-class of Thais. They offer ready-made clothes, cosmetics, toys, and appliances imported from abroad. They are well stocked with restaurants and fast food establishments—all of which seem to do a booming business among Bangkok's avid eaters!

Thai department stores tend to be extremely crowded, cold, and noisy. Many are Japanese department stores which have had to adapt to the local Thai shopping culture. As a result, department stores which initially opened with nice neat behind-the-counter displays with fixed prices now display many goods in typical Thai open-air market fashion—tables in aisles piled high with items and labeled with a special sale sign or guarded by an aggressive salesperson shouting out a sales line, similar to vendors in the traditional markets. It is largely this Thai adaptation to Japanese department stores that makes these places so crowded and congested.

Most tourists do not find Thai department stores of much interest other than as cultural experiences. These stores are primarily designed for the growing Thai middle-class that is increasingly drawn to imported consumer goods and the social status of having shopped at department stores. A few department stores, such as Central, have good book sections and serve wonderful soft ice cream for 5 baht. Some also have handicraft sections, but you may find this section to be too "touristy" for your shopping needs and standards. Except for the handicraft and bookstore sections found in some department stores, you may not want to spend your valuable shopping time in these places.

If you do visit one of these department stores, don't expect to do much shopping. Go for the cultural experience, get away from the heat, or find a bite to eat. The major department stores are:

- **Central:** One of the first and oldest department store chains in Thailand. Still one of the best. Has an excellent bookstore section at their Silom Road branch. Carries a good selection of Thai handicrafts and handmade furniture at their Ploenchit/Chitlom Road and Central Plaza branches.

- **Robinson's:** Similar to Central Department Store. Several large and small branches throughout Bangkok. Largest branches found at the Rajadamri Arcade and on the corner of Silom Road and Rama IV Road.

- **Tokyu:** Large Japanese department store anchoring the Mah Boon Krong Centre. Filled with all types of consumer goods for Thais.

- **Sogo:** Large Japanese department store anchoring the Amarin Plaza. Caters to Thai middle-class with a full range of consumer goods. Another Sogo, located next to the Amarin Plaza and the Grand Hyatt Erawan Hotel, primarily caters to the upper middle and upper classes with famous name brand clothes and accessories—many of which are made locally under licensing arrangements.

- **Thai Daimaru:** Anchors the Rajadamri Arcade. One of the first and oldest Japanese department stores. Similar to other department stores designed for middle-class Thai. Crammed with all types of consumer goods.

- **Galeries Lafayette**: Large French department store anchoring the Peninsula Plaza. An elegant store offering good quality. Includes international brand names such as Christian Dior, Yves St. Laurent, Lancel, and Cacharel.

MARKETS, STALLS, AND BAZAARS

Many modern Thai shopping centers and department stores have characteristics of colorful Third World markets. But certain areas are primarily traditional open-air markets or enclosed markets with vendors selling goods from small stalls. These places are often crowded, dirty, and smelly, especially if they include a fresh food and fish market.

While some visitors love to poke around the Thai markets, taking in the unique sights, sounds, and smells, we have yet to become enamored with these places. After you visit one, you may find you have better things to do with your time. Indeed, such markets are best visited as cultural experiences rather than as shopping destinations for finding quality products. You may quickly discover you need no more than 10 minutes to satisfy your curiosity. Many of these markets are now facing competition from the more convenient and air-conditioned shopping arcades and complexes. The major markets of interest to tourists:

- **Chatuchak Park:** Better known as the "Weekend Market" and located near the Central Plaza Hotel and adjacent Central Plaza Shopping Center. Open every day but most interesting on Saturdays and Sundays (go very early, by 8:30am, to avoid the crowds and get the best selections), this is the largest traditional market in Thailand. Similar to a flee market, it is loaded with every conceivable household item, including food, clothes, pets, plants, and handicrafts. It also includes antique, porcelain, and hilltribe product sections which can yield some good buys on unique items. Many sections of the market are crowded, hot, and smelly, but the market is exotic and thus worth at least one visit. Go for the cultural experience, but don't expect to do much quality shopping here. If you are a pet lover, you may fall in love with the beautiful and inexpensive birds

(Cockatoos at $100), puppies, kittens, and rabbits. Leave them behind since you will have problems getting them back home. If you plan to visit this market, consider stopping across the street at the Jit Pochana Restaurant at 1082 Paholyothin Road. They serve fabulous luncheon buffets in nice indoor and outdoor settings. Eat only **after** visiting the market. Next, proceed on to the Hyatt Central Plaza Hotel and Central Plaza Shopping Center. This could be a good time as your images of the Weekend Market fade in the aftermath of a great lunch and the air-conditioned splendor of the hotel and shopping complex. If you plan to visit only one traditional Thai market, be sure to visit this one. It's one of the most interesting cultural experiences in Bangkok, and you may get lucky and make a few shopping discoveries, especially in the handicraft, antique, porcelain, and hilltribe product sections. For details on this market, see Nancy Chandler's ***Map of Bangkok*** which includes a special color coded "Chatuchak Weekend Market" insert.

- **Pratunam:** An enclosed shopping area overflowing onto the sidewalks and streets at the corner of Phetburi and Rajaprarop Road, just south of the Indra Hotel. This area is promoted to tourists as the Indra Garment Export Center, an enclosed market area with over 500 stalls selling inexpensive ready-made clothes. These are primarily factory outlet shops selling over runs and seconds to the public. Unlike Hong Kong where you can visit garment factories and purchase discounted clothes at factory outlet shops, in Thailand you find this discounted merchandise here at Pratunam as well as at the Weekend Market and the Night Bazaars. You may find the colors, styles, and sizes of clothing at Pratunam inappropriate for you; much of the merchandise is simply dreadful. However, you may also discover some good buys in this area. To fully explore this market, you must get into the interior area behind the shops which face both Phetburi and Rajaprarop roads. You could get lost in the narrow pathways separating one small stall from another. This area specializes in dry goods, such as cheap shoes, shirts, linens, glasses, and a host of household products. This is another one of those cultural experiences which is also crowded. Not as hot or smelly as the Weekend Market, but just as bewildering for many first-time visitors. Not a good place for people who get claustrophobia in small, crowded, enclosed areas. You may find 10 minutes is enough for exploring inside this market. Like the Weekend Market, this one is loaded with inexpensive goods you probably do not need nor want. On the other hand, you may discover some wonderful buys here. Be sure to also explore the shops and sidewalk vendors located just outside the market along Phetburi and Rajaprarop roads. You may also want to wander through the nearby Indra Hotel Shopping Arcade.

- **Thieves Market and Chinatown:** Bordered by Charoen Krung, Yaowarat, Mahachai, and Mitraphan roads. This is an extremely crowded and congested area where you can buy numerous items including jewelry, gold, cloth, antiques, cooking utensils, and colorful funeral supplies. The Pahurat Cloth Market (corner of Pahurat and Chakraphed roads), run primarily by Indian merchants, has a good selection of inexpensive cotton materials sold by the meter. This is a rather crowded and disorienting market but one of the best in Thailand for cotton. Thieves Market (called Nakorn Kasem in Thai and between Charoen Krung and Yaowarat roads at Boriphat Road) is filled with all types of old and new antiques and furniture. This is a excellent place to poke around for Chinese ceramics, bells, bronze drums, carved Chinese panels, and musical instruments. While in Chinatown you can stroll down the famous Sampeng Lane (Soi Wanit 1). Enter directly across the street from the Pahurat Cloth Market (Chakraphet Road) or at the other end on Songsawat Road. This lane is filled with small shops selling numerous household goods, clothes, fabric, jewelry, shoes, tea, etc. If you are looking for gold, the Chinatown area is the place to go. The bright red Chinese gold shops sell gold in all forms, carats, and price ranges. The Ban Mo area (Pahurat Road) is a popular market for diamonds and other precious stones. At night Chinatown is brightly lit, reminiscent of Hong Kong's crowded and neon-blazing streets. Nancy Chandler's ***Map of Bangkok*** includes a detailed section on products, shops, restaurants, and sights in these areas. We highly recommend referring to this map when visiting this area.

- **Banglampoo:** Located along Chakrapong Road, near the National Gallery and not far from Pramane Grounds (*Sanam Luang*) and the Royal Hotel. This is one of Bangkok's larger markets. It is filled with all types of household goods, clothes, fabric, jewelry stores, and food stalls. A very crowded area, it is mainly patronized by local Thai and visitors who stay at the Vieng Tai Hotel.

- **Floating Markets:** Tourists are normally taken to either of two traditional floating markets along Thailand's colorful and muddy canals. The one most tourists see is in nearby Thonburi. However, this is no longer a worthy attraction since today it mainly functions for entertaining tourists. It's highly congested and the tourist shops awaiting the next boat load of tourists sell tacky souvenirs at highly inflated prices. The second and more interesting floating market is at **Damnoen Saduak**, a two to three-hour drive from Bangkok in the province of Ratburi. The market still has an authentic rural atmosphere, but it has become very commercialized for tourists. If you take a tour, you will stop at the tourist shops along the way. These shops are filled with tourist knickknacks. In addition, everything is over-priced—one of the worst tourist rip-offs in Thailand. You will pay 300 percent more for many of the products. Our recommendation: buy a banana or orange from one of the boats, take pictures, and enjoy the terrifying speedboat ride. The same and better products are available in Bangkok at much lower prices. Additional floating markets are being opened for tourists in other areas near Bangkok. If you join a tour group, you may be taken to one of these new areas which should be less congested than the two described here.

- **Food and Flower Markets:** Numerous food and flower markets are also found in Bangkok. One of the most interesting is the **Bangrak Market** at the end of Sathorn Road. In the evening several portable food stalls are set up and the vendors serve numerous tasty rice and noodle dishes. This is interesting to see, but you may want to pass on the food since the dishes are often washed in dirty water—a source for hepatitis. **Thewarat Market**, adjacent to the river on Luk Luang Road near Banglampoo Market and the National Library, is a nice flower market where you can treat yourself to a dozen roses for only US$1.20. The **Samyan Market** (corner of Phyathai and Rama IV Road near Chulalongkorn University), **Pak Klong Market** (adjacent to Memorial Bridge), and **Penang Market** (Klong Toei) are all interesting food markets for individuals interested in such cultural and gastronomic experiences.

- **Night Bazaars:** Within the past two years night bazaars have sprung up around Bangkok's major tourist area—Silom, Patpong, and Suriwongse roads. Centered near the Montien Hotel and concentrated along Patpong Road, but also found along Silom Road and Suriwongse Road, the Night Bazaar consists of over 100 vendors who display their wares on makeshift tables. They primarily sell inexpensive clothes, watches, briefcases, leather goods, audiocassettes, and souvenirs; many are copies or pirated. A festive atmosphere begins around 6:30pm and continues until around 11pm. Since many of the goods are copies of brand name clothes, watches, and handbags, occasionally the police go through the perfunctory motions of raiding this area which gives shopping an interesting air of adventure. The raids usually dampen shopping for one hour or so, and then it's back to business as usual. If you get caught in one of these raids, don't worry. No one will bother you—just the vendors who are engaged in what is ostensibly an illegal activity.

  The Night Bazaar is one of the high points of many individual's visit to Bangkok. The vendors seem to have something for everyone. The Patpong area is the most interesting place to shop given its setting—in the midst of Bangkok's rauchy, neon-blazing topless bars and sex shows (while shopping you'll probably be approached by a tout who will try to sell you—male or female or even with your spouse or friend—on attending his interesting sex show which will probably amaze you for its acrobatics and ingenious choreography!). You will also find smaller but similar bazaar operations at night near some of the other major hotels, such as the Royal Orchid Sheraton, Indra Hotel, and Shangri-La Hotel as well as around Silom Village. Be forewarned, however, that customs in your country may enforce international copyright and trademark conventions by confiscating copies of name brand goods purchased in Thailand's night bazaars and markets. One or two items for yourself or a novelty gift will usually pass customs, although we know of individuals who have had the misfortune of being stopped for just one item. It's best not to wear your purchases when passing through customs. This experience, too, adds an air of adventure to your exotic shopping forays!

CRAFT FACTORIES

Bangkok also has its versions of factory outlets. While most arts and crafts in Bangkok shops come from factories in Chiangmai, a few special craft factories are found in and around Bangkok. You may wish to visit a few of these to observe the craftsmen at work, tour their showrooms, and make direct factory purchases. The major factories welcoming visitors include:

- **Thai Lapidary:** 277/1-2 Rama I Road (214-2641). Large factory, cuts and polishes gems.

- **S. Samran, Bronze Factory:** 304 Phetburi Road (215-8941 or 215-8849). Ask at this showroom to be taken to the nearby factory to observe craftsman at work making bronze items.

- **Supoj Thai Bronze Factory:** Located across the river from Bangkok in Thonburi (302 Moo Baan 8 Soi 20, Rojanasin Suksawat Road, Bangpakok, Thonburi, Tel. 427-2595 or 427-4671. Craftsmen producing numerous bronze items.

- **Bangkok Dolls:** 85 Soi Rajatapan, Makkasan (Tel. 24-5-3008). Produces lovely dolls representing the hilltribes and Thai classical dancers. Includes an interesting doll museum for young and old alike.

- **Niello Ware, Thai Nakorn Company:** 79 Prachatipatai Road (Tel. 281-7867 or 281-3526). Factory producing Thai nielloware.

- **Blue & White Potteries:** Located outside Bangkok on the road to the Rose Garden (Surachia Nuparwan, Oom Noi, Samut Sakhon Province). Family produces excellent quality pottery at good prices.

- **Tao Hong Thai Ceramics:** Located outside Bangkok in Ratburi Province (234 Chedihak Road Ampur Muang). Produces copies of Sung and Ming pottery. You can visit their Bangkok shop on Soi Sarasin.

- **Home Made Silk Factory:** 45 Soi 35, Sukhumvit Road. Displays silk weaving.

OUT OF THE WAY DISCOVERIES

While most of Bangkok's shopping is concentrated in and around major shopping centers and hotel shopping arcades, there are several shops located in hard to find locations. Most of these places are found in residential neighborhoods or in lanes far from the main streets. You will need a taxi or hotel car to get to these places. If you take a taxi, pay a little extra to have the driver wait for you since you may have difficulty finding a cab in these locations. Some of our favorite out of the way discoveries include:

- **Fatima Self Help Center:** Located at 18/65 Asoke Din Daeng Road, this is a popular clothing workshop for expatriates living in Bangkok. Operated by the Catholic Church's Good Shepherd Sisters, the workshop provides training and employment for girls from poor families. They produce a wide range of handsewn items, from pot holders to Christmas decorations. One of the great shopping finds here is the beautiful children's smocked dresses or romper suits which are on display or can be made to order and shipped by parcel post to your home. The Center also produces some lovely handmade Christmas decorations.

- **Lao Song Handicrafts:** Located at 69 Soi 19, Sukhumvit Road (Tel. 253-2948), in the Watana School grounds. Just go through the iron gate and look for the shophouse immediately on the right. This is the main outlet for Lao Song hilltribe handicrafts produced in 800 households of 22 villages in northern Thailand. Sponsored by the Church of Christ, the Lao Song produce lovely stuffed animals, placements, Christmas ornaments, baskets, and pot holders. Many of these designs are now being copied by the House of Handicrafts and the Fatima Self Help Center. Lao Song Handicrafts also exports abroad and has a mail order catalog for those who wish to continue purchasing items once they return home.

- **Bangkok Dolls:** Located at 85 Soi Rajatapan, Rajaprarop (just north of the Indra Hotel), this is a wonderful place to observe the making of the unique and award-winning Thai dolls. While Bangkok Dolls also has a shop at the Peninsula Plaza (Bangkok Dolls Arts & Crafts), it's well worth making the trip to this factory shop to see the selections, museum, and the production process. Appeals to both young and old.

- **Elephant House:** Located at 67/12 Soi Phra Phinit, Soi Suan Phlu, Sathorn Tai Road (Tel. 286-5280), this is one of Thailand's most exquisite antique and home decorative shops. You will find three branch shops, one on the fourth floor of the River City Shopping Complex, another in the Regent Hotel, and another across from the Shangri-La Hotel. However, this is the main shop, which actually consists of two neighborhood shops, each with three floors of unique items. It's the one dealers and collectors are most likely to visit. This shop also has one of the largest collections of Burmese lacquerware in the world. The owner also operates the best Burmese restaurant in Thailand, the Mandalay (23/17 Soi Ruam Rudee, opposite Ruam Rudee Village, Tel. 255-2893).

- **Art Resources:** Located at 142-20 Soi Sueksavitaya, off Soi Silom 9 (Tel. 235-4846), this art and framing shop is difficult to find because it is located off of both Silom Road and North Sathorn Road—few taxis can find it because of the confusing street names. This is the main shop which does outstanding framing work. We have used the services of Mr. Pramote for over 10 years. We take all of our framing work to this shop, and the outcome has always been outstanding. This shop also sells traditional Thai paintings and European art deco bronze reproductions—its two most popular items. Visit his other shop in the Regent Hotel shopping arcade for similar selections.

- **Shinawatra:** Located at 136 Sukhumvit Road, Soi 23 (Tel. 258-0515), this is one of Thailand's largest silk and handicraft shops. The main factory is located in the town of Sankamphaeng near Chiangmai. This shop consists of two buildings across the street from each other. The one building primarily sells cotton clothing. The other much larger building offers silk fabric, clothes, and handicrafts. You can easily spend an hour browsing through these two buildings.

- **Rasi Sayam:** 32 Sukhumvit Soi 23 (Tel. 258-4195). Specializes in Thai handcrafted items, but this is not your typical handicraft, tourist knickknack shop. Offers one of Bangkok's most tasteful selections of handcrafted items produced in numerous villages throughout Thailand. Excellent quality and many unique items. Located in an old Thai house just down the street from Asian Heritage.

- **Asian Heritage:** Located at 57 Sukhumvit Road, Soi 23 (Tel. 251-8274), this is an excellent quality antique and home decorative shop operated from the owner's residence. Not many tourists visit here, but it is popular with many dealers and collectors who are looking for quality items. Since it is not always open, it is a good idea to call before visiting. The owner also operates the nearby Vietnamese restaurant, Le Dalat (51 Sukhumvit Soi 23, Tel. 258-9298), one of Thailand's best.

10 IN SEARCH OF QUALITY

You can have a very rewarding shopping experience by confining your shopping to the Oriental Plaza, River City Shopping Complex, Thaniya Plaza, Peninsula Plaza, Amarin Plaza, World Trade Center, and several deluxe hotel shopping arcades. However, there are many places outside these areas which also offer excellent products and value. Some are shops while others are homes which also function as shops tucked away in Bangkok's maze of side streets and lanes. Some of our favorite shopping discoveries include the following quality shops.

ANTIQUES, ARTS, FURNITURE, CARVINGS, HOME DECORATIVE ITEMS

- **NeOld:** 149/2-3 Suriwongse Road (Tel. 235-8352) and branch shops in the Hilton Hotel Lobby (253-0123, ext. 8684) and the fourth floor of River City Shopping Complex. This is Thailand's premier antique **and** home decorative shop, the place for the truly discriminating shopper with taste and class. Simply fabulous offerings selected by one of Thailand's top antique dealers and 1designers—the soft spoken Mr. Chaiwut Tulayadhan. His decorating skills are well represented in the lobbies of major hotels, such as the Oriental, Shangri-La, Hilton, Siam Inter-Continental, Amanpuri Phuket, and Pansea Phuket as well as in many offices and private homes throughout Thailand and abroad. Chaiwut has an incredible eye for quality and knows how to best display and integrate his selections. Offers excellent quality antiques, arts, mirrors, chest panels, tapestries, furniture, wood panels, lamps and smaller items such as ceramics, lacquerware and baskets; most are Burmese in origin. Gorgeous items which shout quality and will fit into Western decors. Very reliable, very expensive, and very nice. The best shop is the main store on Suriwongse Road. If you are a serious collector of antiques with an eye toward decorating, make NeOld your first stop in Thailand. It doesn't get better after NeOld.

- **Elephant House:** 67/12 Soi Phra Phinit, Soi Suan Phlu, Sathorn Tai Road (Tel. 286-5280) and branch shops on the fourth floor of River City Shopping Complex (234-9365 or 235-2976 thru 9), The Regent Hotel, and across the street from the Shangri-La Hotel. Unique selection of high quality arts, antiques, furniture, and objets d'art from Thailand, Burma, and Cambodia. Designs own handmade furniture using antique opium mats and red lacquer. The Burmese owner/designer-Cherie Aung-Kin—knows quality, speaks excellent British English, and is most helpful. Very reliable. Expensive, but you buy quality and can find one-of-a-kind pieces here. Need to take a taxi to the two main shops off of Sathorn Tai Road—the ones with the most extensive selections.

- **Lek Galleries' Art:** 1310 New Road (Tel. 234-4184). Newly refurbished, this gallery specializes in Burmese and Thai antiques. Large selection of Buddhas, Burmese ceilings and panels, lacquer doors, and attractive smaller pieces such as bells and palaquin hooks. Excellent quality, prices, and service. Very reliable and a joy to work with either in Bangkok or from abroad. Contact either Janya or Pornthep, the husband-wife team that operates this fine shop.

- **The Fine Arts:** First floor of Oriental Plaza (Tel. 2341320-9, ext. 03) and the River City Shopping Complex (#452-454, Tel. 2352972-9, ext. 452-454). Also has shops in other major shopping centers which come under the names of **The Height** (Thaniya Plaza and River City Shopping Complex), **JR** (Thaniya Plaza), and **The Fine**

Creations (opposite the Shangri-La Hotel, #64, Store 14, Shangri-La Hotel Lane). One of Thailand's best and most famous collectors of textiles, Khmer bronzes, and Burmese antiques. Excellent quality. Also produces unique pieces of furniture as well as model ships and boats for discriminating collectors. If you are interested in old textiles, The Fine Arts is the place to go. It is reputed to be Bangkok's biggest dealer in old textiles.

- **Peng Seng:** 942/1-3 Rama IV Road (corner of Suriwongse and Rama IV roads and next to Jim Thompson Silk Company, Tel. 233-1891 or 234-3836). Outstanding quality art and antique store filled with lovely sculptures, ceramics, tapestries, and bronze pieces. Includes an excellent museum on second floor as well as one of the best selections of art books and back issues of major Asia art magazines. Expensive, reliable, a must for the serious collector and well worth a stop to browse.

- **Oriental Commercial House:** Third floor (#314 and 319) River City Shopping Complex (Tel. 235-2966, ext. 314 or 319). Offers a unique collection of Lanna (Northern) Thai arts and antiques. The quality and selections here are outstanding. This is the only shop we know that specializes in the Lanna Thai style. Has two shops near each other. Moderately expensive.

- **Golden Triangle:** Third floor (#302) of River City Shopping Complex (Tel. 234-9365, ext. 301). One of Thailand's most unique quality shops. Excellent selections of hilltribe textiles, silver, and beads. Offers beautifully crafted garments using antique textiles. Nice displays and quality selections and craftmanship throughout this inviting shop. Moderately expensive.

- **Rama Antique:** Second floor of the Oriental Plaza (Tel. 237-5826). This expansive shop is filled with excellent quality Burmese, Thai, and Chinese antiques—chests, lacquerware, mirrors, textiles, tapestries, carvings, beds, boxes, etc. Wonderful selection of quality items. Be sure to explore both adjacent shops as well as the back room of the larger shop. Expensive.

- **Monogram:** The Oriental Hotel, Author's Lounge and adjacent Menam Mall (Tel. 235-1875 or 235-2603). One of Thailand's oldest and most well established antique dealers. Offers excellent quality art and antiques, especially old and new tapestries, statues, silver, and furniture. Expensive.

- **Santi's Art & Antiques:** 174/4-6 Silom Road (Tel. 2354-7027) and branch shops at 178 Sukhumvit Road (Tel. 253-3391 or 253-5417) and fourth floor of the River City Shopping Complex. Excellent quality arts, antiques, and wood pieces from Thailand, Burma, Laos, and Cambodia. Good selection of sculptures and antique Burmese tapestries. Makes excellent quality imitation bronze drums and custom stands. The River City Shopping Complex and Silom Road shops specialize in Burmese antiques; the Sukhumvit Road shop does more with new bronze pieces. Moderately expensive.

- **Asian Heritage:** 57 Sukhumvit Soi 23 (Tel. 251-8274). Beautiful selection of Thai and Burmese antiques, including tapestries, bronze drums, furniture, and carvings. Difficult to find this shop without a taxi and is often closed. Suggest you call before dropping in. Shop is part of family compound. Moderately expensive.

- **Pure Design:** 30 Ruam Rudee Road (off of Ploenchit and Wireless roads, Tel. 253-1719). One of Thailand's best home design and decorative shops. Offers a fine selection of antiques, furniture, and contemporary art. If you are interested in having quality custom work done for your home decorative needs, be sure to contact this firm. Moderately expensive.

- **Taptim Antiques:** 591/1 Sukhumvit Road (Tel. 258-5070). Small shop on second floor of Villa Supermarket (enter through the supermarket and go upstairs). Nice, although limited, selection of quality arts and antiques. Includes lacquer baskets, furniture, mirrors, and tapestries. Moderate prices.

- **Artisan's:** Silom Village, 286 Silom Rd. (Tel. 234-4448, ext. 32). Small and cluttered but good quality shop offering unique antiques and home decorative items. Moderate prices.

PAINTINGS AND FRAMING

- **Art Resources:** 142/20 Soi Sueksavitaya, off Soi Silom 9 (Tel. 235-4846) and the Regent Hotel shopping arcade, Rajadamri Road (Tel. 250-0723). The Silom Road shop does some of the best framing we have encountered anywhere. See the owner, Mr. Pramote, for custom work. Both shops have a nice selection of traditional Thai paintings and bronze sculptures. Moderate prices.

- **Surawongse Gallery:** 287/25-6 Suriwongse Road (Tel. 233-5533) and 3rd floor of River City Shopping Complex. Excellent collection of traditional and modern paintings and sculptures. Good quality and creative framing at reasonable prices.

- **C.V.N. Exotic Ltd.:** 131-3/4 Sukhumvit Road (between Soi 7 and 9). Large collection of traditional and modern Thai paintings. Does inexpensive framing.

- **Amarin Art Gallery:** Third floor on Amarin Plaza. Excellent collection of contemporary Thai oils and watercolors.

- **Petchburi Gallery:** 1807-17 New Phetburi Road (Tel. 251-2426). One of Thailand's largest art galleries presenting the works of leading painters and sculptors. Branch shop on New Road.

- **M.T. Gallery:** Ground floor, Oriental Plaza, 30/1 Chartered Bank Lane (Tel. 234-1320, ext. 12). Offers both traditional and contemporary Thai paintings.

- **Sombat Gallery:** Dusit Thani Hotel (Tel. 233-3611), second floor Royal Orchid Sheraton Hotel (Tel. 234-5599, ext. 3259), and second floor River City Shopping Complex (called Four Art Gallery, Tel. 235-2972, ext. 215). Offers both traditional contemporary Thai oils and watercolors.

SILK AND COTTON

- **Jim Thompson Thai Silk Co.:** 9 Suriwongse Road (Tel. 234-4900) and small branch shops at the Authors

Lounge in the Oriental Hotel and at the Grand Hyatt Erawan Hotel. Offers Thailand's best quality silk and cotton using excellent designs. Includes ready-made clothes, accessories, upholstery material, pillow covers, napkins, placemats, jewelry boxes, picture frames, neckties, and much more. Silk fabric and gift items found at ground floor, and ready-made clothes, neck accessories, and cottons on the second floor. Unfortunately, some of their best colors and designs for upholstery material are only available in Jim Thompson designer shops abroad. Colors and designs for a shop of such quality are sometimes disappointing, especially for garments. Be sure to see their unique neckpieces in the showcase at the top of the staircase on second floor. Very expensive.

- **Design Thai:** Silom Road (next to Central Department Store, Tel. 235-1553). Good quality silk and cotton clothes, fabrics, quilted bedspreads, placemats, toys, and numerous gift items. Includes designer bronzeware and some celadon. Also, look for their shops in Hong Kong and Singapore, which carry other designs. Expensive.

- **Khanitha:** Third floor Siam Shopping Centre (Tel. 251-2933) and branch shops in Oriental Plaza, Ambassador Hotel, the Regent Hotel, and along Suriwongse Road. Good quality and fashionable silk. Includes ready-made clothes and jewelry boxes. If you have 3 days or more, they can make a jewelry box to order. Expensive.

- **Shinawatra:** 94 Soi 23 Sukhumvit Road (Tel. 258-3570). Bangkok branch of Chiangmai silk factory. Two large stores include a large selection of silk and cotton fabrics for clothes and upholstery as well as Thai handicrafts and gift items for tourists. Moderately expensive.

CLOTHES AND TAILORS

- **Pink Poodle:** Oriental Hotel, Author's Lounge (Tel. 236-0400, ext. 3357) and the Siam Inter-Continental Hotel (Tel. 253-0355, ext. 7645). Thailand's most exclusive, haute couture designer shop in a class of its own. One of few shops in Thailand that really understands how to work with fabrics, colors, and designs rather than being preoccupied with only offering the highly overrated Thai silk with its inherent limitations. Uses materials from all over the world, but especially Chinese and Indian silks that work much better for many styles than Thai silk. Designs and prints its own materials. Beautifully designed one-of-a-kind garments for those with good taste and lots of money. The shop European and American VIPs go to for something very special. Very exclusive, very unique, and very expensive.

- **Penny's Boutique:** Peninsula Plaza (#111), 153 Rajadamri Rd. (Tel. 253-4926-7) and Ambassador Hotel, Sukhumvit Rd. (Tel. 254-0444, ext. 1132). Also operates a shop called **Sonja's** in the World Trade Center (A128 Ground Floor, Rajadamri Rd., Tel. 255-9531-2). One of Bangkok's best boutiques noted for quality silks (French, Italian, Chinese, Thai) and expert seamstress skills. Uses lighter weight Thai silks for garments than other shops. If you are interested in having a blouse or dress made in Bangkok, you can't do much better than Penny's Boutique. Expensive.

- **Ajai Zecha** and **A Cha:** Landmark Hotel and Plaza, 3rd Floor (Tel. 252-6911). Two fashion boutiques operated by Miss Rayib Sathabutr, one of Bangkok's talented fashion designers trained in France. Works with Thai silks (mutmee) and textiles. Knows how to turn ethnic designs and color themes into fashionable garments which appeal to many westerners. Good use of colors.

- **Designers' Showcase:** 115/1 Suriwongse Rd. (Tel. 236-2806). Beautifully designed women's garments made from textiles throughout southeast Asia. Ikat garments (mutmee) from Northeast Thailand are especially attractive. Combines both silk and cotton in its garments. Also look for their attractive silk flowers. If you are looking for something "ethnic," this is the place to go. Related to Perry's Tailors on Silom Road, this shop does good seamstress and tailoring work.

- **Choisy:** 9/25 Suriwongse Rd. (Tel. 233-7794). Fashionable designer boutique using Jim Thompson silks and cottons. Offers ready-to-wear garments designed by Western (French) owners.

- **Perry's:** 60/2 Silom Rd. (Tel. 233-9236). One of Bangkok's best tailors. Does both men's and women's clothes, but watch them carefully when doing women's clothes (they are more tailors than seamstresses).

- **Adam's Tailor:** 23/3 Thaniya Road (Tel. 233-7857) and Charn Issara Tower. Good quality men's tailor. Many consider Adam's Tailor to be the best in town. Expensive.

- **C. Fillipo:** Shangri-La Hotel shopping arcade. Another good quality men's tailor. Expensive.

- **River Mark:** Second floor (#238) of River City Shopping Complex (Tel. 237-0077-8, ext. 238). Good quality tailor and excellent service. Moderately expensive.

HANDMADE FURNITURE

- **Sweet Home:** Soi Asoke (Soi 21) Sukhumvit Road or 33 Sukhumvit Road Soi 27 (Tel. 258-3419). Good craftsmanship on all types and styles of wood furniture. View the showroom and discuss your plans using either your pictures and drawings or their book of examples. Reliable but difficult to communicate with salespeople. Get everything in writing and repeat it several times.

- **Gersons:** 21 off Soi Chaisamarn, Soi 4, Sukhumvit Rd. (Tel. 253-1638 thru 41). Produces excellent quality furniture. Reliable.

- **Peter's Furniture:** 157/1 Mahadlck 2, Rajadamri Road (behind Regent Hotel, Tel. 252-6727 or 252-5236). Excellent and reliable.

- **Star House:** 746-52 Sukhumvit Rd., near Soi 34. Produces good quality rosewood and teak furniture. Reliable.

- **Pure Design:** 30 Ruan Rudee Road (off of Ploenchit and Wireless roads, Tel. 253-1719). Produces excellent quality furniture in unique designs for those interested in special home decorative pieces. Produces a wonderful naga (serpent) chair.

- **Elephant House:** 67/12 Soi Phra Phinit, Soi Suan Phlu, Sathorn Tai Road (Tel. 286-5280—talk to Cherie). Produces excellent quality unique furniture pieces using antique opium mats.

- **Corner 43 Co.:** 769 Sukhumvit Road (Tel. 260-1124). Offers some of the most fashionable wicker furniture in Asia. Excellent designs and colors. Will custom make furniture to your designs. Operated by the owner of Taptim Antiques (Villa Supermarket).

JEWELRY, SILVER, AND ACCESSORIES

- **Frank's:** 104 Peninsula Plaza, 153 Rajadamri Rd. (Tel. 254-4528). Beautifully designed jewelry and a favorite shop for visiting VIPs. Specializes in large and elaborate pieces of jewelry that are also very expensive. Related to Joli Jewellery in Amarin Plaza.

- **Bualaad Joaillier:** Peninsula Plaza, first floor, 153 Rajadamri Rd. Exquisite designs, outstanding service, and wonderful shop ambience. Very nice, very expensive, very reliable.

- **Paa:** Peninsula Plaza, first floor, 153 Rajadamri Rd. Excellent quality, good designs, and very reliable. Specializes in fine antique jewelry. Very expensive.

- **Lotus:** Regent Hotel. Exquisitely designed jewelry, especially attractive neckpieces. Unique one-of-a-kind pieces fashioned from gold, silver, precious, and semi-precious stones from all over the world. Many combine old items with additions that make the pieces more exquisite than they were originally. Also have a selection of small decorative items for the home and a selection of textiles. This could easily become your favorite shop! Expensive.

- **Yves Joaillier:** Charn Issara Tower, 3rd floor 942/83 Rama IV Rd. (Tel. 233-3292). One of Thailand's premier French jewelry designers. Produces exquisite designs to your specifications or you can buy from their showcase. Hard to see what's available by looking in the very limited display window. Must go into the shop and talk with the personnel.

- **Merlin et Delaunay:** Novotel Hotel, Siam Square (Tel. 254-3877, 255-6888, ext. 2619). A long established and reputable French jeweler. Produces attractive and imaginative designs. Contact this shop if you also wish to visit their factory.

- **Joli Jewellery:** Amarin Plaza and branch shop at the Menam Mall Shopping Arcade (opposite the Oriental Hotel, 236-7889 and 234-9920, ext. 3455). Good selection of rings, bracelets, necklaces, and pins. Quality rubies, pearls, and diamonds. Excellent service. Stylish designs.

- **Alex & Co.:** 14/1 Oriental Lane (Tel. 234-3908) and branch shop in the Dusit Thani Hotel. Well established store consistently producing excellent workmanship. Specializes in Mikimoto pearls. Designs somewhat dated.

- **Sincere Jewelry:** Dusit Thani Hotel Arcade (Tel. 233-0643) and branches opposite the Narai Hotel on Silom Road (Tel. 234-1241) and on Sukhumvit Road. Excellent quality designs and reliable.

- **Castle of Gems Ltd. Part.:** Dusit Thani Hotel Arcade (Tel. 233-0647 or 233-1130 ext. 2465). Excellent quality jewelry. Will design to your needs.

- **Jim Thompson Silk Company:** 9 Suriwongse Road. Excellent selection of neckpieces using semi-precious stones, gold, and silver. Go to the second floor display case for examples.

- **Uthai Gems:** 23/7 Soi Ruam Rudee (Tel. 252-4365). Designs jewelry to your specifications. Popular with expatriates, especially U.S. Embassy personnel. Very reliable.

- **Peninsula Plaza shops:** Houses some of Thailand's best quality shops on the first floor—**Blue River Diamond, Bualaad, Paa, Frank's, Chailai,** and **Anong Gallery**.

- **Amarin Plaza shops:** Houses several good quality jewelry shops located on the first and third floors—**Tisa Gems, Chavana, D. Diamonds, Vogue Jewelry, Gemsmond,** and **Joli**. Compared to the outstanding Peninsula Plaza jewelry shops, you should find some good quality but more moderately priced jewelry here. More and more jewelry shops are opening in the Amarin Plaza, so look for some new additions.

- **Dusit Thani Hotel:** Has a disproportionate number of Thailand's best jewelry shops, such as **Sincere** and **Cabochon Jewelry**.

HANDICRAFTS

- **Rasi Sayam:** 32 Sukhumvit Soi 23 (Tel. 258-4195). This relatively new shop offers one of Thailand's finest collections of handcrafted items produced in villages throughout Thailand. Look for pottery, carvings, boxes, baskets, ceramics, etc. The emphasis here is on both quality and unique handicrafts and home decorative items. Excellent designs and good value. Perfect place for serious collectors. Moderate.

- **Nandakwang:** 108/3 Sukhumvit 23 Prasanmitr, Prakhanong (Tel. 258-1962). Beautiful cotton woven items that make great gifts or additions to one's home decor. Quality placemats, pillows, boxes, toys, etc. Hard to find this shop in the maze of lanes off Sukhumvit Road, but persist until you find it!

- **Golden Bo Tree East:** 41 Soi 13 Sukhumvit Rd (Tel. 251-0068, 251-9040). This unique shop makes attractive papier mache items. You will find colorful animals, placemats, pots, coasters, jars, baskets, boxes, candle sticks, furniture, and screens here.

- **Thai Home Industries:** 35 Oriental Lane (Tel. 23-4-1736). Nice selection of various Thai handicrafts, including baskets, spirit houses, temple bells, wood carvings, and unique bronze flatware. Service is a little slow, but the products are worth your patience. Moderate.

- **Chitralada Shop:** Top floor of Oriental Plaza and in the Thaniya Plaza. Good selection of hilltribe and Thai village handicrafts, including embroidery, baskets, hats, and boxes. Moderate.

- **Lao Song Handicrafts:** 69-71 Soi 19 Sukhumvit Road. Good selection of hilltribe handicrafts under the sponsorship of the Church of Christ in Thailand. Includes purses, hot pads, tablecloths, placemats, puppets, neckties, Christmas decorations, patchwork, embroidery, and much more. Moderate.

- **Narayana Phand:** In The Mall on Rajadamri Road. This huge two-floor government-run handicraft emporium offers a very large selection of Thai handicrafts for tourists. Everything from woodcarvings to silver jewelry and paintings. Popular place to send tourists for all their handicraft needs. Highly recommended for last minute shopping and for lots of small trip gifts. Be sure to go up to the second floor. Moderate.

- **House of Handicrafts:** Large shop in the Regent Hotel (Tel. 250-0724) shopping arcade and small shop in the Amarin Plaza. Offers a large selection of attractive Thai and hilltribe handicrafts. Moderate.

- **Bangkok Dolls:** Main workshop at 85 Soi Ratapan, off Rajaprarop Road (Tel. 245-3008). Unique collection of handcrafted Thai dolls reflecting numerous ethnic and cultural themes. Great place for both the young and old to visit. Moderate.

- **The Legend:** Third floor of Amarin Plaza (Tel. 256-9929). Unique collection of excellent quality textiles, porcelain, baskets, and pottery. Many one-of-a-kind pieces, similar in quality to those found at Rasi Sayam.

CELADON, BENJARONG, AND POTTERY

- **Prasart Collection:** Second floor, Peninsula Plaza, 153 Rajadamri Rd. (Tel. 253-9772). Specializes in making gorgeous reproductions of Benjarong. The shop has a small inventory which merely represents the type of custom work they can do at their main workshop. And the main workshop is one of Thailand's most interesting museums that houses a fabulous collection of Thai antiques in a large compound which has been designed for preserving Thai arts. If you have time, be sure to visit this unique museum. It's located near Ramkamhaeng University, via Phetburi Road, approximately 40 minutes from the major shopping areas (9 Soi Krungtepkreetha 4A, Krungtepkreetha Rd., Bangkapi). You will be given a 1½-2 hour guided tour of the lovely grounds and museum. Open for individuals from 10am to 3pm, Friday, Saturday, and Sunday. Entrance fee is 200 baht. For more information on the museum, contact the shop at Peninsula Plaza or call the museum directly—Tel. 374-6328 or 374-6384. Very expensive Benjarong reproductions but extremely labor-intensive for highly skilled craftspeople.

- **Celadon House:** 18/7 Sukhumvit 21 (Tel. 258-3920, 259-7744). Large selection of the light grey-green and dark brown-green celadon. Includes numerous decorative pieces, lamps, and tableware. Has a "seconds" section on second floor.

- **Lotus Ceramics:** Soi 3/1 Sukhumvit Road (off of the larger Soi 3, Tel. 253-0044 or 253-2789). Offers a large selection of blue and white pottery.

- **Thai Taworn Brothers Co. Ltd.:** 89/34-35 Rajathavee Cross, Phyathai Road, across from Asia Hotel (Tel. 252-0612). Large selection of Bencharong and blue and white pottery.

BRONZEWARE

- **Siam Bronze Factory:** 1250 New Road (Tel. 2349436). Large selection of bronze items. Will silicon coat upon request.

- **S.N. Thai Bronze Factory:** 157-33 Phetburi Road, Tel. 215-8221 or 215-7743). Large selection of bronze items. Will silicon upon request.

- **Lin Plaza Gems & Thai Silk LP:** Across from Oriental Plaza at 1-7 Chartered Bank Lane (Tel. 233-6592).

Second floor has a good selection of bronze items, from flatware to statues. Good place to buy trip gifts. Also has jewelry and does men's and women's tailoring work at reasonable prices—one of our all-in-one shops.

- **Thai Home Industries:** 35 Oriental Lane, off New Road near the Oriental Hotel (Tel. 234-1736). Offers uniquely designed bronzeware and brass dinner plates.

11 GETTING WHAT YOU WANT

Shopping in Bangkok is especially rewarding if you know the "how," "what," and "where" of shopping in this city's many streets, shopping centers, arcades, and department stores.

PLANNING RIGHT

You should approach Bangkok with a relatively intelligent and flexible plan. Given Bangkok's horrendous traffic situation, **where you stay** will probably be the single most important factor in determining how much you enjoy this city. Believe us. You can easily hate this city if you unwittingly stay in the wrong place. The traffic will quickly kill your enthusiasm for Bangkok as well as Thailand. If you choose a hotel poorly situated in relation to the major shopping centers, you are likely to waste a great deal of time in the traffic trying to go from one shopping area to another. You simply don't need this aggravation by making the wrong hotel choices!

Our recommendation is to stay in one of three major areas where you can easily walk to the major shopping centers or connect with other centers by means of a short taxi ride:

- **Near the World Trade Center/Amarin Plaza/Peninsula Plaza:** The Regent, Grand Hyatt Erawan, Le Meridian President, and Arnoma Swissotel hotels.

- **Along or near the Chao Pyra River:** Oriental, Royal Orchard Sheraton, Shangri-La, or Holiday Inn Crowne Plaza hotels.

- **Near Rama IV and Patpong roads:** Dusit Thani, Montien, and Tawana Ramada hotels.

The Siam Inter-Continental and Novotel hotels near **Siam Center and Siam Square**, the Landmark Hotel on **Sukhumvit Road**, and the Indra Regent hotel near **Pratunam and Rajaprarop Road** are also good choices.

We also recommend staying at some of Bangkok's top hotels. While expensive ($150-$230 per night double occupancy), they are still good buys compared to comparable accommodations in other countries, and you will love Thailand's high quality accommodations and service.

Whatever you do, make sure you concentrate your shopping in one or two areas each day. Trying to cover more than two major shopping areas in a single day will likely put you into the depressing traffic. Take it easy. Plan, for example, to spend a day shopping along Suriwongse, Silom, and New Road. On another day head for the Peninsula Plaza, Amarin Plaza, and World Trade Center areas, and maybe also include Siam Center, Siam Square, and the Pratunam areas. On another day you might want to concentrate only on the Sukhumvit Road area. But don't try to jump from one of these areas to another in a single day. If you do, you'll spend most of your time in the traffic. And you will quickly learn to hate this city simply because you made such choices!

The best approach to shopping Bangkok is to identify the types of items you wish to buy; select your high priority shops in and around major shopping arcades; plan to visit special shops outside these areas; and leave time for serendipity. If you want to take advantage of custom-made clothes, jewelry, and furniture, make sure you bring pictures, examples, or detailed drawings of your designs.

Begin your shopping adventure in the hotel shopping arcades where you will find the best quality products. Start with the Oriental Plaza, River City Shopping Complex, and Peninsula Plaza. After surveying the types of goods available, quality, and prices, expand your shopping area to include shops near the major hotel complexes as well as visit quality shops outside these areas. Hire a car and driver to take you to places like the Elephant House, Pure Design, Shinawatra, Asian Heritage, Rasi Sayam, Lao Song Handicrafts, Fatima Self Help Center, and Bangkok Dolls, which are off the normal beaten tourist path.

BARGAINING

Be sure you bargain for most items you purchase in Bangkok. Shopkeepers expect you to bargain and will give anywhere from 10 to 40 percent discounts. However, certain shops have fixed prices or bargain very little. Department stores have fixed prices, but you may receive a 5-10 percent discount on expensive items, such as jewelry, if you ask for it. Prices also are fixed at Jim Thompson Silk Company, Narayana Phand, and a few other shops. And don't expect much discounting at high quality antique and art shops, such as NeOld, Elephant House, and Monogram. Jewelry shops, on the other hand, can and do give larger discounts. You will receive the largest discounts from vendors in markets who both inflate their prices and can operate on small profit margins given their low overhead. You also can receive discounts on hotels, tours, and guides—but only if you ask and only from certain ones at particular times of the year. In general, the trend in Bangkok is to move toward fixed prices on quality products or to give very minimum discounts.

When you bargain in Bangkok, bargain as you would in other countries, but also try to put some additional degrees of light-heartedness and humor into the process. The Thais are very polite, civil, sophisticated, and fun-loving people who enjoy arriving at mutually satisfactory arrangements. You should never raise your voice or act disgusted or insulted. The Thais tend to be responsive to a nice, easy-going, polite, and humorous negotiation process where everyone keeps a good "face" and arrives at a mutually beneficial arrangement.

Thai shopkeepers tend to be rather fair and honest in contrast to similar merchants in many other countries. We generally don't get or feel ripped-off when we shop in Thailand, but of course we avoid the touts and their shops and are generally careful where we shop. Some of our readers have reported problems with their jewelry and antique purchases, but not because they followed our advice. Indeed, they did just the opposite. Invariably they failed to use good commonsense, and they violated the first rule of good shopping—always shop in reputable shops. Whatever you do, please avoid shopping in places recommended by tour guides, taxi drivers, or anyone who approaches you with a "good deal" recommendation.

SHIPPING

Shipping from Bangkok is relatively convenient although it can be expensive. If you see something you really love and can afford, don't worry about getting it back home. Shops, as well as several reliable shippers, can arrange the air or sea transportation for you. It only takes money—not your time.

Most shops are familiar with shipping abroad. They will pack your goods and take care of all documents necessary for exporting, insurance, and customs. If, for example, you are exporting Thai antiques, these items require special government export certificates. The shop selling the item, or a shipper, can arrange for this certificate.

If you buy several items from different shops, you can request that one of the shops consolidate your shipments or arrange for the consolidation yourself. Expatriates in Thailand regularly use several shippers with confidence. These shippers take the hassle out of making shipping arrangements yourself. Contact any of the following companies for shipping assistance:

- **Hong Kong Transpack:** 59/44 Soi 26, Sukhumvit Road (Tel. 259-0085, 258-6676).
- **Transpo International Ltd.:** 134/31 Soi Athakravi 3, Rama IV Road (Tel. 259-0116, 258-1110).
- **JVK International Movers Ltd.:** 87/43 Patanakarn Road (New Phetburi Ext.) (Tel. 314-7372).
- **Thai International Moving & Storage Co. Ltd.:** 106 Soi Narasri, 21 Ramkamhaeng, Hua Mark (Tel. 314-1517, 314-2520).
- **Schenker (Thai) Ltd.:** 3638 Rama IV Road, Klongtoey (Tel. 259-7640 thru 51).

If you establish a relationship with these shippers, they will work with you through the mail or by fax or telephone to arrange for additional shipments once you return home. This can be a very useful relationship, especially if you later want to import furniture and antiques from different shops. For example, Sweet Home furniture makers regularly use Hong Kong Transpack for their shipping. If you develop a relationship with both of these companies, you will be well positioned to regularly import furniture and other products by long-distance ordering.

Be sure to insure your shipment for both loss and damage. Get all receipts, including a packing list. Normally a sea shipment from Bangkok takes about 8 weeks. However, one of our shipments took about 14 weeks due to unexpected delays with the shipping line that went bankrupt while on the high seas!

12 ENJOYING YOUR STAY

Bangkok and Thailand have much to offer the visitor in addition to shopping. The food is wonderful, hotels are beautiful, service is outstanding, and the sights are truly exotic. We recommend taking time to really enjoy the pleasures of this country.

SIGHTSEEING

The major tourist sights in Bangkok center around the history and culture of Thailand. One of your very first stops should be the fabled **Temple of the Emerald Buddha** and the **Grand Palace Complex.** These two adjacent sites are truly awe-inspiring. Another adjacent site, the **Wat Po** temple complex, with its Reclining Buddha and traditional massages, is also worth visiting. You also can shop in this area for Thai handicrafts. Since the prices tend to be inflated here, bargain hard for as much as 60 percent discount.

Four other temples are especially worth visiting: the **Marble Temple** (Wat Benjamabhopit), the **Temple of the Dawn** (Wat Arun), **Temple of the Golden Mount** (Wat Saket), and the **Temple of the Golden Buddha** (Wat Trimitr). These temples should give you a good overview of traditional Thai architecture and Buddhist art themes found in many of Bangkok's antique, arts, and crafts shops.

Several guided tours with English-speaking guides are available for touring the temples and other sights in and around Bangkok. Most are either for a half-day or full-day. Several tour operators, such as **Tour East** and **Greylines,** offer a variety of programs which can be arranged through your hotel. Most of the tours are relatively inexpensive and are taken in the comfort of an air-conditioned bus or minivan. Our favorite tours are:

- The Temple of the Emerald Buddha, The Grand Palace, Wat Po
- Temple of the Dawn and the Marble Temple
- The Ancient City
- Jim Thompson's House and Suan Pakkard Palace
- Ayuthaya and Bang Pa-in (take the Oriental Queen riverboat one way)
- The Floating Market (Damnuen Saduak only), Nakorn Pathom, and Salt Flats
- The Rose Garden
- Bridge on the River Kwai
- The Rice Barge Cruise

For a good overview of Thai history and culture, visit the **National Museum** which is located next to Thammasat University, across from Pramane Ground and near the Grand Palace. The private **Prasart Museum** (9 Soi Krungtepkreetha 4A, Krungtepkreetha Rd., Bangkapi, Tel. 374-6328, 374-6384, 10am-3pm, Friday, Saturday, Sunday) also is well worth visiting (see earlier description on pages 193-194).

The river and canals are a delight to experience in Bangkok. You can easily rent your own boat and driver for 250 to 350 baht per hour to tour the river and canals or take the numerous river taxis that ply the muddy Chao Phya waters. One of the best on-your-own trips is to rent a boat next to the Oriental Hotel or beside the Pinklao Bridge (next to Thammasat University) for a 2 to 3 hour trip through the canals and along the river. Most drivers know where to take you—just tell them you want 2 or 3 hours with a stop at Wat Arun (Temple of the Dawn). It's easy, fun, inexpensive, and you'll have the flexibility to stop to take pictures, see sights, and shop. One of the best times to take this trip is early morning, before the major shopping arcades and shops open.

RESTAURANTS

If you enjoy eating, you should take advantage of Bangkok's numerous restaurants. Many serve wonderful and inexpensive luncheon buffets in nice settings. Here are some of the best buffets in the city in close proximity to key shopping areas:

Buffet	Location	Shopping Area
■ Giorgio's (Italian/Thai)	Royal Orchid Sheraton Hotel	River City Shopping Complex
■ Lord Jim's (seafood/Thai Japanese)	Oriental Hotel	Oriental Plaza, Oriental Lane, New Road
■ Talay Thong (Thai/seafood)	Siam Inter-Continental Hotel	Siam Centre/Siam Square/Mah Boon Krong Centre
■ Jit Pochana (Thai/Chinese)	1082 Paholyothin Road	Weekend(Chatuchak) Market/Central Plaza
■ Le Meridian Lounge (International)	Le Meridian President Hotel	Gaysorn/Amarin Plaza/World Trade Center, Rajadamri Arcade
■ Tiara Room (International)	Dusit Thani Hotel	Upper Silom Road
■ Window on Silom (International)	Holiday Inn Crowne Plaza Hotel, 981 Silom	Silom Road
■ Le Brasserie (Continental)	The Regent Hotel	Peninsula Plaza

Several other restaurants are also excellent for lunch and make wonderful breaks while shopping. Our favorites include:

- **Trattoria de Roberto:** Patpong 2. Also known as Roberto's. Excellent and reasonably priced Italian food in a pleasant setting. Conveniently located near Peng Seng, Jim Thompson's, and the Montien and Dusit Thani hotel shopping complexes.

- **The Cup:** Peninsula Plaza (Tel. 252-4568). A pleasant international restaurant in one of Thailand's most exclusive shopping plazas. Be sure to make reservations.

- **Thai Pavilion:** Located in the Holiday Inn Crowne Plaza Hotel with an excellent view of Silom Road. Excellent Thai food. Open for both lunch and dinner.

- **Ambassador Hotel restaurants:** Soi 11 Sukhumvit Road. Numerous restaurants and fast food outlets available when shopping in the lower Sukhumvit Road area and Ambassador Hotel complex.

- **Savoury Restaurant:** 60 Pan Road, off Silom Rd. (Tel. 236-4830). Found on the second floor of one of Bangkok's best art galleries—**Artists Gallery**. Open for both lunch and dinner.

- **Sorn Daeng:** Directly to the side of Democracy Monument on Rachadomneon Avenue. Famous Thai restaurant great for people watching and food. Not far from Thieves Market, Chinatown, Banglampoo Market, and the Grand Palace. Good for dinner too.

- **Himali Cha Cha:** Near New Road just off Suriwongse Road. Excellent and inexpensive Indian food in the heart of the Suriwongse-New Road shopping area. The nearby Cafe India (Suriwongse Road, across from the Trocadero Hotel) is equally good.

Your choices for evening dining are numerous, from elegant and expensive French restaurants to local open-air Thai food shops and street vendors. Many are located in major hotels while others are found in the lanes. Some of our favorites include:

- **Normandie Grill:** Oriental Hotel (Tel. 234-8690). One of the world's best restaurants. Wonderful view and service. Elegant and very expensive. Men need a coat and tie. Reservations required.

- **Fireplace Grill:** Le Meridian President Hotel (Tel. 252-9880). Cozy French restaurant serving excellent food with outstanding service. Great for Chateaubriand. Don't miss this one!

- **Ma Maison:** Hilton Hotel. Very elegant Continental restaurant offering superb dishes and service. Considered by many to be Bangkok's best restaurant.

- **Lord Jim's:** Oriental Hotel. Equally excellent for dinner as for lunch. Elegant seafood restaurant with superb view of the river. Outstanding service. Try the fabulous mixed seafood grill.

- **Le Bistrot:** 20/18-9 Ruam Rudee Village (Tel. 251-2523), Soi Ruam Rudee. Considered to be one of Bangkok's top five French restaurants.

- **Le Banyan:** 59 Sukhumvit Soi 8 (Tel. 253-5556). Also considered to be one of Bangkok's top five French restaurants. Pleasant atmosphere.

- **L'Hexagone:** 4 Soi Tonglor 25 Sukhumvit 55 (Tel. 381-2187). Also considered to be one of Bangkok's top five French restaurants.

- **L'Opera:** 55 Sukhumvit 39 (Tel. 258-5605). One of Bangkok's best Italian restaurants.

- **Paesano:** 97-7 Soi Tonson, Ploenchit (Tel. 252-2834). Also one of Bangkok's best Italian restaurants.

- **Hamilton's:** Dusit Thani Hotel. Serves excellent steaks. Open for both lunch and dinner.

- **Regent Grill:** Regent Hotel (Tel.251-6127). Excellent Continental restaurant in a tropical garden setting. Open for lunch and dinncr.

- **Neil's Tavern:** 58/4 Soi Ruam Rudee (Tel. 251-5644). Relaxing atmosphere and serving excellent food. Great for Kobe steaks and seafood.

- **Lee Kitchen:** Fourth floor Thaniya Plaza, Silom Rd. (Tel. 231-2158). Considered by many Thais to be Bangkok's best Chinese restaurant.

- **New Grand Shangrila:** 58/4 Thaniya Road, off Silom Road (Tel. 234-2045). Favorite Chinese restaurant of many expatriates.

- **Mayflower:** Dusit Thani Hotel (Tel. 236-0450). Very elegant Chinese dining. Open for dim sum lunch as well as dinner.

- **Royal Kitchen:** 46-1 North Sathorn Rd. (Tel. 234-3063). One of Bangkok's best Chinese restaurants. Expensive.

- **Jit Pochana:** Soi 20 Sukhumvit Road (Tel. 258-1578) and 1082 Paholyothin Road (Tel. 279-5000). These always reliable Thai restaurants serve some of the best Thai and Chinese food anywhere.

- **Bussaracum:** 35 Soi Pipat 2, off Convent Road (Tel. 235-8915). Excellent Thai food.

- **Lemongrass:** 5/1 Soi 24, Sukhumvit Road (Tel. 258-8636). One of Bangkok's best Thai restaurants. Open for lunch and dinner

- **Thanying:** 10 Soi Pramuan, Silom Rd. (Tel. 236-4361). Another one of Bangkok's best Thai restaurants.

- **Mandalay:** 23/17 Soi Ruam Rudee (opposite Ruam Rudee Village, Tel. 255-2893). Thailand's only Burmese restaurant. Excellent food—much better than you will find in Burma! Operated by the owner of The Elephant House, one of Thailand's best antique and home decorative shops.

- **Le Dalat:** 47/1 Soi 23, Sukhumvit Rd. (Tel. 260-1849). One of Bangkok's best Vietnamese restaurants. Operated by the owner of Asian Heritage antique shop.

- **Dindaeng/Asoke area:** Numerous open air restaurants, such as **Kum Luang** (560 Asoke-Dindaeng Rd., Tel. 246-3272), in pleasant garden and water surroundings. Nice dining experience.

- **Tum Nak Thai:** 131 Rajadapisek Rd., Din Daeng (Tel. 276-1810). Thailand's largest and most unique restaurant. Dishes served by waiters on roller-skates.

Several restaurants also combine a Thai cultural show with Thai food. These establishments are mainly for tourists, but most do a nice job with the food and show and are reasonably priced. Some of the best are:

- **Baan Thai:** 7 Soi 32 Sukhumvit Road (Tel. 258-5403).
- **Pimarn Restaurant:** 46 Sukhumvit Road Soi 49 (Tel. 258-7866).
- **Sala Rim Naam:** Oriental Hotel (Tel. 236-0040).
- **Benjarong:** Dusit Thani Hotel (Tel. 236-0450).
- **Sala Thai**: Indra Regent Hotel (Tel. 251-1111).

ENTERTAINMENT

Bangkok's nightlife remains as lively as ever. Nightclubs, bars, discos, and massage parlors cater to all types of tastes, from classy to sleazy. **Patpong Road** and **Soi Cowboy** (off Sukhumvit Road) are Bangkok's sleazy entertainment areas. In these areas the best deals are the copy watches sold in front of the bars and just watching all the interesting people walk by.

Many of the major hotels and shopping arcades offer good entertainment. Cosy **piano bars** are found in the Le Meridian President (Lounge), Oriental (Bamboo Bar), and Royal Orchid Sheraton (Suralai Bar). Good **discos** are found in the Oriental Plaza (Diana's) and the Dusit Thani (Bubbles) and Montien (Casablanca) hotels. **Big-name entertainment** is usually found at the Dusit Thani Hotel's Tiara Room. The *Bangkok Post* and the weekly tourist publications normally list *"What's Up"* for entertainment during your stay.

Some of Bangkok's best entertainment is on the streets at night. Several areas in Bangkok are transformed into evening **sidewalk bazaars**. Vendors set up portable sidewalk restaurants which spill into the streets while others display their wares, including fruits and vegetables, on a cloth spread over the sidewalk or on tables. These evening merchants sell all kinds of items, such as knives, pins, cooking utensils, and clothes, similar to the daytime merchants found in and around the Pratunam Market. These are interesting areas to do night shopping and to watch a fascinating kaleidoscope of activity. Some of the major night bazaar areas are found at:

- **Patpong-Silom-Suriwongse roads**
- **Banglampoo Market**
- **Pratunam Market**
- **Bangrak Market** (Sathorn and New Road)
- **Sukhumvit Road** (near Soi 1 and railroad tracks)

The Patpong-Silom-Suriwongse roads area is by far the most interesting and lively night bazaar. Some visitors find this to be one of the major highlights to visiting Thailand. Purchasing copy watches, handbags, and clothes in this area is a favorite shopping activity for many visitors. It's definitely a simultaneous shopping and cultural experience!

Bangkok is also a good place to enjoy a haircut, manicure, and massage. The process is enjoyable and includes a shampoo and neck massage and a great deal of attentive service. Try **The Best** at Soi 21 or near Soi 5 Sukhumvit Road and the Menam Mall (Oriental Hotel) for a high-class haircut; expensive, but a wonderful experience. Many of the barbers and beauty shops in and around the hotels are also excellent.

One of the best massages is given by the traditional masseuses at **Wat Po**, next to the Grand Palace and Temple of the Emerald Buddha.

A variety of other massages for men are also available at the numerous massage parlors throughout Bangkok. However, be prepared to loose your innocence in these palatial dens of iniquity which symbolize Thailand's thriving sex trade.

SAMPLING THE TEMPTING SEX

Thailand is well noted as a major male destination for sex—straight and gay. While cheap, tempting, and easily accessible, sex is not a good deal in Thailand. An ostensibly beautiful woman may turn out to be one of Bangkok's infamous transvestites—a shocking revelation and an embarrassing "war story" to take home. Indeed, messing with the local sex is neither good shopping nor a smart health practice; it's Russian roulette of the worst kind—it can kill you. AIDs has arrived in Thailand and with a vengeance; by some estimates, one of every three Thai prostitutes tests HIV positive. Since AIDs is rampant throughout the country, you should avoid sexual contact with the local population. Unfortunately, Thailand has yet to effectively deal with the main transmission villain—widely tolerated prostitution which is institutionalized in its many massage parlors, bars, hotels, and houses of prostitution that employ more than 300,000 prostitutes. Believe us when we say the sex here is simply deadly. You don't need this memory. Spend your money on things you can take home and admire.

PART IV

EXOTIC CHIANGMAI AND BEYOND

13 DISCOVERING CHIANGMAI

Chiangmai is the major city outside Bangkok worth visiting for shopping purposes. Other towns do offer a few local handicrafts, but the selections and quality are limited. In addition, most Thai provincial towns are very small—between 10,000 and 50,000 population—and offer limited accommodations and sightseeing opportunities for travelers. Most towns are government administrative and commercial centers which look similar to one another and are relatively boring places to visit, unless you know someone locally. And those towns which are developing for tourists, such as Pattaya in the Southeast and Phuket in the South, have decided sun and sex themes which are of limited interest to most shoppers.

GETTING TO KNOW YOU

So it's on to Chiangmai if you want to do more concentrated shopping in Thailand. This is Thailand's second largest city after Bangkok with a population of less than 200,000. It is basically a large town boasting a regional university, medical school, a college, a large missionary presence, numerous hotels and restaurants, interesting Burmese influenced temples, charming people, beautiful scenery, and a crowded, congested, and bustling downtown center. It is also Thailand's major handicraft center. It produces quality handicrafts for shops in

Bangkok and abroad as well as serves as the key middleman for coordinating and marketing handicrafts produced by the numerous hilltribes occupying the mountains of northern Thailand as well as the center for beautiful Burmese art brought across the Thai-Burmese border via the rebellious Shan State of Northeast Burma.

Going to Chiangmai is like going to the factory outlets in Hong Kong as well as the woodcarving and artist villages of Mas and Ubud in Bali. You will be going to the production source for Thailand's famous silk, woodcarvings, silverware, celadon, and hilltribe handicrafts. The city and surrounding area consists of several cottage industries run by talented families who continue to pass their trades down from generation to generation. You can visit the houses and factories which produce the goods, watch the craftsmen work, and purchase items from the display rooms or special order to your specifications. The major factories and shops are experienced in packing and shipping to Bangkok and abroad.

During the past 12 years the cottage industries have mushroomed throughout Chiangmai in response to the increasing demand for Thai handicrafts, antiques, and furniture in Bangkok and abroad. The **Chiangmai-Sankamphaeng Road**, for example, is now lined with silver, lacquerware, celadon, pottery, umbrella, furniture, silk, cotton, and antique shops and factories which are open to the public. Here you can observe hundreds of craftsmen at work and visit the display room to purchase the finished products. **Wualai Road** and **Hang Dong Road** are lined with similar craft shops. You will see the same or similar items in Bangkok shops, but prices are less in Chiangmai.

Going to Chiangmai also puts you in touch with the **hilltribes** of northern Thailand and their crafts. The uniquely dressed and exotic looking Meo, Akha, Lahu, Lawa, Lisu, Karen, and Yao tribesmen produce several interesting handicrafts—silver jewelry, boxes, pipes, dolls, textiles, blankets, Christmas ornaments, pillow covers, and much more. The styles and patterns have a distinctive hilltribe look. Red, blue, and black colors along with geometric patterns predominate. In recent years hilltribe clothes have become expensive collectibles used in designing casual wear. Hilltribe clothes are the specialty of some expensive boutiques in Bangkok. In Chiangmai you can buy the separate pieces and have them tailored to your own designs at a fraction of the prices charged in the boutiques.

While it is an interesting adventure to visit hilltribe villages, don't expect to get bargains on hilltribe handicrafts in such villages. Many of the villages have inflated prices just for the wandering tourists; some of their products may be made in Hong Kong or Taiwan. You may do just as well buying hilltribe handicrafts in Chiangmai. In fact, you can buy many directly from tribesmen who come to town to sell their goods in Chiangmai's bazaars at night.

Going to Chiangmai also puts you in touch with Burma and Laos. During the past decade a great deal of **Burmese arts and antiques** have found their way into the markets of Chiangmai and Bangkok. A combination of a stagnant Burmese economy and regional armed rebellions have resulted in Burmese art being sold at ridiculously low prices in order to support rebels who need foreign exchange to purchase Thai goods at the border. Burmese temple carvings, gilded panels, baskets, lacquerware, puppets, and tapestries abound in numerous shops in Chiangmai. Many of these goods are coming into Thailand at an alarming rate. Within the next few years much of the quality art from Burma will be gone—if not already—and replaced by Chiangmai's copies. If you want old Burmese arts and handicrafts, buy now. There will be no tomorrow. A similar movement of antiques and arts from Laos is centered in and around Chiangmai's many shops.

THE STREETS OF CHIANGMAI

Chiangmai is a city as well as a province consisting of numerous villages and towns. The city of Chiangmai was originally a walled city with a moat surrounding it. Remnants of the wall, gates, and moat are clearly evident, and they provide an outline for the city proper. The older commercial, governmental, and residential areas are found within this walled area. But the major commercial and residential areas are located beyond the walls, to the east, north, and west.

The streets and lanes are narrow, and often crowded and confusing for first-time visitors. However, the city proper is very compact and thus relatively easy to walk around, especially along the major downtown shopping area along **Chang Klan** and **Tha Phae** roads.

Transportation within the city is relatively convenient, although confusing to many visitors. Buses regularly run along the major streets as do minibuses, motorized trishaws (*rot tuk tuk*,) and trishaws. The minibuses (*song thaew*) are the major

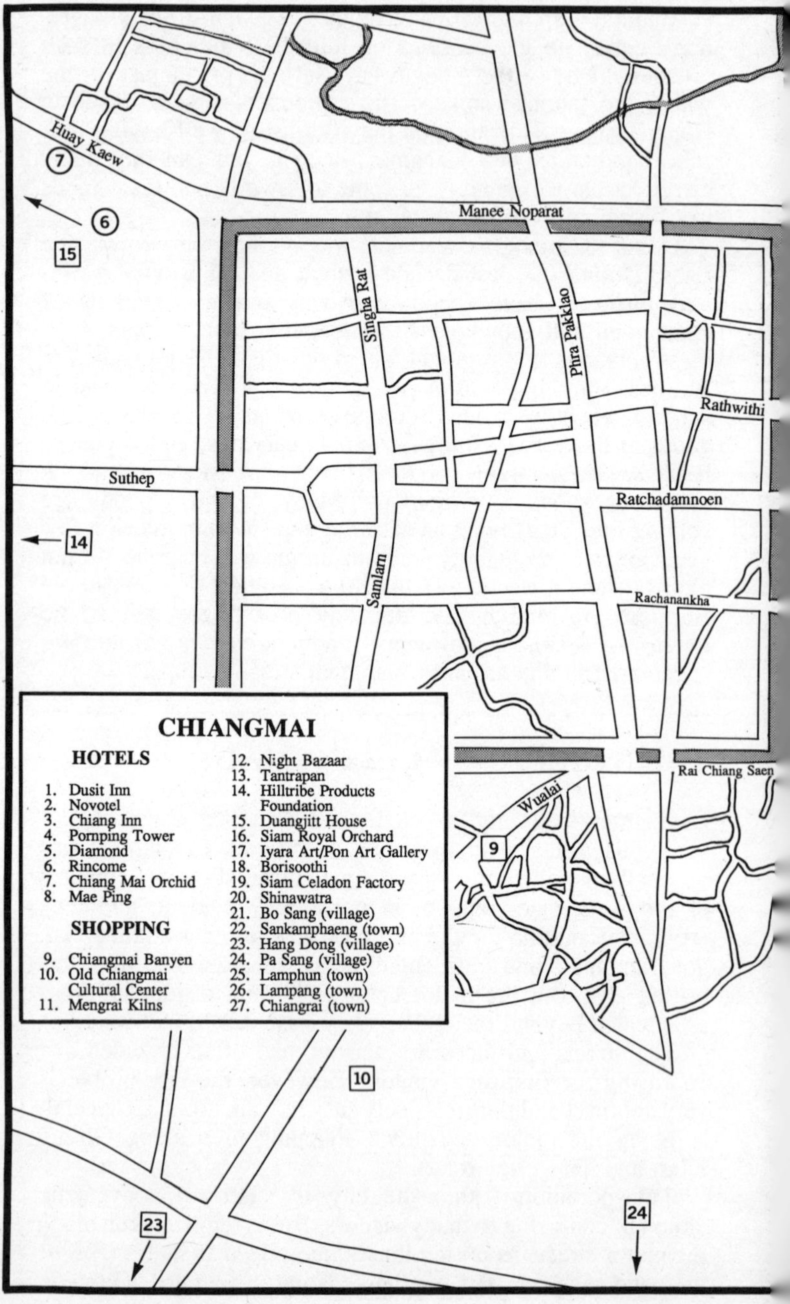
Huay Kaew
7
6
15
Manee Noparat
Singha Rat
Phra Pakklao
Rathwithi
Suthep
14
Ratchadamnoen
Samlarn
Rachanankha
CHIANGMAI
HOTELS
1. Dusit Inn
2. Novotel
3. Chiang Inn
4. Pornping Tower
5. Diamond
6. Rincome
7. Chiang Mai Orchid
8. Mae Ping
SHOPPING
9. Chiangmai Banyen
10. Old Chiangmai Cultural Center
11. Mengrai Kilns
12. Night Bazaar
13. Tantrapan
14. Hilltribe Products Foundation
15. Duangjitt House
16. Siam Royal Orchard
17. Iyara Art/Pon Art Gallery
18. Borisoothi
19. Siam Celadon Factory
20. Shinawatra
21. Bo Sang (village)
22. Sankamphaeng (town)
23. Hang Dong (village)
24. Pa Sang (village)
25. Lamphun (town)
26. Lampang (town)
27. Chiangrai (town)
Rai Chiang Saen
Wualai
9
10
23
24

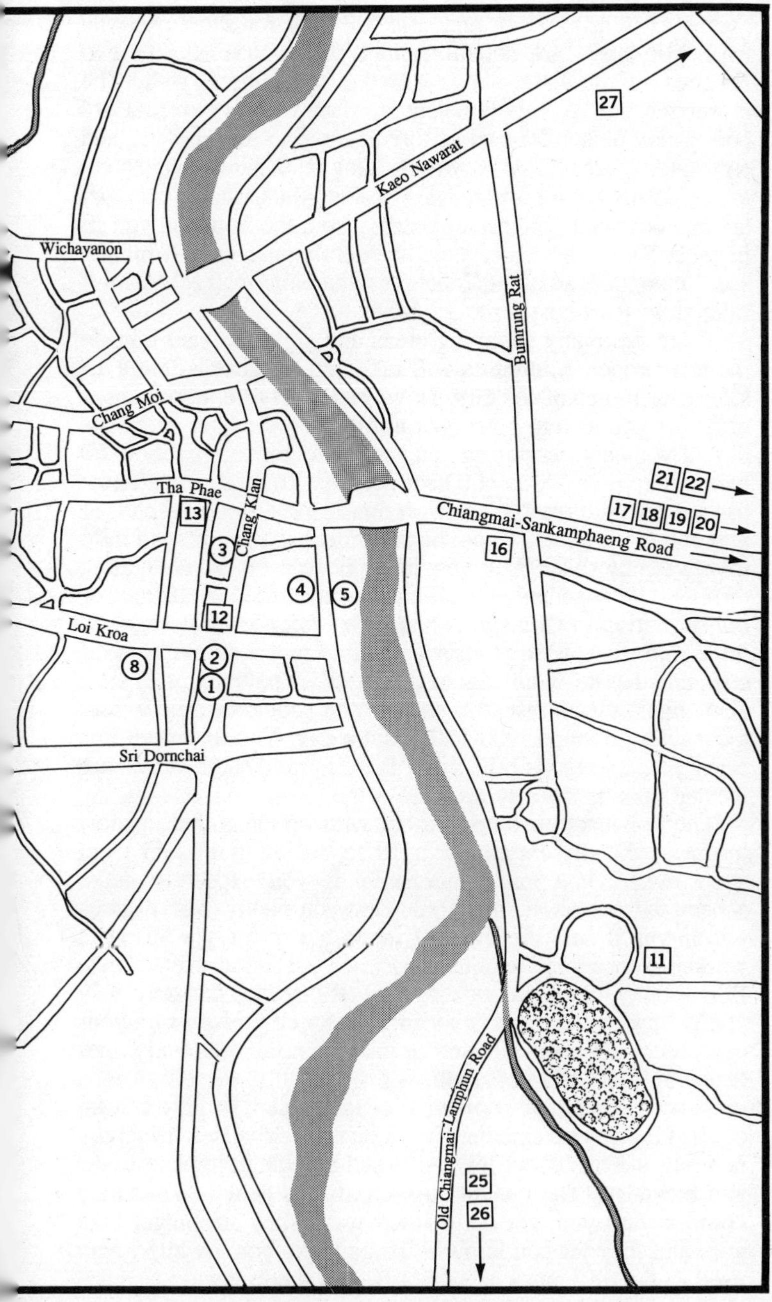
27
Kaeo Nawarat
Wichayanon
Bumrung Rat
Chang Moi
21 22
Tha Phae
17 18 19 20
13
Chiangmai-Sankamphaeng Road
Chang Klan
3
16
4
5
12
Loi Kroa
2
8
1
Sri Dornchai
11
Old Chiangmai-Lamphun Road
25
26

means of transportation and cost 5-8 baht for short one-way trips. Minibuses are actually small pickup trucks with two benches in the back and covered with a metal roof. The motorized and pollution belching trishaws (*rot tuk tuk*) are convenient means for two or three people to tour the city and surrounding area; costs vary depending on distance, but expect to pay 25 to 40 baht for an average ride. The trishaws (*samlor*) are manpowered. The driver peddles from the front and you sit in back. Samlor are an especially charming means by which to see Chiangmai at night. You must bargain for each samlor ride; short trips cost 10 to 15 baht.

There are many shopping areas and sights to visit outside the city proper. Minibuses will take you to areas within a 15 kilometer radius of the city. However, it may be more convenient for you to rent your own minibus by the hour or by the day. If you bargain, you should be able to get one for about 60 baht per hour or 400 to 600 baht per day. You also can arrange for a more comfortable car with driver through your hotel, or rent and drive your own car or motorbike. Chiangmai is fun to tour by motorbike, but you must be careful in navigating through the maddening traffic. We have tried all forms of transportation in Chiangmai and now prefer to rent a car and drive ourselves. Many tourists prefer to rent a car with driver and not hassle with unfamiliar traffic patterns. It's safe, convenient, clean, fast, and cheap. You should be able to rent a car with driver for 900-1200 baht a day. You will need this car if you plan to visit the many factories and shops which are located outside the city proper.

The drawback to renting a car with driver is that in most instances the drivers expect a 10 to 40% commission from shops where you make purchases. If you expect to make substantial purchases, this could cost you plenty. Many shops say if you'll call them they'll send a car for you. This is workable once you are able to narrow your list to a few shops. But initially if you want to survey the scene, the only way you're sure someone isn't getting a hefty commission on your purchases is to drive yourself or take the minibuses (only ones that drop you off and leave).

If you do drive your own car or motorbike, be very careful on the highway outside the city. You must drive defensively—dodging the big 10-wheel trucks and avoiding the pedestrians and bicyclists. The bus and truck traffic is heavy. When they come toward you, get out of their way. They are bigger than you, and they let you know it. It may take you a while to get used to the different types of traffic on the highway.

SHOPPING STRENGTHS AND STRATEGIES

Many Thai products you see in Bangkok can be purchased in Chiangmai at lower prices. Chiangmai is especially noted for its silk, cotton, silverware, lacquerware, celadon, antiques, woodcarvings, umbrellas, baskets, and clothes. In contrast to stores in Bangkok, which have limited selections of many different items, in Chiangmai many stores are very specialized with a wide selection of one or two items only. When you visit a celadon factory and shop, for example, you only find celadon, but it is in many forms: plates, bowls, cups, ashtrays, salt and pepper shakers, chopstick stands, vases, boxes.

When you shop in Chiangmai, you will most likely visit **factories** with shops attached. The normal procedure is to first tour the factory to see the products being made and then visit the showroom where you can make purchases. Since each factory specializes in a particular product, you need a shopping plan which focuses on specific shops. For example, if you are interested in **antiques and woodcarvings**, visit Amaravadee Antiques, Borisoothi Antiques, Chiangmai Banyen, Iyara Art, Pon Art Gallery, the Night Bazaar, Hang Dong, and other factory/shops on Tha Phae, Wualai, Chiangmai-Sankamphaeng, Hang Dong, and Ban Tawai roads. If you are interested in **silk**, plan a trip to the towns of Sankamphaeng and Lamphun as well as the village of Pa Sang. In Sankamphaeng, be sure to visit the Shinawatra silk factory, which also has large branch stores in Chiangmai and Bangkok. If you are looking for **celadon**, you should visit the Mengrai Kilns (31/1 Ratuthit Road), Thai Celadon Company (Highway 107, road to Fang, near Kilometer 6), and Siam Celadon Factory (Chiangmai-Sankamphaeng Road). For **furniture** it's off to several shops along the Chiangmai-Sankamphaeng Road. For good quality **woodcarvings**, visit Letsin, Tawai Antiques, and Golden Antiques along Ban Tawai Road in Hang Dong. And if you want to purchase bamboo and rattan **baskets, mats, and hats**, it's off to the village of Hang Dong, 13 kilometers south of Chiangmai on Highway 108 (Hang Dong Rd.). Refashioned **hilltribe clothes and handicrafts** are mainly found in downtown Chiangmai at the Night Bazaar (Chang Klan Road) and a few shops along Tha Phae Road. If you are looking for **textiles**, be sure to stop at the Night Bazaar and a few excellent shops scattered throughout the town of Chiangmai.

The best way to approach shopping in Chiangmai is to get a good map, a list of names and addresses, and a car and driver to get you from one place to another. Except for strolling down a few streets, such as Chang Klan and Tha Phae, most of your shopping will involve traveling by vehicle between factories and shops.

You should begin your visit to Chiangmai with a copy of Nancy Chandler's ***Map of Chiang Mai***. Similar to her ***Map of Bangkok***, this colorful map gives key shops, hotels, restaurants, and sights around Chiangmai City. You can get a copy of the map in Bangkok or at hotels and bookstores in Chiangmai. Armed with this map, you should be able to navigate your way around Chiangmai with relative ease. TAT's *"Official Shopping Guide,"* the one you should have picked up in Bangkok, lists several recommended shops in Chiangmai. You will also find two monthly tourist publications on Chiangmai: *"Welcome To Chiangmai"* and *"Chiangmai."* Both publications are free of charge and can be obtained in most hotels. They include maps, travel tips, and advertisements from numerous hotels, shops, restaurants, and tour groups.

Most of your shopping will center around four major retail and wholesale shop areas:

- Chang Klan and Tha Phae roads in downtown Chiangmai (street shops and the Night Bazaar).

- Small section of Nimmanhemin Road across the street from the Rincome Hotel.

- Along the 12 kilometer Chiangmai-Sankamphaeng Road.

- Along Hang Dong Road, a 11 kilometer stretch of road south of Chiangmai, and Ban Tawai Road on the outskirts of Hang Dong town.

Additional shopping will be found in special shops and factories in various neighborhoods of the city and in towns and villages within a 20-kilometer radius of Chiangmai as well as along Wualai Road in the southwest section of the city. Unlike Bangkok, most shopping in Chiangmai takes place outside hotel shopping arcades.

Armed with Nancy Chandler's ***Map of Chiang Mai*** and this book and ready with a car and driver, you will be well prepared to make Chiangmai a rewarding shopping adventure. The major shopping areas in downtown Chiangmai are located along **Chang Klan** and **Tha Phae** roads. Here you will find several shops that sell a variety of local goods, from handicrafts to furniture. The huge **Night Bazaar**, between the Dusit

Inn, Novotel, and Chiang Inn hotels on Chang Klan Road, offers a good variety of Chiangmai products at reasonable prices. This colorful and festive area is one you should visit early in your stay. You may want to return there for another night or two.

WHERE TO SHOP

When you go to Chiangmai, you must change your shopping strategy altogether. Chiangmai's shopping facilities and environment are quite different from that of Bangkok's. While in Bangkok much of your shopping centered on shopping arcades, hotel shops, and department stores, in Chiangmai you must go out into the neighborhoods to find particular factories and shops.

Shopping Areas

Chiangmai does have a few good hotel shops, small shopping arcades, and department stores. But for the most part these are not significant areas for shopping in Chiangmai. In Chiangmai you must go to particular towns, villages, and roads where you will find family factories and shops producing quality goods, or you must look for major markets, such as the popular Night Bazaar along Chang Klan Road.

Most of Chiangmai's major shopping is concentrated in five major areas:

- **Downtown Chiangmai:** This area is concentrated along the city's two main streets—Chang Klan and Thai Phae—and centered around the Mae Ping, Novotel, Dusit, and Chiang Inn hotels as well as the city market. Here you find Chiangmai's most popular shopping center —the **Night Bazaar**—which consists of three bazaars: Chiangmai Night Bazaar, Viang Ping Night Bazaar, and Lanna Bazaar. The Chiangmai Night Bazaar, which is housed in a four-story structure, is the largest and best of the three. Some of the most exciting shops selling antiques, handicrafts, textiles, and jewelry are found on the third and fourth floors of the Chiangmai Night Bazaar—a "must visit" area often neglected by visitors who only venture through the first two floors of this bazaar. Here you will find such outstanding shops as **Siam Gallery**, **Chofah Antique**, **Iyara Art**, **Thammas**,

Yanok Treasures, **Paipun's Collection**, **Lost Tribe**, **Baan Je Aim**, and **Classic Lanna Thai** as well as a few shops which do not display names, such as **Lost Tribes**. Along Thai Phae Road look for **Maneesinn**, **Civilize**, **Sawatdee Thapae**, **Ikat**, **Nakorn Sasam**, **Folk Art**, **Phulsawasd Antiques**, **Mungkalu Gallery**, **Chattraporn**, **Nakorn Kasem**, and **Chamchuree**. These shops sell a large variety of handicrafts, textiles, clothes, silver, jewelry, lacquerware, antiques, woodcarvings, and basketry. Don't be surprised if some of these shops have closed recently. The business environment in Chiangmai is very volatile for these types of shops. Shops in the Night Bazaar, for example, continuously change with many leaving and new ones joining the crowd. Occasionally an act of God—fire—further changes the mix of shops.

- **Wualai Road:** Located at the southern end of the city, this road is lined with numerous silver factories as well as shops selling a large variety of handcrafted items. Look for **Noparat Silverware**, **Damrongsilp**, **Ngern Chiangmai**, and **Sterling Silver Ornament Factory** for traditional designed silver items; and **Ban Sanpronon** for a nice collection of baskets, lacquerware, instruments, and textiles.

- **Neighborhood shops:** A few streets in other areas of the city also have some good shops. For example, along **Nimmanhemin Road**, across the street from the Rincome Hotel and near the Chiangmai Orchid Hotel, is a row of very nice quality jewelry, textile, antique silver, clothing, and gift shops well worth visiting: **Duangjitt House**, **P.N. Precious Stones**, **Nandakwang (Homespun Creations)**, **Jinda Needlework**, **Dararat**, **Sbun Nga Collection**, **Sipsong Panna**, and **Sai Thong**. These are some of Chiangmai's best quality shops and a pleasant change from other types of shops found in and around Chiangmai. Just off Nimmanhemin Road, at 188 Soi 9, is **Naenna Studio** (Tel. 217-707) which is operated by Pat Chessman, one of Thailand's leading authorities on textiles. She works with nearby villages in creating excellent quality and uniquely designed silk and cotton materials which are primarily sold for export. Dealers interested in importing unique Thai fabrics will especially want to visit this shop. Pat also conducts textile tours for special groups.

On nearby **Huay Kaew Road**, directly across the street from the Chiang Mai Orchid Hotel, is one of Chiangmai's best silk shops—**S. Shinawatra** (14/4-8 Huay Kaew Rd., Tel. 221-076). It also stocks cotton products and handicrafts.

Along **Bumrung Rat Road** you will find two of Chiangmai's major hilltribe handicraft shops—**Northern Tribal Crafts** and **Thai Tribal Crafts.**

On **Bunmuang Road** (29/3-4) look for **Pong-Pong** for antiques, lacquerware, and Chiangmai's best collection of old opium weights. Just around the corner is **The Loom** (27/3 Rajmanka Rd. and 3rd floor of Night Bazaar) for beautiful antiques and contemporary textiles.

One of Thailand's most unique shops—**Saraphee Silk Lace** at 2 Rajwithi Road (Tel. 214-171)—produces lovely handwoven decorative lace items.

Indigo, a restaurant-shop located at the corner of Old Chiangmai Road and Lampang Road to the south of town, offers a small but unique collection of antiques, furniture, and works of art.

The **Hilltribe Products Foundation** on Suthep Road offers a good collection of hilltribe handicrafts.

Mengrai Kilns at 31/1 Ratuthit Road (Tel. 231-802) produces some of Thailand's best quality celadon.

Siam Royal Orchid Co. at 94 Charoen Muang Road (Tel. 242-282) offers a unique collection of gold plated flowers and semi-precious stones made into attractive and inexpensive neckpieces, earrings, pins, and pendants.

Two of the best collections of woodcarvings, furniture, and home decorative items are found at the huge factory emporiums adjacent to each other (family related) at the intersection of the Super Highway (near airport) and Hang Dong Road—**Chiangmai Banyen** and **Jaifah Chiangmai Lacquerware Co.** (209/3 Super Highway).

One of Chiangmai's major antique dealers—indeed, a powerful force in the antique world throughout Thailand and Burma—is **Amaravadee Antiques** (31/3-4 Nantaram Rd., Tel. 232-156), located just south of Chiangmai Gate and Rat Chiang Saen Road. This extended family also operates a huge antique complex—**Ban Chang Come** (141 Hang Dong Rd.)—a large teak house on the right just before coming to Ban Tawai Road on your left as well as a small shop in the Night Bazaar—**Chofah**.

The Gallery (located on Charoen Rat Road, just south of the Nawarat Bridge, facing the Mae Nam Ping River, and next to the Riverside and Rim Ping restaurants) is a restaurant that also functions as an art gallery. Its changing monthly exhibits represent the best of modern northern Thai art.

- **Chiangmai-Sankamphaeng Road:** We have a real love-hate complex with this major shopping area. One of the most popular shopping areas for tourists, it is highly recommended by local touts who ask exorbitant commissions (20-40%) from shopkeepers which, in turn, inflates prices. In many respects this is Chiangmai's best shopping area. On the other hand, it's also a tourist trap where busloads of tourists are taken from one shop to another by drivers and tour guides who are primarily interested in collecting commissions from shops that charge unwitting tourists high prices. They avoid or badmouth the good shops that don't give them payoffs! Unfortunately, the average tourist ends up in mediocre shops that charge high prices.

This 12 kilometer stretch of road begins at the intersection of the Super Highway east of the city and continues to the town of Sankamphaeng. Both sides of the road are lined with small factories and shops as well as huge factories and emporiums selling everything from traditional handmade Chiangmai furniture to silver, antiques, home decorative items, lacquerware, celadon, silk, and umbrellas. One of Thailand's best and most reliable antique and home decorative shops, **Borisoothi** (15/2 Chiangmai-Sankamphaeng Rd., Tel. 331-777) is located along this road. This is also home for one of Thailand's most famous silk factories—**Shinawatra**. Other good quality shops include **Prempracha's** for cotton, silk, ceramics, woodcarvings, furniture, lacquerware, porcelain, tapestries, silver, and antiques; **Lanna Lacquerware** for lacquer items; **Iyara Art** and **Pon Art Gallery** for antiques, woodcarvings, gables, carved panels, lacquerware, and silver; **Siam Celadon** for celadon; **Kinaree Thai Silk**, **Chiangmai Textile & Garment Center**, **H.M. Thai Silk**, and **Jolie Femme** for all types of silk products; **Chiangmai Treasure Co.** for large carvings and furniture; **Bo-Sang Handicraft Centre** for a large collection of umbrellas, woodcarvings, dolls, Bencharong, lacquerware, baskets, clothes, tapestries, and screens; **Umbrella Making Centre** for beautiful handcrafted umbrellas, dolls, fans, and baskets; **The Emporium of Handicrafts** for a large selection of hilltribe handicrafts; **Siam Gifts** for an excellent range of woodcarvings, tapestries, ceramics, lacquerware, Bencharong, leather, ivory, silver, jewelry, jade, and cloisonne.

- **Hang Dong:** Located 11 kilometers south of Chiangmai, this is Chiangmai's major woodcarving center. However, few tourists ever visit here since they instead are being escorted along the Chiangmai-Sankamphaeng Road by tourist guides and touts who are getting big commissions for steering tourists into shops that may charge two to three times more than the factory/shops in Hang Dong. In fact, many of the shops along Chiangmai-Sankamphaeng Road procure their products for resale from the factory/shops in Hang Dong! Needless to say, you are better off going directly to the source where you will get better prices and have more fun shopping away from the maddening crowds of tourists and touts. The Hang Dong shopping area actually consists of two areas:

  - Factories and shops along both sides of the 11 kilometer Hang Dong Road.

  - One narrow unpaved road—Ban Tawai Road—located on the left just before entering the small town of Hang Dong (look for a small sign with an arrow advertising Tawai Antiques, on the left just before you come to the red and blue flame gas station sign on the right).

  The best antique shop along Hang Dong Road is **Ban Chang Come** (#141), a huge Thai house and antique emporium related to Amaravadee Antiques, Chiangmai's major antique dealer who also controls a large segment of the antique trade throughout Thailand. Ban Tawai Road is lined with numerous woodcarving factories and antique shops offering some of the best home decorative items in Thailand. Indeed, many shops in Bangkok and dealers from abroad purchase their products here. Some of the best factories and shops along this road include **Jarakarn Antiques** (the best antique emporium but hard to find—look for a small sign that directs you to take a right turn on a side road and then cross a small wood bridge), **Tawai Antiques, Letsin**, and **Golden Antiques.** You can easily arrange to have woodcarvings commissioned here and the factory/shops are experienced in shipping abroad (major shipping companies are also located along this road). Prices here are much better than in Chiangmai and Bangkok.

- **Doi Suthep:** Located 12 mountainous kilometers from the city, at the foot of Chiangmai's most famous temple—Wat Prathat—is a shopping center consisting of numerous row shops and vendor stalls selling a wide variety of tourist products. Be careful here. You will find many small stalls selling similar items found in the Night Bazaars in Chiangmai and Bangkok. Prices can be reasonable if you bargain hard. However, some shops charge significantly more than comparable shops in Chiangmai or Bangkok. Beware of nice air-conditioned jewelry shops that may pamper you with friendly service. At **Sawaddee**, for example, we found letter openers that sold for 25 baht in Bangkok selling here for 80 baht! Jewelry was greatly overpriced. One nice shop, the **Jade and Ivory Factory**, is TAT recommended.

WHAT TO BUY

Shops in and around Chiangmai offer a wonderful array of products. You can easily spend three to five days exploring the many shops that offer everything from silk, textiles, and ethnic clothes to jewelry, antiques, furniture, and home decorative items. As noted earlier, Chiangmai is to Thailand what Bali is to Indonesia—the country's major arts and crafts center. Here you will discover the factories and meet the craftspeople that produce the many lovely products displayed in Bangkok's numerous shops.

Jewelry and Accessories

If you are interested in unique inexpensive jewelry and accessories, you should visit the **Siam Royal Orchid** factory and shop at #94 Charoen Muang Road which is located just across the Ping River east of the city. They have a good selection of inexpensive pins, neckpieces, and earrings made from a special gold plating and enameling process using flowers and semi-precious stones. They will make jewelry to your specifications. **John Michael Richardson Co.**, located on the third floor of the Chiangmai Night Bazaar, produces unique costume jewelry, mainly big earrings.

One of the best jewelry stores outside Bangkok is **P.N. Precious Stones** at 95/4-7 Nimmanhemin Road (Tel. 212-368), across the street from the Rincome Hotel. Reversing the normal pattern for most factories and shops, the factory for this shop is located in Bangkok with P.N. Precious Stones in Chiangmai being the only outlet in Thailand. They offer gorgeous gems and jewelry in stylish settings. **Shiraz Co.** at 170 Tha Phae Road (Tel. 252-382) also offers a wide range of gems (rubies and sapphires) and gold and silver jewelry. This small shop is reputed to be very reliable.

Antiques and Home Decorative Items

For antiques, woodcarvings, spirit houses, wood panels, drums, statues, gilded figures, and lacquerware, you should definitely visit the shops and factories along Ban Tawai Road in Hang Dong, Chiangmai-Sankamphaeng Road, and the two emporiums at the intersection of the Super Highway and Hang Dong Road.

Chiangmai's two major antique dealers, especially noted for their quality and reliability, are **Amaravadee Antiques** (31/3-4 Nantaram Rd., Tel. 232-156) and **Borisoothi Antiques** (15/2 Chiangmai-Sankamphaeng Rd., Tel. 331-77). These large shops and factories are well worth a visit during your stay in Chiangmai. Four other antique dealers are also well worth visiting: **Iyara Art** and **Pon Art Gallery**, located adjacent to each other on Chiangmai-Sankamphaeng Road (35/3 and 35/4 Chiangmai-Sankamphaeng Road), **Ban Chang Come** (141 Hang Dong Rd., Tel. 248-628), and **Jarakarn Antiques** (137 Moo 8 Ban La Woo, off Ban Tawai Rd., Hang Dong, Tel. 248-615).

Duangjitt House (985/10 Nimmanhemin Rd., Tel. 215-167) has a very nice collection of antique silver and collectible textiles. This shop also produces lovely handmade paper cards and calligraphy boxes under the trade name **Michi Gallery**, which is located on the third floor of Duangjitt House.

You also will find several antique shops, such as **Chofah Antiques** and **Thammas**, in the Chiangmai Night Bazaar in downtown Chiangmai on Chang Klan Road. One of the best home decorative, antique, and handicraft shops here is **Siam Gallery** (#60, 4th floor, Tel. 242-622, contact Phiboonchai

Sornmai or Richard Dixon). Offering tasteful selections at reasonable prices, this shop is always one of the first we visit in Chiangmai. You're bound to find some lovely home decorative items here. And you are likely to strike up an interesting conversation and share some useful travel tips with other fellow travelers who tend to congregate at this shop between 8pm and 10pm each night.

However, you can easily miss the best shops in the Chiangmai Night Bazaar if you only browse through the first two floors of this building. The antique and home decorative area is found on the **third and fourth floors** of the Chiangmai Night Bazaar. Be sure to climb the stairs to what is certainly the best floors of this building. Other antique shops worth visiting are found along Hang Dong Road and Ban Tawai Road in Hang Dong.

You should also visit the famous **Chiangmai Banyen** at the intersection of Hang Dong Road and the Superhighway. Previously located on Wualai Road, but leveled by fire in 1989, the new Chiangmai Banyen will not disappoint you. It's a huge woodcarving factory, emporium, and museum operated by Mrs. Banyen, one of Thailand's most successful and respected entrepreneurs. Banyen employs over 100 craftspeople who make all types of woodcarvings and decorative items. While more expensive than many other factories in Chiangmai, she does quality work and is very reliable. This is the shop the famous Jim Thompson used nearly 30 years ago to furnish much of his fabulous house in Bangkok. Her children have opened a similar factory and shop next door—**Jaifah Chiangmai Lacquerware Co.** (209/3 Super Highway).

Celadon, Benjarong, and Pottery

Thai celadon is primarily produced in Chiangmai. For good quality celadon pottery, visit the **Mengrai Kilns** at 31/1 Ratuthit Road (Tel. 241-802), across the road from the Chiangmai Gymkhana Club (southwest corner of the city just off the Old Chiangmai and Lamphun Road) as well as their kiln and shop on the Chiangmai-Sankamphaeng Road. Their celadon pieces are lovely and fit nicely into contemporary art collections of pottery. Other celadon factories produce high-glaze celadon dishes and knickknacks. The **Siam Celadon Factory** on the Chiangmai-Sankamphaeng Road (40 Moo 6) has a nice showroom for their wares as does the **Thai Celadon Factory** on Highway 107 (the road to Fang).

Prempracha (224 Chiangmai-Sankamphaeng Rd., Tel. 331-540) produces a wide range of ceramics. They are especially noted for combining celadon and Benjarong—producing color combinations and designs only available in this expansive factory-shop. A good place to purchase lovely gift items.

Thailand's famous blue and white pottery is primarily produced in and around the town of Lampang, which is located approximately 100 kilometers southeast of Chiangmai. You will find nearly 100 factories producing distinct designs in blue and white colors. Some factories also produce celadon and pottery in other colors. The prices are very reasonable, perhaps 30% cheaper than the Bangkok shops selling the same items produced in the Lampang factories.

Baskets, Wicker, Umbrellas

If you are interested in baskets and wicker items, be sure to visit the village of **Hang Dong**, located 13 kilometers southwest of Chiangmai on the road to Mae Klang waterfall and Doi Inthanon (Highway 108) and the village of **Saraphi**, located about 7 kilometers southeast of the city on the road to Lamphun (Highway 106). Look for the wicker fishtraps which make nice lampshades for hanging ceiling lamps. You also will find baskets and wicker items in the **Night Bazaar** and along **Tha Phae Road** and the **Chiangmai-Sankamphaeng Road**. Collectors looking for unique items should visit **Maneesinn** at 289 Tha Phae Road (Tel. 236-586). You will find amongst their exquisite lacquerware some older one-of-a-kind baskets.

Many visitors to Chiangmai like to buy the unique and colorful Chiangmai **umbrellas**. The place to go for such purchases are the umbrella factories and shops in the "Umbrella Village" of **Bo Sang**, located on the Chiangmai-Sankamphaeng Road. Several shops sell their own distinctive style umbrellas. The largest umbrella emporium here is the **Umbrella Making Centre**, located just off the Chiangmai-Sankamphaeng Road at Bo Sang. Just across the road is another large umbrella factory, the **Bosang Umbrella Maker Community**. Nearby you will find the **Sa Paper and Umbrella Handicraft Centre**. The umbrellas at most shops and factories are inexpensive; the small ones make nice trip gifts for children.

Silk and Cotton

If you are interested in silk and cotton, be sure to visit the famous silk town of **Sankamphaeng**, located 13 kilometers east of Chiangmai. Stop first at the **Shinawatra** factory to observe the silk weaving process and explore their sales shop. If you walk down both sides of the main street, you will find several shops that sell silk and cotton material as well as a variety of handicrafts. Since this is a small town, you can easily cover most of the shops in an hour or two by walking along **Mae-On Road**.

Several large shops along the Chiangmai-Sankamphaeng Road offer nice selections of silk and cotton garments as well as fabric. The major factory/shop here is Chiangmai's oldest silk producer—**Shinawatra Thai Silk**. Also look for **Prem-pracha's, H. M. Thai Silk, Kinaree Thai Silk, Chiangmai Textile and Garment Centre**, and **Jolie Femme**. Within the city of Chiangmai, look for **P. Shinawatra Thaisilk's** two adjacent shops across the street from Chiangmai Orchid Hotel.

If you go south of Chiangmai, you will come to the town of **Lamphun** which also is noted for silk. **Pa Sang**, a village located 10 kilometers southwest of Lamphun, is also well noted for cotton weaving. If you visit Sankamphaeng, Lamphun, and Pa Sang, you will cover most of the factories and shops offering silk and cotton.

Clothes and Textiles

Chiangmai is not noted as a fashion center. However, you will find some interesting clothes and textiles here, from refashioned hilltribe garments to silk clothes. One of our favorite shops is **Duangjitt House** at 295/10 Nimmanhemin Road (Tel. 215-167), just across the street from the Rincome Hotel. Here you will discover some very uniquely designed clothing using a combination of traditional ikat textiles and silks fashioned in stylish garments. The **Naenna Studio** at 188, Soi 9 Nimmanhemin Road (Tel. 217-707) produces fashionable export quality textiles that can be used for clothing and upholstery. Several shops in and around the **Night Bazaar**, such as **Classic Model**, as well as along Tha Phae Road (**Civilize**) sell refashioned hilltribe garments. Textile lovers will enjoy **Iyara Art** on the second floor of the Chiangmai Bazaar (#6, Tel. 249-072) as well as **The Loom** at 27/3 Rajmanka Road (Tel. 210-892) and on the 3rd floor of the Chiangmai Bazaar. **Ravipun Batik** at 98/3 Sridonchai Road (near the Chiangmai Plaza Hotel, Tel. 275-323) produces colorful silk and cotton batik fabrics and garments.

If you are interested in hilltribe jackets, contact **Jim Goodman** who works with the Akha tribespeople in producing uniquely designed one-of-a-kind jackets using natural dyes. He can be contacted through **Siam Gallery** in the Chiangmai Night Bazaar (#60, Tel. 242-622) or in care of the Sunshine Guest House (24 Kaew Nawarat, Soi 4).

Several silk shops along Chiangmai-Sankamphaeng Road sell ready-made and tailored silk garments. Some of the largest such shops include **Shinawatra, Kinaree Thai Silk, Chiangmai Textile and Garment Center**, and **Jolie Femme.**

Leather Goods

You will find a few shops and factories as well as vendor stalls selling leather goods. The product range includes handbags, purses, wallets, shoes, and belts. In general, however, we have not been impressed with the quality of Thai leather nor the styles and workmanship. The Thai leather tanning process is still of poor quality. Although the leathers are more supple than we encountered a few years ago, they still lack a finished look and are not particularly stylish. Furthermore, many of the popular tan shoes found in the markets and shops in downtown Chiangmai are made from elephant leather. We urge you to boycott such items. While a few years ago elephants were being killed for their ivory tusks, today many of Thailand's elephants are being killed for their leather—some of which undoubtedly ends up in these shoes. If you are not picky about quality, workmanship, and style, you can pick up some inexpensive leather items in Chiangmai. Several shops in the **Night Bazaar** sell leather goods. Along the Chiangmai-Sankamphaeng Road look for a few factories which both produce and sell leather shoes, handbags, belts, and purses: **San Klang Leather Product** and **Boonkrong Leather Chiangmai**. Most of these shops do not use elephant leather.

Gift Items

Most shops in Chiangmai offer items that will make interesting and lovely gifts back home. We especially like the unique and beautiful selections of woven items—pillows, clothes, tissue boxes, rugs, dolls, placemats—at **Nandakwang** (Homespun Creations) at 95/1-2 Nimmanhemin Road (Tel. 222-261), just across the street from the Rincome Hotel. The items here are both unique and stylish and make lovely gifts appropriate for Western homes. Many shops in the **Night Bazaar** also offer a large variety of gift items. You will have to explore the hundreds of shops and stalls in this area to discover just what you need. A few large shops along Chiangmai-Sankamphaeng Road also offer a large variety of gift items: **Chiangmai Art, Siam Gifts, Shinawatra, Prempracha's, Thai Shop, Bo Sang Handicraft Centre, Umbrella Making Centre, Mesa, Tribal Handicraft Weaving**, and **The Emporium of Handicrafts.** We especially like **Siam Gifts** and **Prempracha's** for their large range of quality items.

Lace

One shop in Chiangmai now produces unique handmade lace items used for decorative as well as garment accessory pieces. **Saraphee Silk Lace** (2 Rajwithi Rd., at corner of Moon Muang Rd., Tel. 214-171) is one of Chiangmai's most unique shops and Thailand's only lace factory. Here you can see the items woven as well as make purchases. It's nice intricate work popular with some Thais, but we have yet to find a place for it in our home or wardrobes. Perhaps you will have some better ideas on what to do with this lovely work.

Silver

Chiangmai also is famous for its silver jewelry and artifacts. The major silver factories with showrooms are located along the **Chiangmai-Sankamphaeng Road** and in and around **Wualai Road**. Of particular interest to many visitors are the intricately hammered silver bowls with unique Hindu and Buddhist scenes. Silver hilltribe jewelry—necklaces, rings, bracelets, earrings—and silver studded hilltribe clothes are also popular. One of the largest silver factories is **Chiangmai Silverware** at 62/10-11 Chiangmai-Sankamphaeng Rd. (Tel. 246-037). Several shops sell silver in the **Night Bazaar** as well as along Chang Klan and Tha Phae roads. **Maneesinn** (289 Tha Phae Road, Tel. 236-586), which primarily sells lacquerware, also offers nice quality antique silver. **Duangjitt** at 395/10 Nimmanhemin Road (Tel. 215-167) also has a very nice collection of antique silver. The nearby **Sibsong Panna** (95/19 Nantawan Arcade, Nimmanhemin Road, Tel. 216-096) has an excellent collection of antique silver.

Lacquerware

Lacquerware is an especially good buy in Chiangmai with prices nearly one fourth of what you will pay in Bangkok.

Several shops on the third and fourth floors of the **Chiangmai Night Bazaar** offer nice selections of lacquerware. However, the best collection of quality lacquerware for sale in Chiangmai is found at **Maneesinn** at 289 Tha Phae Road (Tel. 236-586). Two floors of this shop are crammed with beautiful lacquer boxes and trays as well as baskets. This is one of those "must see" shops for anyone interested in lacquerware. Maneesinn also has a shop on the third floor of the Chiangmai Night Bazaar—**Bai Ploo** (#50, Tel. 236-586). **Ban Chang Come** (141 Hang Dong Rd., Tel. 248-628) also has a large collection of lacquerware. **Borisoothi Antiques** at 15/2 Chiangmai-Sankamphaeng Road (Tel. 331-777) and **Pong-Pong** near the Tha Phae gate both have a few pieces of good quality antique lacquerware. For new lacquerware pieces, several shops along Chiangmai-Sankamphaeng Road produce a variety of lacquerware in a large variety of colors and styles. **Chiangmai Chaiyapruk Lacquerware** (30/1 Bansanklang, Chiangmai-Sankamphaeng Rd.), **Chalerm Lacquerware** (look for sign directing you 50 meters off the Chiangmai-Sankamphaeng Rd.), and **Jaifah Chiangmai Lacquerware Co.** at 209/3 Super Highway (Tel. 235-685).

Furniture

Handmade teakwood furniture is a major cottage industry in Chiangmai. Most of the furniture is produced in traditional Thai styles which may or may not fit well with your home decor. The major factories are located along the **Chiangmai-Sankamphaeng Road**. You may be initially attracted to the first factory on the left—**Tusnaporn**. This famous factory with a huge showroom of handmade teak furniture, elephants, and household items will provide you with a good overview of what most Chiangmai furniture factories produce as well as price ranges. However, be very careful here. Once a reliable shop, Tusnaporn recently has been delisted by TAT for failing to meet TAT service standards. We're not sure what this means, but this shop as well as other shops affiliated with this firm (Thai Shop next door and Sawaddee at Doi Suthep) have reputations for overpricing and promoting high commissions amongst touts and tour guides. Be sure to go here on your own since they do pay guides and touts big commissions; you should expect a significant discount, too. Other furniture factories are found on the left side of the Chiangmai-Sankamphaeng Road. Visitors are welcome to observe the craftsmen and browse through the showrooms. Some of the factories along Ban Tawai Road in Hang Dong also produce furniture, although most of these places primarily produce woodcarvings and home decorative items.

Hilltribe Handicrafts

A variety of Thai, Burmese, and hilltribe handicrafts can be found in many shops in Chiangmai, but especially in the **Night Bazaar**, located between the Dusit Inn and Chiang Inn on Chang Klan Road and around the corner from the Novotel Hotel on Loi Krao Road. We especially like a small stall called **Lost Tribe** in the Chiangmai Night Bazaar. Hard to find (lacks a sign for is located on the corner across from Chofah Antiques on the third floor) and reasonably priced, the soft-spoken owner offers some very unique items from Yao and Akha tribespeople, especially wood carvings, head dresses, jewelry, and shaman items. For a wide range of hilltribe products, you should visit the **Hilltribe Products Foundation** on Suthep Road, located west of the city, just beyond the Chiangmai University Medical School complex and next to the famous Wat Suan Dok. Also, visit **Northern Tribal Crafts** at 121 Bumrung Rat Road (Tel. 245-079), and **Thai Tribal Crafts** at #208 Bumrung Rat Road (Tel. 243-493) in the northeast section of Chiangmai. The **Emporium of Handicrafts** on Chiangmai-Sankamphaeng Road has several demonstration buildings where hilltribes people produce handicrafts as well as shops where hilltribe products are sold. The **Old Chiangmai Cultural Center** on Wualai Road also has several hilltribe craft shops.

GETTING WHAT YOU WANT

Bargaining

Getting what you want at a fair price in Chiangmai requires bargaining and avoiding touts, guides, and drivers. We recommend that you bargain for most things you purchase in Chiangmai, and ask for discounts on hotel rooms and tours. Shops expect you to bargain and typically give 10 to 40 percent discounts. During the off-season, when hotel rooms are plentiful, many hotels will give discounts if you ask at the front desk. Request a business discount and present your business card if asked for it.

Except for buses and minivans which run regular routes, you must bargain for transportation. Most trishaw (*samlor*) drivers, including the motorized ones (*rot tuk tuk*), will reduce their prices by one-third; don't accept the first price quoted unless you feel sympathy for these drivers. Few speak English, so use your fingers or show them the bills or coins you are willing to pay. Most short rides with the *samlor* drivers cost between 10 and 15 baht. Expect to pay 25-30 baht with the *rot tuk tuk* drivers. If you want to go long distances, use the *rot tuk tuks* and minivans which are faster and cheaper than the samlor. Be sure to bargain for all other transportation, especially half-day and full-day rentals of cars and motorbikes.

Avoid the Commission Game

You should also avoid the outrageous commissions now plaguing much of Chiangmai's shopping. This problem is particularly pronounced among the shops along the Chiangmai-Sankamphaeng Road and endemic to tour groups. Many *rot tuk tuk*, *samlor*, minivan, and car drivers as well as tour guides routinely request from shops 10 to 40% commissions on purchases made by individuals they bring to the shops; others may only request 100 to 200 baht for bringing a group to the shop. Consequently, if you are being taken to a shop by a driver or guide, this individual will probably be getting a huge kickback on everything you purchase. The shop, in turn, adds this commission to the price you pay for the goods. If a shop refuses to give the commission, the driver or guide takes future tourists to another more cooperative shop. Unfortunately, nearly 80 percent of the shops along Chiangmai-Sankamphaeng Road have succumbed to this form of blackmail. Shops patronized by large groups of tourists, especially those arriving by tour bus and with drivers, are usually paying the commissions in order to have the customers brought to their shops. Even some of the most reputable international tour groups engage in this practice.

The problem has gotten so serious that it is becoming a crisis of sorts. Prices have become so inflated and the corruption so pervasive that shopping in Chiangmai may become unattractive. Indeed, you may be able to purchase the same items cheaper in Bangkok where you are likely to go into a shop on your own or your driver or guide only requests the standard 10% commission. The 10% commission is the normal going rate in Thailand as well as among touts, drivers, and tour guides in many other countries.

The best way to avoid these commissions is to rent your own car and drive to the various factories and shops in Chiangmai. This is possible to do given the small size of Chiangmai and the ease of finding shops along the main roads. If you drive yourself, you will discover the initial asking price will automatically drop by at least one-third—because you came alone—and you can bargain for another 20 to 40% discount. You can also explore many good shops that most tourists never see because they are told by their guides that the shop is *"no good"* or *"it's closed today"* which translates as *"they don't give me a commission there!"*

Another way to get around the commission game is to call the shop and request that you be provided transportation to visit them. They are more than willing to send a car for you because this means eliminating middlemen who would ask for commissions if they brought you to the shop. You are under no obligation to buy even though the shop has taken the trouble to pick you up. On the other hand, this is an inconvenient and time-consuming way to visit a large number of shops. Some enterprising tourists, who don't want to drive in an unfamiliar town and on the left side of the road, will hire a car with driver for a day or half day to survey the shops—making no purchases or very small purchases as well as noting shops they wish to return to. After returning to their hotel, they call the shops where they have an interest in making larger purchases and let the shop send a car for them.

Alternatively, if you decide to hire a driver, try to communicate that he is not to take commissions. This means you will have to pay him more for his driving services. But this may or may not work to your advantage. If you don't speak Thai, you can't be sure the driver isn't still getting a kickback, even though he may swear *"No, no, no—I don't take commissions."* Also, be aware that some drivers will offer you a *"free shopping tour"* or one that is incredibly cheap—100 baht for four hours! Some tourists think this is a great bargain, equivalent to the proverbial free lunch. They even tell other tourists how they, too, can get a free shopping tour! This is one of those "freebies" you and others are better off not knowing about. Remember, there is no such thing as a free lunch, especially when you are paying for it by other means.

Drive Yourself

You will find driving your own car to be the cheapest way to shop in Chiangmai. You will have the flexibility to explore

Chiangmai-Sankamphaeng Road, shops found in neighborhoods throughout the city, Hang Dong, and several nearby towns, such as Lamphun, Lampang, Chiangrai, and Maesai. You will find several car rental agencies in Chiangrai. We use the reliable **Avis** which is located across the street from the Chiang Mai Orchid Hotel on Huay Kaew Road. Avis also has a desk at the Chiangmai International Airport, adjacent to the baggage retrieval area. It's best to reserve a car from Bangkok (the Avis office is located at the Dusit Thani Hotel) and pick it up as soon as you arrive at the airport. You also can call Avis to have them pick you up at your hotel.

Ship With Ease

You should have no problem shipping goods directly from Chiangmai. Most large shops are experienced in packing and shipping goods to Bangkok as well as overseas. If you are buying many items from different shops, consolidate them at one shop or use an experienced local shipper, such as **Chiangmai Air Cargo Co.** at 234/2 Wualai Road (Tel. 234-705). In fact, you can take your purchases directly to Chiangmai Air Cargo Co. and have them pack them on the spot to be shipped to Bangkok or abroad. Firms such as **Hong Kong Transpack**, which is a branch of a major Bangkok-based international shipper, have offices and shipping services in Chiangmai. Most shops and shippers can send your goods to your consolidation point in Bangkok.

ENJOYING YOUR STAY

Chiangmai is much more than shopping. It is an intriguing cultural area with wonderful sights and a pleasant atmosphere of people, lifestyles, scenery, and climate. Chiangmai has several excellent hotels which we identified earlier in Chapter Four (pages 71-72). TAT maintains a **Tourist Information Office** (105-1 Chiangmai-Lamphun Rd., Tel. 248-604 or 248-607) just south of the Nawarat Bridge on the eastern bank of the Ping River (Mae Nam Ping). This office can provide you with maps and information on local tours and attractions. Your hotel also should have information on various tours within and outside the city. Several tour operators offer a variety of tours to the factories, temples, and sights inside the city and to several locations outside the city, such as the Elephant Training Camp, Doi Suthep mountain, Puping Palace, Doi Inthanon, waterfalls, orchid farms, and caves. You also can arrange overnight trips to the interesting province of Chiangrai and the hill towns of Mae Sariang and Fang or rent a car to explore Lampang and the walled city of Naan.

If you are adventuresome, you can arrange two or three-day trips to the remote province of Mae Hong Son as well as to several hilltribe villages. Three major trekking companies organize a variety of trekking adventures into the hills of northern Thailand. We do not recommend wandering into the hills on your own. You may stumble into sensitive areas populated by rebels, drug dealers, or bandits!

The northern Thai culture differs in many ways from the cultures of Bangkok, central, northeastern, and southern Thailand. For an introduction to the diverse lowland and upland cultures of northern Thailand, you should visit the Chiangmai National Museum, Ladda Land, and the Tribal Research Center at Chiangmai University as well as attend one of the evening dinner-cultural shows, or *khantoke* shows, sponsored by hotels or at the Old Chiangmai Cultural Center.

Chiangmai has several good Thai, Chinese, French, German, English, and Middle Eastern restaurants along with several coffee shops and fast food establishments. The northern Thai food tends to be spicier than the Thai food in Bangkok. Some of our favorite northern dishes include sticky rice (*khao neow*), a curried noodle dish (*khao soi*), and a wonderful—although sometimes blazing hot—pickled pork chile dip eaten with sticky rice or fried pork skins (*namprik ong*). The local raw pork sausage delicacy called *naem* and a minced pork dish called *lap* are very popular, but they can be very hot and may give you a bad case of trichinosis. And watch out for the small green peppers; eat one of these and you may think you are having cardiac arrest! To sample some of these and other northern Thai dishes, you should attend one of the *khantoke* dinner shows or stop at a northern Thai restaurant. Try **Aroon Rai** near the Tha Phae Gate at 45 Kotchasarn Road (Tel. 276-947) in downtown Chiangmai.

For good French and Continental cuisine in charming surroundings, try **Thong Kwon** at the Rincome Hotel and **Le Chalet** on Charoen Prathet Road, just down the street from the Pornping and Diamond hotels and along the Ping River. One of our long time favorites is **The Pub** at 88 Huay Kaew Road (Tel. 211-550), just a short walk from the Rincome Hotel. The food here is both outstanding and inexpensive.

Good Chinese food and seafood are found at the **Jasmine** (Dusit Inn), **White Orchid Restaurant** (Diamond Hotel off of

Charoen Praphet Road), and **Nang Nual Seafood Restaurant** (just off the Old Chiangmai-Lamphun Road in southwest Chiangmai). Other favorite restaurants include:

- **Baan Suan:** Nicely decorated and serves good food. Frequented by tour groups. Located at 51/3 Chiangmai-Sankamphaeng Road (Tel. 242-116).

- **Babylon:** Chiangmai's best Italian restaurant. Located at 100/63 Huay Kaew Road near Chiangmai University.

- **Whole Earth:** Excellent Thai, Pakistani, and vegetarian restaurant located in a garden setting at 88 Sridonchai Road (Tel. 282-463).

- **The Gallery:** This restaurant and bar on the banks of the Ping River is also one of Chiangmai's most interesting art galleries. Located just north of the Nawarat Bridge on Charoen Rat Road and next to other pleasant riverside restaurants such as The Riverside and Rim Ping.

- **Kaiwan:** A garden restaurant near the Rincome Hotel at 181 Nimmanhemin Road. Serves excellent Thai food.

- **Al-Shiraz:** A favorite place for Pakistani, Indian, and Arabic foods. Located at 123-123/1 Chang Klan Road (opposite the Night Bazaar).

The buffets at the Chiang Inn and Chiang Mai Orchid Hotel are good values although the selections are more limited than those in Bangkok. For the adventuresome, try **Kaithong Restaurant** for jungle food. Located at 67 Kotchasarn Road (Tel. 276-584), this restaurant serves such unusual dishes as cobra, python, crocodile, hare, and mixed jungle steak.

LOOKING BACK

Four days in Chiangmai should be enough to visit the major factories and shops as well as do some basic sightseeing in this interesting area. Your shopping experience in Chiangmai will probably be more of an adventure than your shopping in Bangkok. To be effective and truly enjoy shopping in Chiangmai, you must develop a different shopping strategy which is most appropriate to the structure of shopping and transportation in Chiangmai. You will do less walking and more vehicular traveling between shops and factories.

You should enjoy the change of pace, the pleasant climate, and the friendly and gracious people in and around this northern city. You will find many items you saw in Bangkok, but you also should discover many gorgeous antiques and handicrafts not available there. Above all, you will be encounter quality goods, unique items, and reasonable prices.

Chiangmai should become one of your major shopping highlights in Asia. Chiangmai—the window to Burma, Laos, hilltribes, and the history and culture of northern Thailand—will once again confirm the wisdom of shopping in exotic Thailand!

14 BEYOND THE CITIES

While you will find few major shopping opportunities outside Bangkok and Chiangmai, some towns do offer interesting shopping adventures. In northern Thailand the towns of Chiangrai, Maesai, Lampang, and Lamphun—all located within a one to three hour drive from Chiangmai—are worth visiting for shopping and sightseeing. If time permits, you may also want to visit Mae Hong Son, located near the Thai-Burmese border, a 11 hour drive or 40 minute flight from Chiangmai. Ayuthaya, the former 17th century capital of Thailand, is located 86 kilometers north of Bangkok. While it is a major tourist destination for individuals interested in visiting Bang Pa-In Palace and the ruins of the former capital, it offers some unique shopping opportunities. Pattaya, a popular resort southeast of Bangkok, can be reached within three hours driving time; it has a few interesting shops. Phuket, a major beach and island resort in southern Thailand, also offers shopping opportunities for those who primarily visit this lovely area for sun and surf.

Each of our "beyond Bangkok and Chiangmai" locations are essentially small towns with populations of less than 60,000. Shopping is confined to either the central business district or to shops and factories on the outskirts of town. In each town you should be able to complete your shopping within one to four hours.

GETTING THERE

Getting to these locations is relatively easy. Since they are popular tourist destinations, each town is accessible by air, rail, bus, or car. Tours are regularly organized to the popular towns of Chiangrai, Ayuthaya, and Phuket. However, it is relatively easy and convenient to rent a car with driver or, if you are a bit adventuresome, drive your own rental vehicle in these towns. In northern Thailand, for example, you may want to rent a car in Chiangmai and from there drive to Maesai, Chiangrai, Lampang, and Lamphun and then return to Chiangmai. This circle trip, including sightseeing and shopping, can be done in two to three days. If you include Mae Hong Son, it's best to fly. In fact, you can take an early morning flight into Mae Hong Son, hire a car and driver to see the major sights and shop, and then take the late afternoon flight back to Chiangmai where you will still have time to shop Chiangmai's Night Bazaar. This makes for an interesting one-day trip.

The easiest and fastest way to get to Pattaya is by car. You may want to rent a car with driver to visit Pattaya. If you leave early in the morning from Bangkok, you can see the major sights and shop, and return to Bangkok the same day. However, many visitors prefer staying over in Pattaya for one or two nights.

You will probably want to fly to Phuket and then rent a car upon arrival at the airport. In Phuket driving allows you to venture into a few nearby provinces, such as Phang-nga.

You may want to rent a car with driver in Bangkok to visit Ayuthaya or join one of the regularly scheduled tours to this province and town. Driving in and around Bangkok is much less convenient than driving to "up-country" provinces, towns, and villages.

CAUTIOUSLY SHOP THE HINTERLAND

Please do not venture beyond Bangkok and Chiangmai with the expectation of finding great bargains and quality goods. If you do, you will be disappointed as you waste your precious travel time. The "good stuff" is either in Bangkok or Chiangmai, with Bangkok by far offering the largest range of the best quality products. What you will find in these other towns are a few unique items, such as blue pottery in Lampang and stone sculptures and antique ceramics in Ayuthaya, and some interesting historical and cultural sites. Better still, you will get to see a less urban and more picturesque Thailand than had you just confined your visit to Bangkok and Chiangmai.

If you do shop beyond Bangkok and Chiangmai, please be careful where you shop and whom you trust with your money and purchases. Most shops and merchants outside Bangkok and Chiangmai speak little English and they are not experienced in packing and shipping abroad. Some travelers report shipping problems with purchases they made in the Thai-Burmese border town of Maesai. However, they forgot the golden rule for shopping in border towns:

> Expect scams to readily operate and unscrupulous merchants to prey on tourists who mistakenly think *"I'll really get a super deal at the border."*

Most border towns are transient towns with populations engaged in all types of legal, illegal, and unethical practices. Remember, if it's too good to be true, it probably is. At the same time, some well-meaning shops agree to do things for buyers—which are considered routine for merchants in Bangkok and Chiangmai—but in the end they are incapable of performing. For example, some tourists buy Buddhas—which are illegal to export from Thailand without proper government permits. Obtaining the permits is an expensive and time-consuming process centered in Bangkok. The buyers expect the shop to ship the items to their home address. When their purchases do not arrive in a few weeks, they then write letters of complaint to the shopowners who, in turn, don't read or write English. It is simply foolish to expect shops in such towns to perform these tasks and then further expect them to communicate with you in English. Our advice is simple and sensible: **hand carry from shops all items you purchase outside Bangkok and Chiangmai.** You can take them to a reliable shipper, such as Chiangmai Air Cargo in Chiangmai or Hong Kong Transpack in Bangkok, and have them pack and ship everything with the expectation you will receive your goods. **Never ever leave your purchases with a shop in the smaller towns.** To do so invites disappointments. If you purchase a Thai Buddha, for example, be aware you may never get it out of Thailand, regardless of what an enterprising shop-keeper may lead you to believe. If you purchase gems or jewelry in out-of-the-way places, especially border towns, make sure you know what you are doing. An ostensible US$5,000 ruby may turn out to be a beautiful US$25 synthetic spinel! These are expensive lessons you do not need to learn the hard way.

CHIANGRAI

Chiangrai, the capital of Thailand's northern most province which borders both Burma and Laos, is a small sleepy provincial town located 180 kilometers northeast of Chiangmai. It can easily be reached within three hours driving distance via a scenic and good paved, yet mountainous and winding, road. Leave Chiangmai's noisy and polluted rush hour traffic by 7am and you will be in quiet downtown Chiangrai by 10:30am.

Chiangrai is becoming one of the north's most popular tourist destinations. Tour buses leave Chiangmai every day to take tourists into Chiangrai's land of the "Golden Triangle." Famous for its colorful hilltribe peoples, opium warlords, and Shan rebels from Burma, Chiangrai reminds one of Chiangmai 20 years ago. The pace of life is slow, traffic is sensible, air and noise pollution are minimal, and the people are both friendly and curious. The area is inherently fascinating because of its natural beauty, diverse population, and history of opium, warlords, rebels, and ancient kingdoms. While one of the most popular tours is to the "Golden Triangle" area northeast of Chiangrai town, which became famous as a center of opium production in the 1970s, Chiangrai still retains its reputation as one of Southeast Asia's major opium growing regions—complete with opium warlords, couriers, and middleman who engage in an extremely profitable, adventuresome, and deadly trade.

Shopping in the province of Chiangrai is primarily centered around the provincial capital of Chiangrai, the border town of Maesai, and the Golden Triangle area near Chiangsaen. The town of Chiangrai is a good place from which to explore Maesai and the Golden Triangle area as well as the ancient town of Chiangsaen. While hotel and restaurant facilities are not as deluxe as those found in Bangkok, four relatively new deluxe hotels and resorts have opened during the past three years in anticipation of a coming surge of tourism to Chiangrai. Within the city of Chiangrai are the deluxe **Dusit Island Resort**, **Little Duck**, and **Rimkok Resort**. First-class hotels include the **Wiang Inn** and the **Wangcome Hotel**. Most tour groups stay at these hotels and resorts which also function as the social centers for the local elite. The hotels have good restaurants as well as small gift shops. In the Golden Triangle area, just west of Chiangsean, is the superbly located and beautifully appointed **Golden Triangle Hotel** which overlooks the Mekong River where Burma, Laos, and Thailand meet.

Shopping in Chiangrai should take no longer than two hours. A relatively small and compact town, most of the downtown shops are within easy walking distance from the Wiang Inn and Wangcome Hotel. The main shopping streets are the intersecting streets of **Paholyothin, Ratanacate**, and **Tanalai.** You will find numerous restaurants and shops lining these streets. However, most shops are filled with consumer goods of little interest to tourist. Especially at night, these are interesting shops to browse through to get a sense of what's popular with the local community.

You will find two silver, antique, and craft shops in downtown Chiangrai worth visiting. **Chiang Saen** at 869/96 Pemavipat Road, just off Paholyothin Road (Tel. 713-535) is Chiangrai's best antique and handicraft shop. Its three floors are filled with hilltribe clothing, silver, baskets, Buddhas, ceramics, puppets, and lacquerware. The shop has an excellent collection of good quality baskets and Lanna Thai Buddhas. The prices here are also very good—beautiful US$100 baskets in Bangkok sell for US$35 here. Across the street at 869/145 Pemavipat Road is **Chiang Rai Silver Ware** (Tel. 714-764). This shop has a similar range of silver items found in its other shop (Bor Sang Silver Ware) at the village of Bo Sang just off the Chiangmai-Sankamphaeng Road in Chiangmai.

One of the major shopping attractions on the outskirts of Chiangrai is the **Chiangrai Handicraft Center** (Tel. 713-355), which is located 3 kilometers north of the city, on the road (Phaholyothin) to Maesai and Chiangsaen. Easily recognized by a huge ladle in front of the factory-shop, this is one of the largest handicraft centers in northern Thailand. It's an excellent place to stop and view the making of pottery, ceramics, and silk and cotton material. The showroom is filled with good quality ceramics, clothes, Bencharong, woodcarvings, silver, flowers, dolls, lacquerware, puppets, jewelry, paintings, jade, and Burmese products. This is also a good place to purchase a map of Chiangrai. All prices here are fixed.

MAESAI

The town of Maesai is by far the major shopping attraction in the province of Chiangrai. Located 50 kilometers directly north of the town of Chiangrai, Maesai is one of Thailand's major border crossings with Burma. Visitors from all over Thailand —tourists, traders, and itinerate travelers—come here to enjoy the interesting peoples and shop to their heart's content. However, only Thai and Burmese citizens are permitted to cross the border at this point. Other citizens can only look over the river and check point and wonder what life is like on the other side. Thais tell us there is not much to see or do, so you probably aren't missing out on much. The most interesting side of the border is in Maesai—where you can do some interesting shopping at excellent prices—if you are very careful!

Maesai is the type of town you might expect to find at a major border crossing where a very poor country meets a relatively well developed country—somewhat dusty, worn, but busy with people crossing to and from the border in search of products and profits. The Thai side of the border is the prosperous side whereas the Burmese side is relatively poor, although better off than most Burmese towns and villages. Burmese traders continuously stream across the border to buy basic Thai consumer goods that are difficult to find in poverty-stricken Burma. Thai tourists, in turn, cross the border to purchase traditional medicines and food stuffs as well as witness what life is like on the other side.

Most shopping in Maesai is concentrated along the main street adjacent to the border crossing. Here you will find numerous antique, handicraft, and jewelry shops as well as street side vendors and hawkers selling products from Burma. It is a good area to just stroll up and down the street, take pictures from the bridge, visit numerous shops, and watch the colorful tribespeople crossing the border and bridge from Burma. You can even have your picture taken with the cute tribal children who are real professionals at posing for tourists —and politely asking for payment afterwards. Indeed, "people watching" is as much fun as shopping for inexpensive items from Burma.

The shops and vendors in Maesai primarily sell products from Burma: gems, jewelry, silver, antiques, lacquerware, tapestries (*kalagas*), puppets, and a variety of other handcrafted items. If you know how to bargain—expect 20 to 60 percent discounts—prices here are some of the cheapest in Thailand. In fact, many dealers from Chiangmai, Bangkok, and abroad purchase their antiques, gems, and handicrafts directly from the same shops and vendors you will encounter in Maesai. For example, expect to pay anywhere from one-fourth to one-half the price you would pay in Bangkok for a Burmese tapestry (*kalaga*) found in abundance in the shops of Maesai. A *kalaga* selling for US$250 in Bangkok and US$150 in Chiangmai goes for US$80 in Maesai—and a surprising US$1000-2,000 in North America and Europe! Burmese puppets that sell for US$50 in Bangkok and US$30 in Chiangmai sell for US$10 in Maesai and US$300-500 in North America and Europe. The prices are so cheap that you may find it difficult to restrain your shopping urges.

The reason prices are so cheap here is that Burmese labor is some of the cheapest in the world. Given the devastated nature of the Burmese economy, the Burmese at this border crossing willingly trade their valuable antiques and handcrafted items for the much desired Thai consumer goods. Especially in the case of the *kalagas*, which involve weeks of intensive skilled labor, you will be shocked at such cheap prices for these works of art. Our advice for shopping in Maesai is to buy now since you may never see these prices—and perhaps the products—again.

We do not have specific recommendations for shops in Maesai. The reason is that most shops and vendors are located next to each other within 150 meters of the border crossing. They all seem to carry the same items. All you need to do is go from one shop and vendor to another to compare products and prices. Once you find something you like, do comparative shopping among the various shops and vendors. As you bargain over prices, play one shop and vendor off on the other by mentioning that you can get the same item from another shop or vendor for much less. The competitive nature of this shopping environment will ensure you a good price on many products.

Be forewarned, however, that some shops and vendors may misrepresent their goods. A few shops, for example, sell gold and lacquer hats that were ostensibly once worn by Burmese soldiers. Some shops will tell you these are *"very old—100 to 200 years"* and try to sell them for US$100-200 each. Don't believe a word they say. These hats may look old, but most were made yesterday; other more honest shops sell them for US$16. Consequently, do your comparative shopping and be skeptical of claims about antiques. The same is true for gems and jewelry. Maesai is notorious for selling fake gems at genuine stone prices. Many a tourist has left Maesai believing they had purchased a valuable gem at an unbelievably cheap price. And yes they did get something unbelievable—the gem rather than the price. While you can get good deals on gems at Maesai, please know what you are doing before you make such a purchase. In general, street vendors with mobile carts do not generate a great deal of confidence in any product we might buy that costs more than US$20. If you spend more than US$100 from one of these vendors, don't be surprised if you later learn they were literally "fly-by-night" merchants who sold you an under US$20 item at a truly "unbelievable" price!

One shop along the river—**Mengrai Antique**—is noted for its wide selection of Burmese antiques. We have found this shop to be reliable although some of our readers report problems with purchases not being shipped. However, we **always** take our purchases with us and would **never** trust this or any other shop in Maesai to ship our goods. There are simply too many problems involved in such a transaction. Mengrai Antique is one of the largest shops in Maesai—three dusty and cluttered floors of antiques and handicrafts. Here you will find an excellent selection of woodcarvings, hilltribe costumes, textiles, antiques, bells, rain drums, lacquerware, and puppets. This shop alone is worth a trip to Maesai.

But be your own judge. We're not comfortable making recommendations in Maesai because of the frontier atmosphere of shopping here. You can easily get cheated here if you don't know what you are doing. Remember, this is not Bangkok or Chiangmai—it's a border town where everyone is out making money on the local border and tourist trade.

To be on the safe side, we recommend starting your shopping at **Mengrai Antiques**. Look over their product selections; ask about prices, but expect to get at least a 20% discount; and then compare their products and prices with other nearby shops and vendors. Two adjacent shops—**Mala Antique** and **Chai Siam**—also offer a large range of antiques, handicrafts, and jewelry. Chances are you will eventually return to Mengrai Antiques to do much of your buying. This shop also sells those US$100-200 "antique" warrior hats for what they are really worth—US$16—which is indeed an "unbelievable" price!

Maesai also has a jade shop—**Thong Tavee Jade Factory**. Similar to other jade factories, you can observe the jade carving process and then shop at the factory shop. The shop also sells jewelry and silver. And like other jade factories we have visited, prices here seem very high and the quality is not the best. If you purchase anything here, make sure you get a huge discount—nothing less than 60%. We found prices on jewelry to be about 200% higher than retail shops in Bangkok.

You will also find some shopping opportunities among hilltribe peoples. Several Yao villages sell handcrafted items from stalls near the Hill Tribe Development Center which is located 16 kilometers southwest of Maesai. While a few items are indigenous to the Yao, such as embroidered hats and bags and opium scales, most of the items are imported from shops in Chiangmai. Be sure to bargain with the Yao, expecting to receive 20 to 50% discounts on most items offered. We don't recommend wandering around too much in this area. We discovered a Rolls Royce and several other extremely expensive cars parked in out-of-the-way-places and speculated about their origins in the heart of opium country. Sometimes it is not good to know too much!

THE GOLDEN TRIANGLE

The popular Golden Triangle area is located northeast of Chiangrai town or directly east of Maesai. It takes about one hour to get there by car from Chiangrai town. There's not much to see or shop for here. The ancient town of Chiangsaen is small a quaint town fronting on the Mekong River. It has a few temple ruins dating to the 13th century when Chiangsaen served as a kingdom in northern Thailand. In downtown Chiangsaen you will find one shop (90 Limton) that makes T-shirts, bags using Lao designs, and souvenirs to supply shops near the Golden Triangle Hotel.

The major shopping area is located nine kilometers west of Chiangsaen near the Golden Triangle Hotel and the marker certifying this to be the "Golden Triangle" area. Here you will find numerous small shops, restaurants, and guest houses catering to the growing tourist trade. More than 30 shops sell souvenirs, gift items, antiques, T-shirts, lacquerware, silver, pipes, masks, bags, clothes, puppets, gems, and costume jewelry. Two of the better shops in this area are **Phukham** (in front of the Phukham Guest House) and the **Golden Triangle Souvenir** (fronts on river). Three kilometers further west is the **Wanglao Handicraft Center** where you can observe the traditional weaving process and purchase textiles, black pottery, and bags. Remember, these are tourist areas, so bargain hard for everything you plan to purchase.

LAMPANG

Lampang is a surprise to many visitors. A town of approximately 40,000 people, it is located about 150 kilometers south of Chiangrai and nearly 100 kilometers southeast of Chiangmai. Once a sleepy provincial capital best noted for its horsecart rides and intriguing Burmese temple architecture, today Lampang is a bustling town which is beginning to offer visitors several shopping options.

Since Lampang is not on the normal tourist itinerary, tourist facilities here are limited but more than adequate for an overnight stay. The two major first-class hotels—**Asia Lampang Hotel** (229 Bunyawat Rd., Tel. 217-844) and **Tipchang Lampang Hotel** (54/22 Thakrao Noi Rd., Tel. 218-078) offer above average up-country accommodations, complete with restaurants and nightclubs. Restaurants are numerous throughout the city.

You are well advised to approach Lampang by first stopping at the **Lampang Tourist Center** (Tel. 318-823), located adjacent to the Lampang Provincial Hall (*Sala Klang*) in the heart of town. There you can view a display of products available in Lampang, acquire maps and brochures, and ask questions of the personnel who staff the center. Also in this area you will find several vendors selling tourist knick-knacks. The town's major market is located only a half block away. Like many other town markets in Thailand, this one is filled with the usual local consumer goods as well as fresh fruits, vegetables, and meats.

Lampang is noted for producing blue and white ceramics, woodcarvings, and wood furniture and home accessory items. Lampang's blue and white ceramics are found in numerous shops in Chiangmai and Bangkok. Lampang also produces a distinctive cloisonne which compares favorably with Chinese cloisonnea.

Over 50 blue and white **ceramic factories** are found in Lampang. Some of these you may wish to visit. Three of the largest export factories—**Lampang Silpa Nakon**, **Kittirote**, and **Sang Arun**—are located near each other along the major highway that passes through the town, **Phaholyothin Road**. One of our favorite ceramic factories and shops is **Chour Lampang Earthenware** at 583 Paholyothin Road (Tel. 217-443). They produce a uniquely designed elephant planter with a green ceramic interior—one of the most unusual and interesting items we encountered in Lampang and one that could be exported abroad. You will also find some lovely Bencharong and celadon here as well as porcelain cups, bowls, plates, tea sets, and small ceramic animals. This shop is a little difficult to find since it does not have a sign in English. However, it is on the right-hand side of the road as you go along Phaholyothin Road on your way into the town of Lampang. You will see the ceramics on display in the front of this open shop. Another excellent ceramics factory is **Indra Ceramics** at 382 Lampang-Denchai Road, km. 1 (near Yonok College, Tel. 221-189). Along with the traditional blue and white ceramics they produce some lovely green and peach colored ceramics. They also produce a wider range of products than most factories—pots, plates, napkin rings, and animals.

Lampang is especially famous for its **woodcarvings**. The villages of Mae Tha and Ban Luk are well noted for carving large animal figures—elephants, deer, bears, giraffes, lions, masks, horses, and humans—from monkey-pod wood. They also produce much smaller items. Indeed, many shops in Chiangmai and Bangkok buy their carvings from these villages. Indeed, a visit to these villages will give you a fascinating introduction into both family and village woodcarving traditions in Lampang. Each village household is engaged in producing their own carved figures. You can purchase non-commissioned items here or have your own carvings commissioned. The villages are located approximately one hour driving distance southwest of the town of Lampang. Keep in mind that large pieces of wood may crack when taken to dryer climates.

Lampang is also home to one of Thailand's most important **wood factories—Siam Rich Wood Co.** The factory is located at 304 Super Highway (Tel. 218-448), approximately one kilometer north of Phaholyothin Road, adjacent to the first bridge you cross. The factory does good quality work using teak, pine, rubber, beech, and oak woods. Under contract to produce Scandinavian-type wood products for three companies in the United States—magazine racks, tables, chairs, wine racks, bread boxes, cutting boards, coasters, computer disk storage units, ice chests—Siam Rich Wood Co. also operates a small gift shop which is open to the public. The prices here are very good. You may want to stop here to purchase a few gift items. All of their products integrate nicely into contemporary Western homes.

LAMPHUN

The town of Lamphun is only 40 kilometers southeast of Chiangmai. If you are returning to Chiangmai via Chiangrai and Lampang, you will most likely pass by this town on the Superhighway. Take a left off the main highway and go into this small provincial town. It offers some shopping opportunities as well as a small but interesting historical museum—**Hariphunchai Museum**—in downtown Lamphun.

Lamphun is noted for its cotton and silk weaving and basketry work. The town of Lamphun itself has a few shops selling these items. However, the major shopping area is a small town within Lamphun province called **Pa Sang**. Located half way between Lamphun and Chiangmai—approximately 20 kilometers in each direction—Pa Sang has one main street with several shops selling cotton and silk garments, throw rugs, comforters, dolls, pillows, bags, hats, stuffed animals, woodcarvings, and baskets. Most of the items are produced in nearby villages. However, some of the woodcarvings are produced in the Lampang village of Ban Luk. Since we are not impressed with either the quality or styling of the products found in Pa Sang, we cannot recommend making a special trip here. If you are on your way to Chiangmai from Lampang, or vice versa, you may want to stop here along the way. But don't expect to do quality shopping here. You are much better off shopping in Chiangmai and Bangkok for your cottons, silks, woodcarvings, and handicrafts. Lamphun does have a few interesting temples worth visiting.

MAE HONG SON

Located 368 winding mountainous kilometers (10-12 hour drive) or a 40-minute flight northwest of Chiangmai, Mae Hong Son is an interesting provincial town located near the Burmese border and in the heart of hilltribe and opium country. It's best to take the flight from Chiangmai which departs daily. If you are in a hurry, you can take the early morning flight and return to Chiangmai late in the afternoon. Unless you are interested in trekking or exploring hilltribe villages (Shan, Karen, Lahu, Meo), there's not a great deal to do in Mae Hong Son. It has some beautiful Burmese style temples and a quaint remote small town atmosphere. You can easily arrange for a car and driver to take you around town as well as visit a few hilltribe villages within 50 kilometers of town and still have time to shop in downtown Mae Hong Son. Once you arrive at the airport, ask one of the porters for information on a car and driver. They can refer you to a tour operator who is near the airport area. Unfortunately, the airport does not have well organized tourist information services. If you ask around, someone will soon assist you.

Shopping in Mae Hong Son is primarily confined to a few handicraft and souvenir shops. One shop, **Thai Folk Arts and Crafts Center**, located just outside town, has a small collection of locally produced hilltribe dolls, lacquerware, pots, wicker furniture, and hilltribe clothes. Within town you will find six handicraft shops in a two block area selling the same types of products—lacquerware, gems, jewelry, clothes, and textiles. The attractive Burmese lacquer boxes are especially good buys—30 baht (US$1.20) in Mae Hong Son, but 150 baht (US$6) in Chiangmai, 350 baht (US$14) in Bangkok, and US$35 in last year's Neiman Marcus catalog!

Again, Mae Hong Son and other northern towns outside Chiangmai are not major shopping destinations. While they do produce some interesting local handcrafted items, they mainly offer interesting historical and cultural sites and friendly small town atmospheres not found in Thailand's larger cities. Plan to visit these places primarily for rest, relaxation, and curiosity rather than for shopping.

AYUTHAYA

Ayuthaya, located 86 kilometers north of Bangkok, is the former capital of Thailand that was sacked by the Burmese in 1767. Today, it is a bustling provincial capital hosting thousands of tourists each year who come to visit the interesting ruins and tour the summer palace at Bang Pa-In. At the same time, Ayuthaya offers some unique shopping opportunities for those who have the flexibility to get around the city and surrounding area on their own.

Since most foreign tourists go to Ayuthaya with a tour group, they have little opportunity to do shopping outside the areas catering primarily to tour buses. Nonetheless, you can do some good shopping while on a tour, especially near one of the major tour bus stops—Wat Phra Si Sanphet. You may want to rent a car and drive yourself to Ayuthaya. However, be forewarned the traffic from Bangkok to Ayuthaya can be horrendous and frustrating. You may want to rent a car with driver instead. One of the best, and most picturesque, trips is the daily boat-bus combination tour from the Oriental Hotel (Tel. 236-0400, 236-0420, ext. 3133). You can either arrive or depart Ayuthaya via an air-conditioned luxury cruiser, complete with a buffet luncheon.

There are three major shopping areas worth visiting in Ayuthaya: Bansai, Wat Phra Si Sanphet, and Si Sanphet Road.

Bansai, located a few kilometers outside the town of Ayuthaya, is home for the **Royal Folk Arts and Crafts Center**. Under the patronage of Her Majesty the Queen, the Centre trains students over a three to four month period to produce a wide range of handcrafted items. Organized similar to a college campus, each building specializes in the training and production of specific handcrafted items. You will find students producing wood and rattan furniture, baskets, leather goods, toys, display fruits, stuffed animals, and bamboo items. One area is devoted to glass blowing whereas another area is a center for producing traditional Thai paintings. You will also find a small row of thatched huts on a canal where you can purchase items produced at this training center. The quality and prices are good, and many of the items are unique. You can also purchase similar items in the **Chitralada** shops in Chiangmai, Bangkok, and Pattaya. These shops are also under the patronage of Her Majesty the Queen. The major problem here is that the center cannot produce enough products to satisfy the increasing demand. At present few tourists visit the center, although you are welcome to visit. Admission to the center grounds costs 10 baht. If you are visiting Ayuthaya, this stop is worthwhile. You will be able to see the production of handcrafted items as well as do some interesting shopping.

The major tourist shopping area in the town of Ayuthaya is at Wat Phra Si Sanphet. Most tour buses stop here so visitors can see this beautiful temple. Adjacent to the temple is a large market area where more than 30 shops and stalls have been erected. Most of the shops and stalls sell the same items—baskets, hats, bells, instruments, fans, jewelry, woodcarvings, knives, dolls, windchimes, bronzeware, and placemats. Much of this area is filled with tourist kitsch. However, you will find one antique shop here that sells a large range of what appears to be authentic antiques, although we don't know if their claims are true. We especially like the unique ceramic coasters which ostensibly come from the bottoms of old ceramic bowls. This is one of the few shops we know of in Thailand that has a good range of such coasters. But be forewarned that this and other shops in this area have inflated prices for the tourists. Other shops less frequented by tourists sell the same ceramic coasters for 60 baht whereas the shop here sells them for 300 baht. Our advice: take a short walk to Ayuthaya's third shopping area.

The third shopping area is located within a five minute walk of Wat Phra Si Sanphet. Several shops along **Si Sanphet Road** sell a large range of antiques, ceramics, stone carvings, bronzeware, and woodcarvings, and paintings. Few tourists visit this area because the tour buses only stop at Wat Phra Si Sanphet. This is unfortunate because the selections and prices are much better than at the other tourist shops. If you are with a tour group, the easiest way to find this shopping street is to directly face Wat Phra Si Sanphet, turn around 180 degrees, and walk straight ahead for 5 minutes toward King Uthong Monument. You will quickly come to this street as it is adjacent to the monument. From the shops you can see Wat Phra Si Sanphet and the tour buses. We especially like the large range of selections at **Arun-casem Antique** (79/3 Si Sanphet Rd., Tel. 251-193). This shop is crammed with stone sculptures, woodcarvings, ceramics, and Bencharong. One of the major specialties of this and other shops along this street are stone carvings. If you wish to have a figure commissioned, the shops will be more than happy to assist you with your request. The prices are good and the workmanship is excellent. While you would not want to air freight such heavy items home, they can easily be shipped by sea freight since sea freight charges are figured on the basis of volume. **Porntip Shop** at 79/3-5 Si Sanphet Road (Tel. 251-507) also has a nice selection of blue and white ceramics, jars, woodcarvings, and canvas paintings. This is where you can buy those 300 baht ceramic coasters for 60 baht!

PATTAYA

Pattaya, located within three hours driving distance southeast of Bangkok, is one of Thailand's popular resort destinations. It has all the amenities expected of seaside resorts—fine hotels, open-air restaurants, beach facilities, water sports, and numerous resort shops. Pattaya also has numerous bars and entertainment establishments geared toward all sexual persuasions, fantasies, and age groups. While Pattaya tries to appeal to families, it has a well deserved reputation for being Thailand's center for "beach, beer, and broads." It's party-time along the beach at night, and especially when U.S. Navy ships periodically unload hundreds of sailors who find more interesting things to do than go shopping in this beach resort. It is a combination of the French Riviera, Acapulco, Daytona Beach, and Patpong Road all rolled up into one. Pattaya offers good quality family resort amenities along with honky-tonk sex and sleaze. You may or may not like this place. It's very different from such resort areas as Hua Hin, Cha-am, and Phuket.

The easiest and fastest way to get to Pattaya is by car, although buses regularly shuttle between Bangkok and Pattaya. With a car you can easily get around Pattaya and its outlying areas, especially Jomtien Beach which is 9 kilometers south of Pattaya.

Most shops are found along the main streets—Central Pattaya Road, South Pattaya Road, and Pattaya Beach Road. The largest concentration of hotels, restaurants, and shops are found along Pattaya Beach Road. Here you will find numerous small shops and vendors selling typical resort items—T-shirts, souvenirs, copy watches, postcards, sunglasses, purses, wallets, and inexpensive clothes similar to those found along Patpong and Silom roads in Bangkok. The prices here are relatively good compared to Bangkok, especially if you bargain hard. It's also fun shopping, similar to the night bazaar along Patpong Road in Bangkok, for copy watches, clothes, and leather goods.

Some of the best shops along Pattaya Beach Road include **Chitralada**. Located next to P.K. Villa Hotel, this small shop offers good selections of colorful and nicely designed handicrafts, bags, straw hats, and clothes. Many are made in Her Majesty the Queen's training project in Bansai, Ayuthaya. **Thaipan**, which is also found in Bangkok on Suriwongse Road, offers three floors of nice silk, cotton, bronze, and toy products. This is the largest of three branch shops in Pattaya. Be sure to visit the third floor which has dresses, stuffed toys, bronze, and brass items. Next door is **World Gems**, one of Pattaya's nicest, friendliest, and most entrepreneurial jewelry stores. They offer loose stones as well as nicely designed jewelry. Other jewelry stores along this road include **Ma Belle**, **Royal Gems**, **T. Gems**, **Lucky Gems**, **Ben's Jewelry**, **Quality Gems**, and **Pattaya Lapidary**.

Other shopping areas worth visiting are centered in and around the resort hotels. The **Royal Cliff Beach Resort** has a shopping arcade with a few shops offering handicrafts, jewelry, and ready-made and tailor-made clothes.

Approximately nine kilometers south of Pattaya, along the rapidly developing Jomtien Beach, is the new **Ambassador City Jomtien**. This is one of Asia's largest hotel and shopping complexes which when completed in 1994 should have 3650 rooms, a convention center seating 5,000, 80 shops, and 34 restaurants! Built by the same owner of Ambassador City in Bangkok, it's one of Thailand's most ambitious resort and convention projects. Stay tuned for the next five years on the development of this complex. Some observers have doubts about its future success. It is likely to benefit from Thailand's nearby Eastern Seaboard area which continues to undergo rapid development with new factories and port facilities making this Thailand's hottest economic development area. For now, shops are just beginning to open—and struggle—at the shopping arcade within the Ambassador City complex. Numerous other shops and vendors are opening along the adjacent Jomtien Beach area which has been virtually transformed over the past few years with new condominiums and hotels.

PHUKET

Phuket is one of Thailand's most popular tourist destinations. Located some 900 kilometers south of Bangkok, Phuket is an island, town, and a province. Increasingly tourists are discovering the many pleasures of this west coast island with its generous offerings of sun, surf, sand, and seafood on the Andaman Sea.

Tourists primarily go to Phuket for the beaches. During the past 10 years numerous tours, restaurants, and first-class and deluxe hotels have sprung up to give Phuket a first-class tourist infrastructure and a well deserved international resort reputation. You will find some wonderful hotels here, such as the **Phuket Arcadia, Dusit Laguna**, and **Amanpuri**.

But Phuket also offers shopping opportunities for visitors who do not plan to visit Chiangmai or have limited time in Bangkok. Most of Phuket's shops and emporiums sell woodcarvings, handicrafts, silk, cotton, and antiques imported from Chiangmai and Bangkok. Indeed, some enterprising entrepreneurs from Chiangmai have opened handicraft emporiums—similar to the ones found along Chiangmai-Sankamphaeng Road in Chiangmai—in and around the town of Phuket. Prices, of course, are higher in Phuket for the same items you will find in Chiangmai and Bangkok. In addition, the cost of labor in Phuket is high compared to other areas in Thailand.

At the same time, shops in Phuket offer several unique locally produced items. The major products include pearls, beach wear, batik, and shell items. The pearls are especially attractive and can be good buys if you know what you are doing. The colorful Phuket batik is both distinctive and attractive.

Downtown Phuket

Shopping in Phuket is mainly found in the downtown area along Phang-nga, Rasda, and Phuket roads, at handicraft emporiums outside the town, and in a few resort hotels. Downtown Phuket should be one of your first stops on the island. Here you will find a very helpful **Tourism Authority of Thailand** office at 73-75 Phuket Road (Tel. 212-213). A good place to start shopping is at the corner of Yawaraj Road and Phang-nga Road. Start at **Puk**, an antique, handicraft, and souvenir shop located at 7-9 Phang-nga Road (Tel. 211-434). Both sides of this street have several shops of interest to tourists. **Voravuth** (#5), for example, offers antiques, souvenirs, *kalagas*, nielloware, bronze items, spirit houses, jewelry, and woodcarvings. **Nightingale Shop** (11-13 Phang-Nga Rd., 2nd floor, Tel. 212-837) is one of Phuket's nicest boutiques; you should be able to find some great gift items here, from bronzeware, batik, and bedspreads to tablecloths, pewter, and napkin rings. Other shops along Phang-nga Road worth visiting are the **Silk House** (#17), **Shell Shop** (#29), and **Native** (#80).

Rasda Road parallels Phang-nga Road. This street is lined with numerous souvenir, handicraft, silk, and jewelry shops. Starting at the intersection of Phuket Road and Rasda Road, you will come to the **Pewter Center** which sells silk and cotton along with pewterware. Next door is **Natural Pearl** which offers a large variety of strung and unstrung Phuket pearls as well as loose stones. **Chan's Antiques** offers a good selection of *kalagas* and woodcarvings from Chiangmai. **Rawai Shell** (#91) has a large selection of shells, including windchimes and lamps made from shells. Other shops along this road offer similar items: **Sea Pearl**, **Cotton House**, **Phuket Reminder**, **Phuket Souvenir Center**, **Sea World**, and **Phuket Gallery**. **Phuket Pearl** (#55) is one of the largest souvenir shops in Phuket offering a wide selection of shell items, pearls, pewter, and handicrafts from Chiangmai.

Just off of Rasda Road is the **Phuket Shopping Center**. Here you will find a department store as well have several small boutiques and shops along the street. **Pan Sea Boutique**, for example, offers a good selection of beach wear, *kalagas*, books, batik, and woodcarvings. You will also find a few tour companies located in this area.

You'll also find a few other shops outside these two major streets worth visiting in downtown Phuket. **Phuket International Lapidary** at 22-24 Deebuk Road (Tel. 215-876) is a large two-story jewelry and handicraft emporium. This is a good place to visit if you want to get an overview of quality and selections available. In addition to finding rubies and sapphires here, this shop also carries Phuket pearls which sell between 14,000 and 34,000 baht per string. However, their jewelry is not particularly stylish. While the first floor is devoted to gems, jewelry, and pearls, the second floor is filled with silk, leather, pewter, jade, and clothing items.

Phuket Ho Ryo Do at 7/38-40 Chao Fa Road is another handicraft shop which is located outside the city center. If you travel south of Phuket town, you will pass by this shop on your left—or on your right as you enter town. This shop offers everything from silk, pewterware, and masks to lacquerware.

Handicraft Emporiums and Centers

Two large handicraft emporiums—**Native Handicraft Center** and **Cheewa Thaicraft**—modeled along the lines of those found along Chiangmai-Sankamphaeng Road in Chiangmai, are found along the road to the airport—Thepkrasattri Road. These emporiums basically carry the same handcrafted items—woodcarvings, furniture, silver, silk, ceramics, Phuket batik, bronzeware, *kalagas*, dolls leather goods, shell boxes, windchimes, silverware, masks, fans, lacquerware, umbrellas, dolls—but at twice the prices you might pay in Chiangmai. If you don't have a chance to visit Chiangmai, these are excellent places to visit. However, if you have been to Chiangmai, these emporiums are more of the same except for some of the local products included in their collections, such as shell items, windchimes, and Phuket batik.

One of the best collections of quality Thai handicrafts is found at the **Thai Village** which is located just off the road to the airport. This is a Thai cultural show and demonstration area, but the shopping section is very nice. Over 25 shops offer a wide range of excellent quality textiles, leather goods, pewter, batik, clothes, shell items, baskets, purses, paintings, umbrellas, *kalagas*, and puppets. One stall selling *mutmee* textiles from Khon Kaen has some of the most attractive such materials we have found anywhere in Thailand. If we had only one place to shop for handcrafted items in Phuket, the Thai Village would be our choice. The admission fee to this village is 150 baht which also includes the show.

If you are on Vichitsongkharm Road, you might want to stop at **Gold Park**. This restaurant and handicraft shop has a good collection of silk, ready-made clothes, bronzeware, bags, jewelry, lacquerware, textiles, woodcarvings, blue and white ceramics, hilltribe clothes, and baskets—all from Chiangmai. This is a very expensive shop, especially if you have recently arrived from Chiangmai and know the prices on comparable goods. Nonetheless, Gold Park has a nice selection of handcrafted items.

Hotel Shops

A few of the major hotels in Phuket also have souvenir and gift shops. The most exquisite collection of jewelry, antiques, and decorative items is found at the **Amanpuri Hotel**, Phuket's classiest and most expensive hotel. This hotel has two hard-to-find shops. The sundry shop is located to the left of the pool while the shop with the most exclusive collection of jewelry and antiques—"The Gallery Shop"—is found under the bar. You may have to request that someone get a key to open this shop which seems to have irregular hours. However, it's worth the trouble. This shop carries a collection of jewelry and antiques from three of Bangkok's most exclusive shops: **The Golden Triangle**, **Lotus**, and **NeOld**. Taken together, these three shops represent at the Amanpuri Phuket's best quality shopping. If you can't visit these three shops in Bangkok, be sure to visit the shop at this hotel. The sundry shop also sells beachwear, jewelry, woodcarvings, and baskets. The jewelry, especially the silver earrings, are nicely designed and reasonably priced. The major problem of shopping here is the hotel security. You may or may not get into the hotel grounds. Our advice: dress like you are loaded with money; maybe the guards won't ask you many questions!

Other hotels with a few good shops and small shopping arcades include the **Dusit Laguna** and **Phuket Arcadia**. However, these are not the type of shops you would make a special trip to visit. If you happen to be in the area of these two fine hotels, you might be interested in browsing through their souvenir and jewelry shops.

15 RESOURCES FOR SHOPPERS, TRAVELERS, AND IMPORTERS

Preparation is the key to enjoying any shopping adventure. In Chapter Two we recommended several additional travel books as well as package tours to Thailand. As we close this volume, let us review resources and make some additional recommendations to assist you in planning your trip. For serious shoppers who also wish to import Thai products for business purposes, this section presents some tips for buying wholesale and importing Thailand's many products.

TOURS

We normally travel to Thailand on our own with great success. Indeed, this book reflects our own independent style of travel. However, like budget travel, on-your-own travel is not for everyone—especially when you have limited time and it becomes more inconvenient and expensive than joining a tour. We have nothing against organized tours nor do we have a vested interest in promoting any particular tour group. We do know there are many excellent tour groups providing fine travel services to Thailand. We do not hesitate recommending these services because we know that most of these groups use excellent hotels, include a good variety of local travel experiences, and are very reasonably priced compared to what it might cost you if you put together your own trip. Furthermore, we have heard many good things from people who have taken such tours to Asia. Therefore, we wish to draw your attention again to our recommendations on tours in Chapter Two.

ASIAN PRODUCT SHOPS

In addition to conducting comparative shopping as outlined in Chapter Three, you may wish to visit a few local stores selling Thai products to get a better idea of the range and quality of products offered in Thailand. In most major cities you will find stores selling arts, antiques, and handicrafts from Thailand. Neiman Marcus and Bloomingdales in the U.S., for example, are major buyers of Thai handcrafted items. In fact, during the writing of our regional Asian volume we discovered a new Southeast Asian shop located a few miles from our home. Offering a fine collection of Thai, Burmese, and Indonesian arts and antiques, this is one of the best shops we have found outside of Asia which offers a wide range of excellent quality Thai products:

BANANA TREE
1129 King Street
Alexandria, VA 22314
Tel. 703/836-4317

For anyone from the Washington, DC area planning to visit Thailand, this is a "must see" shop to browse in prior to departing for Thailand. You may also wish to revisit this shop after returning home; it may look different to you after having shopped in Thailand. The Banana Tree owners recently have begun taking tours to Thailand where members have a chance to shop for quality Thai products while also seeing the many sights in Bangkok and Chiangmai. If you are interested in possibly joining an upcoming tour, give them a call or write to the above address.

Other U.S. cities, such as New York, Seattle, San Francisco, and Los Angeles, also have a few shops specializing in Thai products. Check your Yellow Pages as well as survey Asian arts and crafts magazines for names, addresses, and telephone numbers. ***Arts of Asia***, a magazine published in Hong Kong, for example, carries ads from many of the best quality shops in North America, Europe, and Asia.

IMPORTING

If you are in or plan to get into the trade, you can easily arrange for importing Thai products. Indeed, many entrepreneurs do a lively business selling Thai jewelry, antiques, art, handicrafts, and home decorative items. You will find most shops identified in this book also work with businesses abroad. Some even have export offices where you can purchase items at wholesale. Inexpensive jewelry wholesaling for US$3-10 but retailing in Thailand for US$25 and abroad for US$25-50, for example, is available at wholesale prices from several shops along New Road in Bangkok (near the central post office). Look for such shops at **Yoo Lim Gems Co. Ltd.** at 1180 New Road. Other nearby shops also wholesale arts and antiques. You will see signs on the doors of these establishments that state "Wholesalers Only." For more expensive jewelry, visit any reputable lapidary, such as **Thai Lapidary** at 277/122 Rama I Road (Tel. 214-2641), and they will be more than happy to work with you on a wholesale basis.

If your interests include arts, antiques, and home decorative items, such shops as **NeOld**, **The Elephant House**, and **Lek Galleries' Art** work directly in supplying many dealers from abroad. Most other shops can make similar arrangements. All you need to do is ask if a shop works with dealers. Chances are most shops will say *"yes."*

If you are interested in importing a wide range of Thai products, one of the best places to visit is the **Department of Export Promotion's Exhibition Hall** on Rachadaphesi Road. This building has several on-going exhibits geared specifically to those interested in importing Thai products. Depending on when you visit, the product range can include everything from jewelry and handicrafts to packaging materials and semiconductors. Department personnel at the Exhibition Hall can provide you with details on exporting from Thailand.

If you are looking for inexpensive clothes, be sure to visit the **Indra Garment Export Center** on Rajaprarop Road, just adjacent to Pratunam and the Indra Hotel. Since the major Thai clothing manufacturers sell garments here, you will get a quick overview of the types of clothing products available for export.

One of the major sources for arts, antiques, and home decorative items is Chiangmai. Dealers from both Bangkok and Chiangmai regularly visit this city to do their buying. Some shops work with a single supplier or factory which custom makes their products to their own particular designs. Others buy off the same markets, such as the **Night Bazaar**, you and others will visit while touring Chiangmai. Great dealer contacts can be made by contacting shops on the third and fourth floors of the **Chiangmai Night Bazaar**. Some of the best places for wholesalers are the numerous shops lining Baan Tawai Road in **Hang Dong** as well as several shops along **Chiangmai-Sankamphaeng Road**. For blue and white ceramics and attractive wood products visit the many ceramics factories and **Siam Rich Wood Co.** in Lampang.

Shopping can be a wonderful adventure, either at home or abroad, if it is done with knowledge, a sense of adventure and good taste, attention to detail, and an emphasis on quality. When you shop in exotic places, you will unfold a new world of exciting shopping that may well change the way you organize your travel, view the world, and enjoy your life. In the end, that is what travel is all about!

INDEX

C

D

E

TRAVEL AND SHOPPING RESOURCES

If not available at your local bookstore, the following "Impact Guides" to shopping and traveling in exotic places can be ordered directly from the publisher. Complete the following form (or list the titles), include your name and mailing address, enclose payment, and send your order to:

IMPACT PUBLICATIONS
4580 Sunshine Court
Woodbridge, VA 22192 (USA)
Tel. 703/361-7300
FAX 703/335-9486

All prices are in U.S. dollars. Orders from individuals should be prepaid by check, moneyorder, or Visa or MasterCard number. If your order must be shipped outside the U.S., please include an additional US$1.50 per book for surface mail or the appropriate air mail rate for books weighing 20 ounces each. We accept telephone and FAX orders (credit cards).

Qty.	TITLES	Price	TOTAL
___	*Shopping and Traveling in Exotic Asia: Hong Kong, Thailand, Malaysia, Indonesia, & Singapore*	$16.95	______
___	*Shopping and Traveling in Exotic Hong Kong*	$12.95	______
___	*Shopping and Traveling in Exotic Indonesia*	$12.95	______
___	*Shopping and Traveling in Exotic Thailand*	$13.95	______
___	*Shopping and Traveling the Exotic Caribbean*	$13.95	______

____	*Shopping and Traveling the Exotic Philippines*	$12.95	______
____	*Shopping and Traveling the Exotic South Pacific: Australia, New Zealand, Papua New Guinea, Fiji, and Tahiti*	$14.95	______
____	*Shopping in Exotic Places: Hong Kong, Korea, Thailand, Indonesia, and Singapore*	$14.95	______
____	*Shopping and Traveling in Exotic Singapore and Malaysia*	$13.95	______
____	*Shopping in Exciting Australia and Papua New Guinea*	$13.95	______

SUBTOTAL $ ______

Virginia residents add 4.5% sales tax $ ______

Shipping/handling ($3.00 for first book and $.50 for each additional book) $ ______

International surface shipments add an additional $1.50 per book. $ ______

TOTAL ENCLOSED ----------$ ________